Literary Structures
edited by John Gardner

KINGSHIP

& COMMON PROFIT
in
GOWER'S

confessio amantis

By Russell A. Peck

Foreword by John Gardner

SOUTHERN ILLINOIS UNIVERSITY PRESS

CARBONDALE AND EDWARDSVILLE

FEFFER & SIMONS, INC

LONDON AND AMSTERDAM

Library of Congress Cataloging in Publication Data

Peck, Russell A
   Kingship & common profit in Gower's Confessio amantis.

   (Literary structures)
   Includes bibliographical references and index.
   1.   Gower, John, 1325?–1408.   Confessio amantis.
2.   Gower, John, 1325?–1408—Religion and ethics.
3.   Social ethics in literature.   4.   Kings and rulers in
literature.   I.   Title
PR1984.C63P4   821'.1   78–8984
ISBN 0–8093–0801–0

To *Ruth Demaree Peck*

CONTENTS

FOREWORD

LIKE OTHER BOOKS in the Literary Structures series, Russell Peck's *Kingship and Common Profit in Gower's "Confessio Amantis"* is a close study of a literary masterpiece, a study intended not for specialists—though specialists will find it illuminating—but for literary generalists, that is, for teachers not primarily concerned with poetry in Middle English, for graduate students, or for anyone interested in increasing his understanding and appreciation of great poetry. It may at first glance seem a trifle odd that anyone should call the *Confessio Amantis* a masterpiece, or give it a place in a critical series devoted to the essential poetic works of our civilization (such works as—to mention both studies already published and studies forthcoming in this series—the epics of Homer, Virgil's *Aeneid,* Dante's *Divine Comedy,* and Milton's *Paradise Lost* and *Paradise Regained*); and it must of course be granted that John Gower's *Confessio* is not a work of that class.

Yet the poem is far more important—and far more elegant—than its present unpopularity with critics would suggest. So far as we can make out, no one doubted, from Gower's time to Shakespeare's, that the poem was a masterpiece. Its failure to hold up reflects not stupidity or bad workmanship on the part of John Gower so much as our own loss or abandonment of the central attitudes and ideals that informed Gower's character and time. Such failures are common. Think of the decline in the literary stock of Petrarch's *Africa,* Apollonios Rhodios' *Argonautica,* or the works of Tasso, Ariosto, or Prudentius. Every work of literature requires retranslation, reinterpretation, from age to age if it is to keep its first lustre. As George Steiner points out in *After Babel,* we

can hardly read even Jane Austen—even Noel Coward—without a
dictionary. Even the greatest works at times fall out of fashion, as Virgil
and Milton are out of fashion today and as Shakespeare was out of
fashion for more than a century. We tend to suppose, with foolish
arrogance, that we have outgrown the supposed great poets of a
former age. One hears very little good said of, for instance, Tennyson,
and much less good said, these days, of Dante Gabriel Rossetti. We say,
more wisely than we know, "we cannot read them." So no one could
read Apollonios Rhodios, century after century, until suddenly there
came around an age much like his, and such writers as John Barth and
Donald Barthelme—sophisticated, cynical, crafty, "exhausted"—
whose ways of thinking and writing were so similar to those of Apollonios as to spark a revival of interest (at the moment still young) in the
cranky Alexandrian master.

Russell Peck's contribution to the Literary Structures series is a
brilliant shining up of just such a tarnished and half-forgotten major
work. *Kingship and Common Profit in Gower's Confessio Amantis* sympathetically revives the poem's intellectual and moral context, recap-
tures the aesthetic (different from our own) on which the poem de-
pended for its elegance and beauty, and thus returns the poem to its
place as one of the great poetic statements of its time.

Professor Peck teaches medieval literature at the University of
Rochester and has published numerous articles in the field.

John Gardner

Bennington, Vermont
February 1976

PREFACE

Be war of wylffulnesse • lest wondris arise.
    —mum and the sothsegger

IN THE LATTER HALF of the fourteenth century, England, despite its
relative economic prosperity, witnessed an unusually large number of
stresses and threats to its social and ideological stability. When Chaucer
laments that in these chaotic times "the world hath mad a permu-
tacioun / Fro right to wrong, fro trouthe to fikelnesse,"[1] he addresses
himself to what must have been an almost universal feeling. The very
fabric of human society seemed in danger of becoming unwoven.
Seldom had the state seen worse times. Though it had survived three
severe plagues (1349, 1361, 1369), it lived under the constant threat of
recurrent outbreaks. But worse than the plagues was the plethora of
human pestilences, those wonders of which the Sothsegger speaks,
where men greedily turn themselves into beasts to despoil their own
land.[2] The costly wars with France, which had once galvanized a sense
of national pride, even nostalgic splendor, had degenerated into an
excuse for rich men to become richer. Though the Good Parliament of
1376–77 brought to trial many offenders and exposed the kinds of
fiscal profligacy which burdened the nation, such exposures were not
conducive to restoring confidence in the leadership of the country.
The senility of Edward III, the death of the Black Prince, and then the
rule of a boy-king under a factious regency came at a time when
England needed as never before a strong, clearheaded, and public-
minded leader. Heavy taxation, the Peasants' Revolt, and the continuous infighting of the aristocracy with its intrigues and assassinations
which culminated in the overthrow of Richard II, demonstrated vividly

the failure of secular leadership. As the Sothsegger puts it,

Now, Richard þe redeles • reweth on ȝou-self,
þat lawelesse leddyn ȝoure lyf • and ȝoure peple boþe;
for þoru þe wyles and wronge • and wast in ȝoure tyme,
ȝe were lyghtlich ylyfte • from þat ȝou leef þouȝte,
And from ȝoure willffull werkis • ȝoure will was chaungid,
And rafte was ȝoure riott and rest • for ȝoure daieȝ weren wikkid,
þoru ȝoure cursid conceill • ȝoure karis weren newed,
And coueitise hath crasid • ȝource croune for euere![3]

   But if deceit, covetousness, riotous living—in short, singular profit at
the expense of the commonweal—seemed to characterize secular leadership, the church set an even worse example. Never in England's
history as a Christian nation had the people been more generally
disaffected with the church as a worldly institution. To many Englishmen, even many churchmen, the Avignon papacy, in its efforts to
maintain itself as a strong worldly power, seemed aptly designated by
the derogatory metaphor "Babylon." The official church seemed
wholly devoted to strengthening its administrative system without
much care for the spiritual needs of its people. Earlier in the century,
after the papacy's attack on the spiritual Franciscans, William of Ockham had debated with Pope John xxii over the question of ecclesiastical poverty, a dispute which led the papal representatives into the
awkward position of insisting that Christ Himself was a man of wealth.
The pope went so far as to declare excommunicate anyone who maintained that Christ had no worldly possessions. Though Ockham's political writings were condemned, they were well known in England and
had some influence on men like Wyclif in their subsequent formulation
of criticism against the worldliness of the church. It took lots of money
to maintain the papacy along the lines advocated by Boniface viii, who
had declared the pope temporal ruler over all earthly lords, and although that dream was far from being realized, John xxii was bril-
liantly efficient in raising money.[4] But to churchmen of less worldly
ambition, his fiscal policies, policies which would be followed for the
next several generations, seemed nothing less than avaricious extor-

tion. The selling of church offices, the selling of "expectancies" of church offices, the levying of annates (half a year's salary) to be paid by newly appointed ecclesiastics, the claiming of first fruits during vacancies, the imposing of income taxes on the clergy which were in turn levied from their flocks, the selling of pardons and indulgences, the imposing of heavy fines on clergymen who failed to adhere to the new policies—these remained the points of criticism against papal administration throughout the century and gave support to the assault on church corruption by Wyclif and his followers. Wyclif's attack on the papacy led to his challenging of the whole church hierarchy, even the priesthood itself, and the sacraments to which it claimed exclusive rights of dispensation.[5] At first his attack, like Ockham's, was directed primarily against the worldliness of the church: the pope should abandon worldly goods and follow Christ in evangelical poverty; a worldly pope should be deposed; obedience to the pope should be contingent upon his conduct; and so on. Later, after the schism, his reservations became even stronger: only Christ can ordain priests; no priest has power of absolution; the church has no power to mediate between man and God. Wyclif was not a lone figure in his criticism of church policies. The cry for reform came from all sides, from laymen and churchmen alike. The schism, with its two popes using their powers not to support the needy but to attack each other, threatening and excommunicating those men or nations who did not support them, made a mockery of what had once been a solemn example. Attempts such as that of Boniface IX to provoke England once again to attack France or to promote "crusades" against the pope's opponents were too much for even papal supporters like Archbishop Courtenay to stomach.[6] In short, the church was in a state of chaos. Many a poor soul must have felt besieged, like Chaucer's poor widow Mabely,[7] by rapacious churchmen, whether summoners, friars, or pardoners.

Yet despite these unsettling facts of political and ecclesiastical life, England was experiencing growing pains of a different kind—pains of economic expansion and a vaguely discomforting awareness of a new universal, very different from any feudal principal, which might bind society together, namely money.[8] The beginnings of capitalism, with the development of banking systems, and the rapid growth of cities and their intricate systems of trade brought worldly success to men other than high churchmen or aristocracy, enough success to distract attention from the fragile stability of the first two estates. But such new wealth and power created contradictions and threats of their own. A philosophy of materialistic pragmatism was even more alien to medieval moral sensibilities than two popes or the problem of replacing a willful king.

Plagues, an irresponsible aristocracy, corrupt churchmen, popular uprisings, repression of dissent by both church and state, a legion of avaricious fiends loosed upon all areas of society who would willingly murder for the widow's mite—such decadence provoked responses, and the literature of protest against the times is vast.[9] With the integrity of leadership called sharply into question it is no surprise to find writers of this period bent on moral retrenchment. In times of confusion people tend to become morally conservative. Ethical conservatism in writers like Gower and his contempories manifests itself in several ways: *1]* a turning backward to scrutinize the past from which the present troubles derive; *2]* a turning inward to study one's own psychology; and *3]* a heightened awareness of the individual's involvement in larger social issues. One finds these traits in most of the literature of the time, especially in that of the major authors.

The marked tendency of English writers of the later fourteenth century to hearken after sources or to turn to the classics for story material involves more than literary fashion or mere antiquarianism. It reflects an uncertainty about dealing with the present and an attempt to rediscover a vital mythology by renovating the past. This psychological process of regenerating the past will be a main consideration in Gower. Time, it would seem, has degenerated; yet its history holds a key to present dilemmas. Earlier in the century the courtly attempts to revive Trojan legends and reemphasize England's descent from Brutus had added a dignity and glory to the enterprises of young Edward III's entourage.[10] In view of the distraught conditions of the state in the latter part of the century, however, attitudes toward such traditions were decidedly more ambivalent. Chaucer, the Gawain-poet, and Gower all appraise the "noble" lineage with a more jaundiced eye. But they still study that material. If London is "the toun of newe Troye"[11] it seems as precarious as the old Troy, and perhaps as doomed. Treachery, rather than glory, might well be the gift inherited from that ancient society. The Troy story is, of course, only one segment of history which Gower's generation reassesses in order to get a perspective on themselves. They also draw heavily on Roman history and—especially Gower—on the Old Testament.

But what is more striking about his generation of writers than their reassessment of the present from the vantage of antiquity is the persistence with which they turn their study of society into questions of psychology. They seem preoccupied with the working of the human will. The search for origins and resolutions often becomes an inward quest, undertaken and plotted according to the urgings and divergings of the will. Even if the quest is not an inward journey but a wandering about middle earth, as in the romances or *Piers Plowman,* the focus of attention is likely to be on the operation of the will as the protagonist's desires qualify his decisions. It might be observed that many of the principal theological questions debated by the generations of scholars following Aquinas centered upon the operation and efficacy of the will. This is especially true of the English theologians (e.g., Duns Scotus, William of Ockham, and Robert Holcott, with their emphasis on the primacy of the will, and Thomas Bradwardine, Richard Fitzralph, and John Wyclif, with their emphasis on the contingency of the will upon God's power). The intensity of these studies marks an important step in the direction of humanism. The heart of the dispute concerns the relationship of will to grace in man's quest for salvation. But it also touches upon the whole question of man's responsibility in governing his behavior. The topic of free will and man's involvement in shaping his destiny was not, however, restricted to ivy-covered towers. William of Ockham complained that "laymen and old women" would tackle theologians on questions of free will and contingency.[12] The arguments of St. Augustine and Boethius were widely known on these topics. So too were Aristotle's observations on personal governance in the *Ethics.* What is remarkable is the frequency with which the governing of the will becomes the central concern of popular literature. Essays on the education of the good king (i.e., the well-governed will) appear in the name of the Philosopher (Aristotle), along with dream vision literature and romances which probe the subtlest adventures of the will as it searches out its jurisdiction. Whether the poem be *Piers Plowman*, *Pearl*, one of Chaucer's dream visions, or Gower's *Confessio Amantis* (to mention only a few), the will is either a protagonist or a guiding (perhaps troubling) concern of the protagonist. Sometimes, as in *Wynnere and Wastoure* or the alliterative *Morte Arthure*, the question will be posed in terms of what constitutes good kingship, the true king being the one who can govern his will rightly. In other poems, like *Troilus and Criseyde* or *Patience*, the question turns on the protagonist's manipulation of his desires. The "wondris" which arise in these poems (to borrow again the Sothsegger's phrase, though I might have drawn upon the opening of *Piers Plowman* or any *chanson d'aventure* where the persona sets out "wondres to here") originate in the fantasies willfully engendered by the minds of the protagonists. As fantasies are conceived and dealt with, whether in the mind or in the realm of romance, they are not unlike the perverse events of history which men, in their misrule, perpetrate upon society. But whether in real life or in fiction, to understand these wonders one must understand the workings of man's will.

A third feature of these fourteenth-century poems which reflects the uneasy times in which they were written is their heightened awareness of social involvement. Even when their plots explore the governing of the will through some sort of mental journey, they seldom end with a simple recognition of personal limitations. The last step, beyond psychological reordering, is outward, away from the self and back into society. To put it another way, in addition to the study of personal kingship (right governance of will), these poems also are likely to acknowledge a need for common profit, perhaps through a display of the benefits which good personal rule makes possible for the whole society, or at least the show of a willingness to enter again into the lives of other people. It is not enough simply to "find oneself." One encounters this second leg of the journey again and again in the quest literature of the period, in *Sir Orfeo,* in the king's return to his court; in *Sir Gawain and the Green Knight,* where the hero rejects the Green Knight's invitation to stay in his court in order to return home; in *Sir Gawaine and the Carl of Carlisle,* where the Carl's wilderness abode is converted into a civilized place which benefits all of Arthur's court, even the presumptuous Sir Kay; and in the exquisite short romance *Emare,* which turns the Constance story into a tale of governing the will to regain lost kingdoms and common profit for all. Similarly, in the dream visions, we generally find the protagonist not only awakening at the end but compelled to move back into the sphere of mankind where nothing remains simple.

The English poet during this period who most systematically studies the ills of his society and theorizes their basis in personal behavior is John Gower. My goal in this study is to examine in detail the complex plan of moral reform which Gower enunciates in his *Confessio Amantis* as a remedy for the ills of his time. Though Gower entertained questions of moral reform in the *Mirour de l'Omme* and the *Vox Clamantis,* the *Confessio,* with its psychological chronicle of the wanderings of Amans, who is a figure for the wayward will, provides fullest insight into the intricacies of Gower's philosophy. What seems to me most needed at this time in Gower studies is a penetrating analysis of what Gower sees the issues to be and a demonstration of how the numerous tales in his long poem hold together and support both the poem's loose plot and the poet's strongly moral intention. In composing my discussion I have set for myself several guidelines: *1*] I have tried to deal with what seems to me to be the heart of Gower's moral purpose in the poem. *2*] I have tried to keep my analysis simple, though not to the detriment of Gower's interweaving of ideas through his multiple analogies. Gower himself professes simplicity in the poem, though the ease of his ideas is deceptive. *3*] I have kept my argument brief. I have not, for example, allowed myself the luxury of discussing fourteenth-century English social and political history or speculated about events to which Gower may occasionally allude. He himself is not so much concerned with specific incidents as he is with the clarification of moral attitudes toward degenerate behavior. Though he is casual with his historical

facts, he is earnest with his principles and generalizations.   4] To show
the subtlety and self-consciousness with which Gower shaped his argument I have often turned to his sources to show how he alters
materials to make his central theme more coherent.   5] Finally, I have
tried to keep the style of my essay clear and lively (earnest in game),
which is the way Gower suggests his argument is to be understood. In
short, I have tried to write a study of Gower's major poem, a poem
among the most important of the fourteenth century, which will be
useful to the general reader of medieval literature (not simply the
specialist), the friends of Chaucer who would like to broaden their
acquaintance with the writings of that time.

IT IS REASSURING to find colleagues and associates who are willing to let
you share your ideas with them and courageous enough to criticize
them as well. I wish to express special thanks to Rowland Collins,
Thomas Hahn, Linda Flowers, Theresa Coletti, and to an unnamed
reader for the care, patience, and useful suggestions they offered me
after reading my manuscript in a late draft. Their astute criticisms
saved me from many errors. I also owe a note of appreciation to Gayle
Hamilton, William Soll, Mary Maleski, and Francis Hildahl for helpful
comments of various kinds, and to John Gardner for encouragement at
a time when I most welcomed it. Finally, I thank the Danforth Foundation for an E. Harris Harbison Award which gave me the means for
time off to write the book.

Russell A. Peck

Dacre, Ontario
September 1977

INTRODUCTION

SEVERAL years ago, George R. Coffman suggested Gower's most significant role as a man of letters was that of a philosophical social commentator: "We shall have to wait until we come to Milton before we find another English writer who, to paraphrase Macaulay, treats 'the whole field of man's religious and moral nature, . . . the purposes of Providence in dealing with him' and 'the method which should be followed by man in order to reconcile himself to God.' Like Milton also he seems to record his spiritual biography in his works. . . . He was interested, not in philosophical thought, . . . but in a philosophy of living."[1] It is certainly true that virtually every work Gower wrote touches on his philosophy of life. John Fisher, his modern biographer, observes: "The most striking characteristic of Gower's literary production is its single-mindedness. . . . In a very real sense, Gower's three major poems are one continuous work."[2] The *Mirour de l'Omme,* the *Vox Calmantis,* and the *Confessio Amantis* recurrently explore the individual's responsibility within the larger social context. Gower's Latin works, especially the *Vox Clamantis,* the *Tripartite Chronicle,* and *O Deus Immense,* strike forthrightly at problems arising out of misgovernance of the three estates. Gower was a fearless critic of men in high places—whether they be king, pope, or archbishop—and precise in exacting behavior of them commensurate with the ideal of their offices. He was wholly committed to the welfare of mankind. Fisher has commented on the prominence of social concern in Gower's writings: "What distinguishes Gower's views from those of many of his contemporaries, and places him among the progressive thinkers of his day, is his emphasis upon legal justice and regal responsibility for all the estates, defined in terms of 'le bien commune,' 'bonus communi' [*sic*], or 'the comun good,' depending upon the language in which he happened to be writing. . . . Gower emphasized this concept more than any of his contemporaries."[3] Fisher notes that the idea is classical in origin and prominent in the writings of the early church fathers. It was revitalized in the twelfth, thirteenth, and early fourteenth centuries by John of Salisbury, Thomas Aquinas, Augustinus Triumphus, and William of Ockham, and was a topic of both civil and canon law.[4] But although the topic was commonplace by Gower's day, in view of both the church and state's avaricious disregard for the common good, his assertions carry the weight of a foredoomed prophecy.

Gower's concern with the commonweal is not that of a political scientist. His approach to society is preeminently humanistic. As moral philosopher and social critic, he directs his attack against men, not the office itself. (*Cf. Vox Clamantis,* Prol. to Bk. iii.23–26, where he defends adamantly the feudal concept of the three estates.) His goal is not to undermine social structures but rather to show the faults of men who corrupt them. Like so many writers of his day, he focuses on questions of volition. In the *Mirour de l'Omme,*[5] for example, as Gower progresses through his analysis of estates and offices his emphasis steadfastly falls upon the responsibility of each member of society to the other. The pope and his court should be defined by what they can do for Christendom (not by the revenues they can extort), bishops by their responsibilities to their dioceses, pastors for their curacy, knights by their obligation to defend "le commun droit" (23610). Lawyers should stop fleecing people and work for "le bien commun" (24341; 24345), as should teachers and artisans (25501 ff.). Viscounts, bailiffs, and "questours" should uphold "la loy commune" for "proufit de communalté" (24818–23), and merchants should serve "le commun proufit" (25260) instead of trying to get all the lucre for themselves through their deceits ("triche"). The point of the elaborate review of the state of the world— the genealogy of all the progeny of sin and the catalog of decadent social institutions—is not to lament bad times at hand. "Siecle" (Time), though often accused of evil, is not to blame. Neither are the stars, the elements, or random events. The ills of the times originate with man himself (27361). But so does hope, as the life of Mary and the Incarnation of Christ make clear (27481 ff.). All social issues resolve themselves in the personal lives of men.

What is unique about Gower's social commentary is its insistent correlation of social criticism with a benevolent psychology of personal ethics. He seems always mindful of man as a double entity, both social and individual. When exploring man's individual psyche he turns to metaphors of state; when criticizing the state he conceives of a common body. The manifestations of human happiness, whether personal or social, are mutually dependent. Neither form of happiness can be fully realized without the other. Gower's notion of social structure is thus interwoven with his theory of ethics, psychology, and theology. In *Vox Clamantis,* for example, where he admonishes King Richard that a ruler is personally responsible for the moral welfare of his state, his ideology and the rhetoric through which he presents moral issues is kin to that of *Confessio Amantis,* where the persona Amans is likewise told that he is a king who should take better care in looking after the common interest of himself in his individual and social parts. In both works, kingship is viewed as a form of maturity. It is balanced rationality. Woe to the kingdom ruled by an "undisciplined boy" *(Rex, puer indoctus)*[6] whether that boy be a Richard II or a wayward Amans.

The key to Gower's encyclopedic moral philosophy is "comun profit," by which he means the mutual enhancement, each by each, of all parts of a community for the general welfare of that community taken as a whole. It applies to the community of faculties within an individual man as well as the state of England with its individuals and its three estates. Each part has its natural rights. If one part deprives another, not only does the deprived part suffer from the onslaught but the oppressor is diminished too, for he loses the benefit of his larger self which he has affronted. To diminish another is to diminish oneself. Conversely, if one is capable of taking joy in another's success, and promotes that success for "l'onour et le commun proufit" *(Mirour* 12905), he will himself grow and find a joy as great as his own successes hold.

Gower believed that mankind shares a common, God-given nature which is to be respected even beyond human offices, which were, after all, established only by men. He distinguishes between natural law, which is by definition good since it reflects God's expressed intent even before the Fall, and positive law, which reflects social agreements after the Fall in an effort to deal with human nastiness. Positive law, being that which man "posits," is often subject to error simply because men usually rule according to expedient and private motives. Such law is valid only insofar as it has man's support and answers man's needs. Common profit and a healthy, productive society depend upon good governance according to both kinds of law. Kings were instituted by men after the Fall as an expedience for preserving peace and the common rights of men.[7] A king's security lies in ruling well. If he rules badly, he will be overthrown. This attitude toward rebellion is not a condoning of revolution, however, any more than misery is an excuse for neurosis. It is simply the consequence of a situation to be avoided. A king must understand all law—natural, positive, and even divine law. Above all, he must act justly.

O Rois, si estre voes parfit,	*O King, if you wish to be perfect*
Fai ce pour quoy tu es eslit,	*Do that for which you are chosen,*
Justice au pueple fai donner;	*Have justice done to the people;*
Ly Rois qui par justice vit	*The king who lives by justice*
Ja n'ert du guerre desconfit.	*Will never be undone by war.*

Mirour 23077–81

Insofar as the state reflects the constitution of individual man, however, wherewith Reason holds the office of king over the rest of the body and its faculties, there does seem to be a natural justification of kingship, at least by way of analogy.[8] It is man's God-given nature to be kingly and behave justly. To Gower's way of thinking the state reflects man, not man the state. He will, of course, discuss man by means of metaphors of the state, but he does so cognizant that such rhetoric offers a useful way of recalling an original truth by reversing an analogy so that the mind moves from an outward manifestation toward an inner truth. We work backward to make right our upside-down perspective.

Although Gower's Latin and French works treat extensively of man's responsibilities to his various estates, the *Confessio Amantis* gives fullest voice to his ideas on man's moral obligations. The related motifs of kingship and common profit inform not only the subject matter of Gower's English poem but, as we shall see, even its structure and rhetoric.[9] The *Confessio* is deliberately a simple poem, a "tale plein withoute frounce" (VII.1594), written "with rude wordis and with pleyne" (VIII.3122). In his discussion of Rhetoric in Book VII (1507–1640), Gower stresses the power of words to assist man in virtuous behavior. Perverters of words are enemies of the state, as Ulysses (whose eloquence persuaded Antenor to betray Troy) and the accomplices of Catiline (who would have deceived Rome) illustrate. Gower would "do my trewe peyne" (VIII.3121) not for the sake of eloquence or "curiosite," but for the state of England. In the poem's final Latin epigram Gower calls the poem his *liber purus,* a book without alloy. Its singleness of purpose and true intent constitute part of its theme.[10] The epigram directs the book to the poet's political hero, Henry, Earl of Derby. This poem, in the rude English of the people, would speak plainly to all Gower's fellow Englishmen, common and noble, in the hope of the true rhetorician "the comun profit forto save" (VII.1609).

Like many fourteenth-century English writers, Gower was extraordinarily sensitive to what we call persona—what he thought of as the poet's voice. In *Vox Clamantis* he professed to speak in the voice of "John," the prophet crying in the wilderness,[11] and imitated the tone of his namesake, John of the Apocalypse. The *Vox Clamantis* was addressed to learned men, especially men like Thomas of Arundel, Archbishop of Canterbury, to whom the final version was dedicated.[12] Yet by the 1390s it must have been painfully clear to Gower that a writer cannot effect social reforms in an academic treatise. Reform can come only from the people themselves. In the *Confessio* we hear a different voice crying, that of a common Englishman speaking the common language. Perhaps the *Vox Clamantis* might provoke a man like Arundel to enforce the laws of the church. But in the *Confessio* Gower appeals not to the officers of the land but to the officers of the soul. He would reform society not by laws but by reshaping the hearts of men. The people's voice is a rhetorical necessity to the *Confessio Amantis*.

Gower was profoundly disturbed by the Peasants' Revolt which occurred while he was finishing his writing of the *Vox Clamantis*. The seminal motive behind the *Confessio Amantis* is to make Englishmen conscious that they are one people in religion, state, and person. In the *Confessio* his persona is still one crying in the wilderness, but now the wilderness is that of romance, where a cupidinous Amans cries out in a self-imposed exile. The effect is charming rather than vituperative, though the ultimate goal is not far removed from that of the more ostensibly pious Latin works. Through the popular genre of romance, Gower reaches toward a wider audience to remind men that they share one great tradition and one common nature. If they become like the house divided against itself, they are doomed to fall, both individually and collectively.

Professor Coffman quite rightly refers to the *Confessio* as Gower's *summa moralis*.[13] The poem explores God's plan and demonstrates that it works. Gower gives minute attention to moral process. It is his hope to show men in troubled times how to reclaim their right estate. His plot of a fallen lover whose willfulness has bereft him of Reason exemplifies the behavior of a state without its king. Amans' plot defines the reeducation, the disciplining, of all fallen men. Gower's structure must be sufficiently elaborate to explore both the personal and social sides of the analogy, so he frames the lover's plot with didactic attacks on corruption within the religious and secular institutions of his day. During the confession itself, Amans' priest, Genius, often "digresses" into diatribes which recall or further develop specific criticisms laid out in the Prologue. But it is important for the reader of the *Confessio* to recognize that for Gower the broad social criticism and the personal woes of the lover are part of one and the same plot. Repeatedly Gower had stressed in his earlier writings that man is the cause of his own dilemmas.[14] He makes the point again at the outset of the *Confessio*. It is the kernel of truth out of which the whole Prologue and subsequent poem spring. Because of the interconnectedness of God's creation, no creaturely act is totally private. A crime against oneself is a social crime, and a crime against society is a deprivation of self.

The *Confessio Amantis* is insistently didactic, but not narrowly so. Though he obviously cannot teach all things, Gower would, nonetheless, include all aspects of human knowledge within the poem's purview. He will as best as he is able show how all things pertain to each other in man's fundamental quest for self-composure. So broad, in fact, is the intent of Gower's poem that modern readers have had difficulty comprehending synthetically the various facets of Gower's plan and have preferred to talk of his "structural blunders," his "long digressions," the irrelevant or gratuitous prologue, his "unsuccessful coda," or his bungling of courtly love traditions.[15] But Gower is a more skillful craftsman than readers have generally allowed. There are, no doubt, flaws in Gower's artistry, depending upon what kind of critical standard one chooses to judge him by. He is not a modern poet. He does not share our notions of literary economy, realism, or organic unity. But he knew what he was doing in the *Confessio Amantis,* and he did it with considerable polish. It is one medieval poem in which we have strong evidence of careful revision and correction.[16] By exploring the themes of kingship and common profit within the work, I hope to be able to demonstrate the congruity of subject in Gower's poem with its various forms of statement. My attention shall be directed toward the ethical bias of his theme and will deal with matters of structure, language, and source as they pertain to the theme. For the most part I shall proceed according to the chronology of the poem.

KINGSHIP AND COMMON PROFIT

in Gower's

confessio amantis

Figura, seu repręsentatio de septem pctis mortalibus,
.s. Supbia, auaricia, luxuria, ira, gula, iuidia, & accidia

PROLOGUE

THE PROLOGUE to the *Confessio Amantis* tells little about what kind of poem will follow. There is no indication of a confession systematically ordered around the seven deadly sins, no reference to the Boethian quest for peace of mind, nor any mention of Amans, Venus, or her confessor-priest Genius. There is not even an announcement that tales will be told. In what way, then, does the Prologue introduce the poem? Consisting of five expository sections, each set off by a Latin epigram, the Prologue establishes the poem's main topics. I shall deal with each of the five sections separately, though at the outset it might be useful to anticipate a few of the main conceptual metaphors which Gower introduces, particularly those which pertain to time, place, and the mind.

The Prologue establishes the analogy between the greater world and the "lasse world" (947).[1] The greater world is both the macrocosm and human society at large. The lesser world is individual man, whose obligation it is to maintain a harmonious perspective on both of his greater dimensions. This is no easy task for he knows that the analogies exist mainly in the minds of men, at least as far as men themselves are concerned. Civilization, as well as sanity, involves a fragile balance. If the analogies within the Creator's plan are to hold valid for man, he must use his mental faculties carefully. He must know how to govern his estates well, and he must recognize that he is both a community of his own as well as part of a larger community. Both kingship and common profit are thus, for Gower, psychological as well as political concepts.

A modern reader of the *Confessio Amantis* would do well to keep in mind the traditional model of faculty psychology which stands behind Gower's vocabulary for the mind's behavior. Insofar as the mind is a "lasse world," St. Augustine, the most influential spokesman on the subject, saw in its aspects and behavior a reflection of the Trinity.[2] That is, the mind's faculties are three—Memory, Intellect, and Will. Like the persons of the Trinity, each faculty refers to each severally, but each is uttered by all three.[3] Memory is the holding faculty; Intellect is the discerning faculty; Will is the loving faculty. God's mystery lies in the simultaneity of His Memory, Understanding, and Love. The human mind is like God only as in a glass or enigma.[4] Man, living amidst temporality, seems able to remember, understand, and love things, but only separately. For example, Augustine describes a man discussing a complex problem of geometry. That man also happens to be an excellent musician. But while he is concentrating on his geometry, his knowledge of music is stored and momentarily forgotten in his memory, even though he knows and loves music. He cannot know and do all things at once.[5] For him, everything is always in process of time. He is perpetually obliged to put things together. This obligation to coordinate and balance rationally one's limited perceptions lies at the heart of most of Gower's moral principles.

Love is a crucial faculty in that it is the combiner and unifier of the other two faculties. It is the motivating desire.[6] Everyone loves according to that which he loves. Thus for man, much of his loving is a mere parody of truly virtuous love. Yet even sin reflects something of the true process of love, if only dimly or in reverse. Augustine suggests that the process of knowing follows a pattern: first the mind approaches outwardly sensible things, then discovers in the experience things pertinent to the inner man in order to approach contemplation of things eternal.[7] That is, the mind turns outward, then inward, then transcends itself. The middle step is the crucial one. The mind is eager to know and love itself, so much so that it sometimes forgets that even self-knowledge must be transcended. Love of self for the sake of self is Narcissism, a parody of self-knowledge. Without thought of the ultimate goal, it is a kind of forgetfulness, a misunderstanding, a myopia. Such a confusion is usually the result of a rebellious Will's assuming a sovereign position over Memory and Intellect to exact some private end.

All three terms and their attendant implications and patterns of intellection are necessary for understanding the "matiere" of Gower's poem. "Love" and "Will" are of the same category and perform as the motivator in his scheme. He does not use the precise term "intellect." Often he uses the word "Wit," which was the common Middle English gloss on *intellectus*, though usually he relies on the more general term "Reason," which along with Memory and Will, completes his trinity of mental faculties. As the reader gets further into the *Confessio*, he will find Genius invoking Memory even more frequently than Gower does in the Prologue, as he tries to help Amans to know himself better by subduing his Will to proper balance. That process of releasing the mind from Narcissistic fantasy is begun in the Prologue, however, as Gower enjoins his audience to draw into remembrance the "tyme passed" (94) when "the lif of man" was lived "in helthe" (96). The healthy mind knows that its temporal limitations and spatial confinements are resolved through the analogy with the Creator, for, in His eternal memory, the Creator is beyond time and space.

Sin is that which upsets the analogy. Gower equates it with division of that which should not be divided. Understood as part of his theory of political and psychological organization, it is an aggressive act for singular profit at the expense of the commonweal (849–1053). The result of such mental or social fragmentation is confusion and alienation, both temporal and spiritual (851–55). Selfishness destroyed the Golden Age and has flourished ever since. Gower uses Nebuchadnezzar's dream of the monster of time in the book of Daniel to epitomize the process (585 ff.). The monster, with its head of gold, chest of silver, belly of brass, and legs and feet of steel and clay crumbling into powder, is significantly in the shape of a man, for as Gower explains, the corruption of time is the consequence of man's severance from God: "Al this wo is cause of man" (905–66).

This idea of man's accountability is crucial to the plot of the *Confessio*. As men become increasingly forgetful of their original harmonious position in God's scheme they become more like the divided and

crumbling feet of the monster, which, Gower suggests, represent the
latter days of war and civil strife as well as the schism within the church.
The more men ignore common profit to pursue singular ends, the
more they forget their common nature and hate each other. We shall
see Gower's definition of sin as division and confusion dramatized in
the main part of the *Confessio*, as Amans, that "lasse world," tears himself
apart in his willful desire, unable to remember a wholesome self. The
confused lover's plot will be the reclaiming of his lost sense of common
nature through a sorting out of limited perspectives. Without a proper
sense of God, man is lost both temporally and spatially. He does not
know who or where he is. This problem of man's relationship with his
divine center defines what Gower sees as man's need for right "remembrance," whereby an individual puts time and place back together in his
head. Gower's theory of mental stability hinges on the operation of
Memory, Wit, and Will. And insofar as poetry helps man to sort out his
mind it too has a moral function in Gower's scheme.

The first part of Gower's Prologue discusses books, explains Gower's
reasons for writing in English, and dedicates the poem to Henry of
Lancaster. The initial Latin epigram consists of an apology and an
exhortation:

> Torpor, ebes sensus, scola parua labor minimusque
>   Causant quo minimus ipse minora canam:
> Qua tamen Engisti lingua canit Insula Bruti
>   Anglica Carmente metra iuuante loquar.
> Ossibus ergo carens que conterit ossa loquelis
>   Absit, et interpres stet procul oro malus.

[*Sluggishness, dullness of perception, little leisure, and scant
application, all these plead extenuation for me, least of poets, for
inditing somewhat slight themes. In that tongue spoken on the
Island of Brutus, and aided by the English Muse, I shall offer my
songs. It has not, therefore, been my intention to cover over with
pretty words a lack of inner substance in my verses; and may a
vicious expounder of them never discover the gold that lies hidden
there.*][8]

Suffering from the same limitations all fallen men experience, the poet invokes the good intentions of his audience. The fact that he writes in English, he explains, is a sign that his intent is not to cover over lack of substance with loquaciousness. He will be plain and direct.

Books enable men to discourse with others of different times. Such discourse serves mankind in a double capacity. It teaches men of past times, thus freeing them from captivity to the present, and it shows them by example how to write about our own time.

> Of hem that writen ous tofore
> The bokes duelle, and we therfore
> Ben tawht of that was write tho:
> Forthi good is that we also
> In oure tyme among ous hiere
> Do wryte of newe som matiere,
> Essampled of these olde wyse
> So that it myhte in such a wyse,
> Whan we ben dede and elleswhere,
> Beleve to the worldes eere
> In tyme comende after this.
>
> *(1–11)*

This initial passage justifies both the method and content of what follows. The many tales from ancient authors, the scientific matter from Aristotle and his redactors, the moral treatises and wisdom literature which Genius will so often cite—all are part of the available booklore of antiquity to teach men where they came from and where they presently are. Combined with present experience, such matters help men explain themselves to future generations and to each other. Books thus bind men of all times together.

Books form a crucial link in Gower's understanding of human community. As he explained in *Vox Clamantis,*

> Scripture veteris capiunt exempla futuri,
> Nam dabit experta res magis esse fidem.
>
> *(Prol.1–2)*

*[Writings of antiquity contain examples for the future,
For a thing known by experience will afford greater faith]*

In the *Confessio* Gower conscientiously writes for his own people and for future generations as well. As he explains at the end of the poem in its Latin epilogue (II, 478), he would please the people of Britain forever *(perpetuis annis)*. He sees himself as a social commentator and a preserver of what is good. His theory seems to be that a healthy nation, if it hopes to live coherently and with mutual understanding, must hold knowledge of the past in common. Gower says he will write "of newe som matiere," but by examples of old. His idea of new matter based on old ideas is like Chaucer's notion of poetry as "newe corn" from "olde feldes" in the *Parlement of Foules* (22–23). Like Chaucer, Gower adheres to the hallowed rhetorical principle of combining "sentence and solaas." His poem will follow a "middel weie" (17); it will be a means to an end, its subject treating "somwhat of lust, somwhat of lore" (19), but always with an eye toward the public welfare. His poetry will be one way of answering the corruptive effects of time and sin.

When we get into the main part of the *Confessio* we shall see how Genius' tales help Amans reclaim his lost heritage. But more important, these tales will in a pleasing way recall that whole lost heritage back to the mind of Gower's audience. Amans will be only a vehicle for the more significant task of cultural regeneration. In such days at the end of the fourteenth century when England was confused and divided and when all values seemed "welnyh . . . al reversed" (30), Gower felt his task to be urgent. By describing the ills of society in conjunction with a plot based on the long hallowed Boethian journey of the mind homeward from exile, Gower hoped to illuminate a pathway back to right order. In this respect he is indeed "moral Gower," who writes his book "for Engelondes sake" (24). He writes in the common tongue so that all his people may hear, share, and understand.

Gower suggests that writing is good for the writer as well as the audience. For both writer and audience it demands an ordering of the mind. Order is essential to a well-governed estate, whether psychological or political. Gower keeps before him the image of the Golden Age when poetry and well-measured behavior were synonymous. In more virtuous days, he asserts, writing was more prized than now:

> be daies olde,
> Whan that the bokes were levere,
> Wrytinge was beloved evere
> Of hem that weren vertuous.
>
> (36–39)

This bookishness, a characteristic of many medieval writers,[9] runs throughout the *Confessio Amantis* and is a mark of Gower's classically oriented humanism. Beloved books keep men mindful of the moral, historical, and physical dimensions of their lives, despite the disappointing vicissitudes of fallen nature and real life. If a man is wise, he will look to books, books of old and books remade by present authors, to recover that ancient perspective necessary for a stable society. Like Chaucer, who refers to books as "the key of remembrance,"[10] Gower argues that from books,

> What wysman that it underfongeth,
> He shal drawe into remembrance
> The fortune of this worldes chance.
>
> (68–70)

Orderly books enable him the better to deal with the fallen world's irregularities.

The first version of the *Confessio* (ca. 1390) lacks this tribute to books. (First version lines noted by asterisk.) It tells instead how Gower wrote his poem at the request of King Richard, whom he met while boating on the Thames (24–92*). In that version the poet uses the occasion to rehearse his allegiance to the king, hoping that the King of Kings will grant "his corone longe stonde" (32*). Gower turns his expression of allegiance into an epitome of a true subject's right relationship with his liege lord (25–28*), thus adding an important touch to the theme of kingship and common profit which he is preparing to develop. After the pleasing autobiographical account of the meeting on the river he talks further about his poem, praying that it be well received and

shielded from malicious attack. He mentions a long illness which complicated his complying with the king's request and notes that despite
the hardships his book is written

> in such a maner wise,
> Which may be wisdom to the wise
> And pley to hem that lust to pleye.
>   (83–85*)

Readers have occasionally lamented that this charming passage was
deleted from Gower's later recension of the poem, but the revision tells
us much about the progress of his thought and his attitude toward his
book and the society to which it is addressed in the early 1390s.

The revised version of the Prologue is exactly the same length as the
original (68 lines deleted, 68 lines added). Perhaps Gower's plan was to
substitute the new passage for the old, the exact same length making it
possible to excise the lines to be replaced in extant copies, replacing
them with the new. If this is the case, it suggests more than revision; it
amounts to obliteration. The content of the new passage is markedly
different from the nostalgic autobiography of the first. Instead of
explaining that the book was written "for king Richardes sake" (24*),
Gower now writes "a bok for Engelondes sake" (24). Instead of praising
the king, the poet laments that the land now stands "in worse plit" than
ever it suffered in "olde daies passed" (55 ff.). The pessimistic tone,
with its ominous stress upon the strife and division in the land, reflects
his total disenchantment with Richard. His eulogy on books becomes
part of that pessimism as the poet implies that books are the only place
where worthy princes may be found. The idea of the persona's allegiance to his lord, which had been an important feature of Gower's
first version of the Prologue, he salvages at the end of this section of the
recension with a brief dedication to Henry of Lancaster (81–92), whom
he addresses as "myn oghne lord" (86). By paying tribute to his feudal
lord the persona reaffirms his sense of right order within the larger
world of social domain, as he had done with Richard in the first version.
The passage effectively links Gower's discussion of the realm of books
with that of the realm of states: Henry is "ful of knythode and alle

grace" (89), with power to join virtues of the past with the present. He is Gower's "wys man," a man who respects ancient wisdom and yet is near the center of present policy. Gower, it appears, even as early as 1392 was wondering what the state of England might be like if Henry were king instead of Richard. But the placement of the passage at the end of this section, and its juxtaposition with the lamentable condition of the present rule, creates an effect nearer to desperation than optimistic hope. Gower indicates that he will treat more extensively the idea of a virtuous ruler later in the poem (cf. 77–80, which anticipates Bk. VII), though he does not specifically attack Richard. There will be sufficient places elsewhere in the poem to speak out against the kinds of incompetence which provoked the mood of disenchantment in the recension.

Critics have sometimes looked upon Gower's shift of allegiance from Richard to Henry as a lack of courtesy and loyalty, and even as crass expedience. But such does not seem to me a fair assessment. Richard's increasingly arbitrary behavior as king, his choice of self-aggrandizing counselors, and his high-handed exploitation of the state while carrying out his personal struggle with the great men of the realm brought criticism from all sides.[11] Gower's position is similar to that of the Lancastrian apologist Henry Knighton, who argued in his attack on Richard,

> From ancient statute and a precedent of times not long past which might be invoked again, though it was a painful thing, the people have an established principle that if, because of evil counsel of any kind, or silly obstinancy, or contempt, or singularly impudent willfulness or irregular behavior, the king should alienate himself from his people and refuse, despite the sane advice of the lords and most celebrated men of the realm, to be governed and regulated by the laws, statutes, and praiseworthy ordinances of the realm, but would impudently exercise in his insane counsels his own singular willfulness, then it is allowable for them, with common assent and with the consensus of the people of the realm, to depose the king himself from the royal throne and to raise to that throne in his place someone near at hand from the royal family stock.[12]

Such seems to be Gower's political sentiment exactly. Repeatedly he will admonish the offender of justice, regardless of station, by reminding him of the voice of the people and stress the evil of willfulness and false counsel. As we shall see, the main body of the *Confessio* will reenact the search for true counsel, as the lover through his confession exemplifies for the reader the loss of kingdom which inevitably ensues when one indulges in self-flattery.

The heart of Gower's Prologue is his estimate of the three estates (pts. ii–iv), where he shows the duplicity and chaos which result when man loses his sense of the divine center. Part Two begins with an epigram on kings and temporal rulers.

> Tempus preteritum presens fortuna beatum
>   Linquit, et antiquas vertit in orbe vias.
> Progenuit veterem concors dileccio pacem,
>   Dum facies hominis nuncia mentis erat:
> Legibus vnicolor tunc temporis aura refulsit,   5
>   Iusticie plane tuncque fuere vie.
> Nuncque latens odium vultum depingit amoris,
>   Paceque sub ficta tempus ad arma tegit;
> Instar et ex variis mutabile Cameliontis
>   Lex gerit, et regnis sunt noua iura nouis: 10
> Climata que fuerant solidissima sicque per orbem
>   Soluuntur, nec eo centra quietis habent.

[*Present fortune has forsaken the blessed past and overturns ancient ways. In former times, when a man's looks declared his thought, concord and love gave birth to peace. In those days a single-colored light shone in the laws; in those days the ways were filled with justice. But now concealed hate paints a face of love. Beneath feigned peace, a call to arms is covered. The law acts like a chameleon, fickle and varied; new kingdoms, thus new laws. Times that once were most sound are thus dissolved throughout the world, their centers not at rest.*][13]

Repeatedly Gower will utilize this trope of antiquity from his Latin epigram to impress upon his reader the need for a well-ruled man to free his mind from momentary fetishes in order to regain a more balanced mental climate. *Climata* (11), which Professor Geier translates as "times," might also be understood as an astronomical reference to the earth's climatic zones (torrid, temperate, frigid).[14] In this sense Gower suggests that the quiet center, the temperate zone, is no longer quiet; the balance, which he will later emphasize in his discussion of Aristotle's golden mean (end of Bk. v), is gone. Gower starts his discussion of kingship with the "former age" in an effort to "drawe in to my mynde / The tyme passed" (93–94). Perhaps by considering a time of good health, plenty, riches, and strength, a time when knights valued their good name and kings appreciated and honored their privilege to rule, when people stood in "obeissance under the reule of governance" (107–8), when justice and peace kissed, and charity was their companion—perhaps through such consideration we as audience can better lay hold on the discrepancy between our communal aspirations and the discordant events of present reality. Gower's discussion is a pastiche of conventional moral dicta: in antiquity hearts matched countenances, love was without envy, and "the word was lich to the conceite / Withoute semblant of deceite" (113–14). Although the passage may seem cliché, to scorn it as derivative would be to miss the point. For Gower's purpose the account must be familiar. His *liber purus* must embody the basic model of the society's aspirations.

This process of encompassing in the mind "the tyme passed" in order to regain a balanced perspective is perhaps the most fundamental proposition in the *Confessio*. Man learns from the consequences of his actions; history teaches him those consequences. The problem as Gower understands it is not that the image of the ancient ideal is faded and worn, but that it is too seldom recalled. The good king must keep it ever present in his thought. With Christ as his model he should maintain open counsel and heed the voice of the people. Gower invokes the king of kings as his model as he prays,

> Amende that wherof men pleigne
> With trewe hertes and with pleine,

> And reconcile love ayeyn,
> As he which is king sovereign
> Of al the worldes governaunce,
> And of his hyhe porveaunce
> Afferme pes betwen the londes
> And take her cause into hise hondes,
> So that the world may stonde appesed
> And his godhede also be plesed.
>
> (183–92)

A true king should be, like Christ, a man of peace. This Christian model of true governance provides the reader with a standard for judging every king and his kingdom throughout the *Confessio*. Gower elaborates the idea in Book VII where the poem concentrates exclusively on the education of the king. Then in Book VIII he dramatizes it further in the education of Apollonius. In the conclusion to the *Confessio* the kingly model becomes the standard for every man, as Amans, sobered by age, realizes his own personal sense of kingship and domain within the larger context of common profit. When the *Confessio* concludes with its prayer for England, we must understand that although we seem to have moved beyond the private concerns of the lover, we have not abandoned the theme of love. Rather we have entered into a new definition of love as Amans discovers how deeply he is involved in the welfare of his whole community.

In contrast to this peaceable image of the ideal kingdom of past time, Gower begins his assessment of present time with an image of an upside-down tree.

> Now stant the crop under the rote,
> The world is changed overal,
> And therof most in special
> That love is falle into discord.
>
> (118–21)

The kingdom once fruitful now suffers a fruitless, smothered existence. Order is reversed. The confusion is recorded by "the comun

vois, which mai noght lie" (124). Gower sees the disorder of the wayward state as primarily a crime against the common people. The voice
of common man is the voice of God. As Gower puts it in *Vox Clamantis:*
"Vox populi cum voce dei concordat."[15] That voice of common profit
must be heeded. People must act as a community to redress disturbances
caused by selfish interests.

> Althogh a man be wys himselve,
> Yit is the wisdom more of tuelve;
> And if thei stoden bothe in on,
> To hope it were thanne anon
> That god his grace wolde sende
> To make of thilke werre an ende,
> Which every day now groweth newe.
> *(157–63)*

Gower notes that in his own day, no peaceable kingdom based on wise
counsel exists to fulfill men; instead, a cancerous war thwarts all seg-
ments of society. Christ is, Gower points out, the ultimate answer to
man's dilemmas; only the Prince of Peace can restore the Garden. But
men seem so bent on selfish goals that "love is fro the world departed, /
So stant the pes unevene parted / With hem that liven now adaies"
(169–71). By love Gower here means charity (i.e., right order), not the
fruitless parody of true love by selfish men. Unfortunately, in these
days (i.e., fourteenth century) men can only pray to the keeper of all for
mankind's amendment and peace. Earthly kings and lords seem little
able to set the right example.[16]

Gower's assessment of the deficiencies of the temporal rulers leads
directly into his criticism of the church, then the commons. In excoriat-
ing the second estate's failure to recognize and remedy the problems of
men, Gower is even more severe than he had been in his attack on the
nobility. As he had done in his discussion of the first estate, he evokes a
former age, when the church in its pristine condition followed the
model of Christ. What immediately strikes one in Gower's juxtaposition of the ideal with the actual is the contrast between a strong spiritual
commitment to charitable behavior and the practical (amoral) con-

siderations of a worldly court. For the past century the church had been embroiled in a debate over the secular rights of the church. Gower places himself staunchly in opposition to the papal publicists who argued that the one earthly sovereign to whom all others owed homage was the pope.[17] Such emphasis, he felt, distracts the priesthood from its proper concern. His ideal churchman is essentially nonpolitical. He should seek wisdom rather than earthly authority. He should be studious, but the "substaunce" of his "Scole" should be the pursuit of God rather than the befooling of his wit with "erthly werkes, / Which were ayein thestat of clerkes" (199–202). The seeking of "erthly werkes" through the auspices of church office is, to Gower, a form of simony, a commitment to accidence which wastes substance by perverting holy estate to "Lumbard" values.

Gower's criticism of the church's worldliness adheres to that of John of Paris, William of Ockham, Marsilius of Padua, and John Wyclif in their attacks on the papal publicists.[18] Later in the *Confessio* he will cite the Donation of Constantine as the beginning of the downfall of the church (end of Bk. ii) and will single out Boniface viii, who brought to a crisis the controversy on papal sovereignty, as a particular villain in that his greed for power resulted in the Babylonian Captivity and ultimately the Schism (ii.2950 ff.). In the Prologue, Gower views the Schism as the principal manifestation of the present church's degradation, since it exposes so blatantly the worldly ambition of churchmen perversely redefining their holy offices to compete with earthly lords. They would levy taxes to maintain armies and incite war rather than act as counselors of peace. The two competing popes are the most sinister of all in that they not only set a powerful (in this instance, negative) example, but they also possess the authority to enact laws ("lawe positif") to advance their schemes, have power to coerce others into adhering to their schemes through jurisdiction, rights of appointment, and excommunication, and claim the right to tax and belabor the clergy whom they should be helping. Later in the Prologue, Gower will define sin as "modor of divisioun" (1030). Here, at the head of the church, where we might hope to find a stearsman of "Petres barge" who ever turns his ear to Christ and lives a life "sobre and chaste and large and wyse" (235 ff.), we find instead bitter division, the epitome of sin.

Gower uses the abortive Norwich Crusade of 1383 to illustrate the corruptive effects of the schism upon society at large. Since he deals with the crusade only by allusion and innuendo, it would perhaps be helpful to review briefly the historical details upon which his criticism rests. In March 1381 Pope Urban vi (the Roman pope) issued two bulls to Henry Despenser, Bishop of Norwich, giving him powers to grant indulgences to those who took part in or made contributions to support a crusade against the antipope Clement vii, and to dispense clerks to take the cross.[19] The privilege of the cross in effect made those so endowed direct subjects of the pope, temporarily exempting them from the justice of their lords and civil law and placing their property and person under jurisdiction of the church.[20] Since contracts and obligations between creditors and debtors were annulled when one took the cross, the appeal of such a "privilege" to the irresponsible and the resentment it might cause among the preempted can readily be understood.

Gower speaks out against crusades in several places in the *Confessio*. Perhaps his animosity stems from the Norwich Crusade, a situation which focused his hostilities toward the church charading in Caesar's robes. The political complexities of this particular campaign were extraordinarily convoluted. Charles vi of France and the duke of Burgundy had seized Bruges in November, 1382, thus effectively hampering the English wool trade.[21] Charles supported Clement vii's claim to the papacy. So did the Spanish king Juan I of Castile, with whom the English had been at war over the past several years. John of Gaunt was eager to return to Spain to support that campaign after the earl of Cambridge's expedition had ended in failure.[22] He succeeded in getting a bull (*Regimini Sacrosante*, 1382) from Urban declaring the king of Castile schismatic. Both he and Bishop Despenser thus found themselves "jockeying for advantage"[23] with Parliament to gain support for their "holy wars." The Commons favored the Norwich venture over Gaunt's on five grounds:[24] *1*] It was felt that the bishop's crusade might attract more voluntary revenues because of the great devotion of the people who would support holy church ardently in hope of salvation; *2*] the bishop's crusade would support the alliance with Flanders which was necessary for the realm and the wool trade; *3*] the campaign would relieve Gascony, which Charles was harassing, by diverting the French efforts to the north;   4] by diverting the French northward the duke of Lancaster's campaign in Spain might fare better even without his direct support. A fifth point which worked against Gaunt's project was the opposition to his leaving the country so soon after the Peasants' Revolt, for it was feared that he might be needed at home.

At first the plan seemed (by one standard, at least) a splendid success: the people lent their support. The fourteenth-century chronicler Henry Knighton, who, like Gower, was indignant about the Norwich fiasco from beginning to end, tells how churchmen collected vast sums from all manner of people—high and low, and especially from women, who fervently gave gold, silver, precious baubles, necklaces, rings, dishes, pieces of cloth, spoons, and other trinkets, on the promise of absolute remission of sins not only for themselves but for the dead. "And thus," Knighton laments, "the secret treasure of the realm which was in the hands of women is gambled away"[25] on this bishop's crusade. McKisack stresses the "extraordinary enthusiasm . . . significant of the prevailing mood of national hysteria" with which the crusade was launched.[26] Knighton tells how angels from heaven were promised to descend from the clouds to accompany the souls absolved in purgatory up into heaven.[27]

But though the fund raising, with all its pious excitatoria, more than filled the coffers, once underway the crusade was almost immediately a failure. Despenser was no military strategist; he did not even have a clear goal in mind. Was his campaign a *chevauchée* or a crusade? He wanted to reopen the wool trade, but to do so his army would be attacking Flemish towns which were loyal to Urban, though subjected to France. He sailed from Sandwich on 16 May 1383, sacked Gravelines, and captured Bourbourg, Dunkirk, Nieuport, and Dixmude. He then seems to have become confused. Some advised attacking Artois to get at the real Clementists; others favored pressing on to Bruges to save the wool trade. The count of Flanders, with whom he had now joined forces, wanted to recapture Ypres in hopes of better defense against renewed French attacks. So Despenser, without siege weapons, laid siege to Ypres. By this time Charles brought up his army, and the bishop beat a hasty retreat in disarray back across the channel. Margaret Aston notes that within five months after setting out on his glorious crusade Despenser was again before Parliament, this time facing impeachment, while the French had not only retaken all the towns he had occupied but were threatening Calais itself.[28]

Gower's concern is not with the failure of this particular campaign nor with the incompetence of its leadership. His chagrin lies in the whole operation which makes a mockery of what holy church should be, a mockery provoked by the pope himself, who behaves more like Antichrist in his power struggles than the redeemer. Gower compares the war-mongering pope with a brigand adventurer, juxtaposing him to an ideal pope of olden days who would not descend to Lombard values or the manipulation of bishoprics or the use of papal decrees for selfish ends at the expense of the people (206–11). Instead of "aventure of armes and of brygantaille" (213), simony and the manipulation of laws to "make were and strif / For worldes good" (248–49), the pope and all churchmen should set their study on Christ who "him self hath bode pes" (243). When churchmen abandon their appointed role of peacemaker and vie with kings for wealth, they are guilty of a near-sightedness which, as Gower will later explain, is the efficient cause of sin. "The heven is farr, the world is nyh" (261), they opine, as they myopically mislead the pious, playing upon their hopes and superstitions to support a foolish war. The sad result is that the prayers of the people are turned to curses (261–78). The church, which should bring men to health and common profit, seems committed to pestilence and strife.

Gower marvels at the openness with which the evil in the church manifests itself.

> And forto loken over this,
> If Ethna brenne in the clergie,
> Al openly to mannes ÿe
> At Avynoun thexperience
> Therof hath yove an evidence,
> Of that men sen hem so divided.
>
> (328–33)

But even more strange is man's inability to perceive so evident an evil or know what to do about it. While the divided papacy attacks itself over false concerns, instead of being alarmed or demanding reform, the clergy follows suit, fostering "delicacie" for its "swete toth" (325), while the needy are ignored. "Between two stoles lyth the fal" (336), says the proverb; so it is with the people under the care of these false pastors, who tear and destroy their sheep rather than salve their wounds (390 ff.).

Not only does organized ecclesiastical crime such as the Norwich Crusade deceive the people; such corruption lends support to heresies like "this newe Secte of Lollardie" (349).[29] Though Gower's position against the papacy's insistence upon earthly sovereignty shares much with Wyclif, who also deplored the worldliness of the pope and condemned the Norwich Crusade,[30] he is adamantly against the Lollard movement, which in its puritanical piety is as much at odds with the common good as the corrupt papacy. But if the papacy set a true example, perhaps this counterextreme would never have been spawned. Instead of attacking the whole hierarchy of the church, including the sacraments, as Wyclif did, Gower takes a middle way. Reform constitutes rediscovery of the old virtues. The ideal clergymen of former days led exemplary lives, committed to helping the less fortunate. They were

> chaste in word and dede,
> Whereof the poeple ensample tok;
> Her lust was al upon the bok,
> Or forto preche or forto preie,
> To wisse men the ryhte weie
> Of such as stode of trowthe unliered.
>
> (228–33)

Such book learning and preaching for the sake of common profit is not to be confused with that of the Lollards', however, who devote themselves to biblical exegesis which undermines the old religion.

> It were betre dike and delve
> And stonde upon the ryhte feith,

> Than knowe al that the bible seith
> And erre as somme clerkes do.
>
> (352-55)

But neither should learning be wasted in such debates as those in defense of papal sovereignty, which Gower sees as an idle waste of time. The issues are moot and ignore the real needs of the society. Yet men of talent, nonetheless,

> argumenten faste
> Upon the Pope and his astat,
> Wherof thei falle in gret debat;
> This clerk seith yee, that other nay,
> And thus thei dryve forth the day,
> And ech of hem himself amendeth
> Of worldes good, bot non entendeth
> To that which comun profit were.
>
> (371-77)

Either use of learning, that of the Lollards or that of the publicists, is foolish insofar as it misses the real purpose of ecclesiastical office, namely, pastoral care. True wisdom, which all priests should seek, requires a delicately balanced perspective, the best of intentions, and a humble willingness to serve.

Gower ends this section of the Prologue on a chilling note as he calls for God to pass judgment on the priesthood.[31] He seems to have little hope that the clergy will reform itself, having become so deeply mired in its pride and avarice. Like Langland, he seems doubtful that there will be any great wave of social virtue. That is all the more reason why he appeals so earnestly to individual conscience for reform. If there is to be hope for a new society it must begin there.

The fourth section of the Prologue addresses the common people.

> Vulgaris populus regali lege subactus
>   Dum iacet, vt mitis agna subibit onus.
> Si caput extollat et lex sua frena relaxet,
>   Vt sibi velle iubet, Tigridis instar habet.

Ignis, aqua dominans duo sunt pietate carentes,
Ira tamen plebis est violenta magis.

(I, 18)

[The commons, while lying subjected to the king's law, will bear
its burden like a gentle lamb. If it raises its head and if law
should loosen its bonds, then, when the people commands by
its own self will, it has the look of a tiger. Fire competing with
flood for rule knows no loyalty. But the wrath of the mob is
more violent still.]

The Peasants' Revolt left Gower with a profound respect for the power
of the mob. This is, of course, not to say that he saw the mob's rule,
though powerful, even inexorable, to be in any way admirable. He saw
rather an abomination greatly to be feared. He did not place the blame
for their rage solely on their own shoulders, however. The fault lay
largely with the foolish leaders of the state, even the king himself, who
failed to uphold the responsibilities of their offices. Gower's political
position extends to his view of man's personal governance as well. By
analogy, one's will is not entirely at fault if it rebels under abuse,
oppression, or irresponsible behavior perpetrated by one's other mental faculties. Such rebellion is almost inevitable for fallen man. It will
take the grace of the Lamb to restore peace on earth. But Gower is not
without hope. The will naturally loves God, even in its confusion. Wit
and memory, if rightly ordered, can help discover why.

In discussing the third estate here in the Prologue, Gower focuses,
therefore, on individual responsibility. Failure of state and church is no
excuse for the commons to revolt. One should not blame the world.
The confusion grows out of individual man himself. Only individual
man can shape his own destiny. Even though church and state may be
corrupt, man may at least still govern himself. As we shall see, that self is
one kingdom which only he can justify. Moreover, the larger community of men can succeed only when its individual members behave with
individual dignity. Common profit does not impinge upon personal
integrity. Rather, it is the fruit of personal fulfillment.

Gower concludes his Prologue with an account of Nebuchadnezzar's
dream about the degeneration of time. The meditation on time serves

as a broad context within which to understand how the three estates got so confused in the modern era. The problem is largely the result of man's limited perspective. In his willfulness he has mistaken his momentary needs and wants for absolute values. The epigram for this section compares the fickleness of the world to a dice game: "Sicut ymago viri variantur tempora mundi, / Statque nichil firmum preter amare deum [Like man's image, the world's seasons vary, and nothing stands firm except the love of God]" (I, 21, lines 5–6). As Gower then turns to the biblical account, he juxtaposes to the "eterne remembrance" of "the hyhe almyhti pourveance" (585–86), Nebuchadnezzar's monster of fallen time which lies stretched across the "stage" (603) of this world. Gower deemed the monster's image to be so important to his idea that he included a drawing of it looming over the sleeping persona as his frontispiece to the Fairfax 3 manuscript.[32] Moreover, he draws upon the same biblical passage in the Latin prose note appended to the end of the *Confessio,* which briefly names and describes his three major writings. There he singles out the dream on degenerate time and his discussion of kingship as main points of the *Confessio,* which he calls his *Anglico sermone,* though the principal theme, he says, has as its fundamental concern love and the mad passions of lovers ("amorem et infatuatas amantum passiones fundamentum").[33] In the larger view, mankind's history is like the fallen monster seen by Nebuchadnezzar. From the perspective of the "lasse world," the history of man's personal life is perhaps akin to the frenzied will which confesses so plaintively in Gower's poem. Either way the effect is monstrous.

Gower attributes the temporal degeneration of history to the selfish factions of men bent upon singular profit. His version of Nebuchadnezzar's dream goes far beyond the biblical account, tracing the deterioration right up to his own time. Each period surpasses the former only in its greed. The present age is represented by the crumbling feet of the monster, an age of "erth and stiel" in which

> The comun ryht hath no felawe,
> So that the governance of lawe
> Was lost.
>
> (795–97)

Even the spiritual realm has been corrupted, and venom is mingled with the earthly activities of "holy cherche" (858–59). So divided is the world that it seems set on destroying itself: "Where as the lond divided is / It mot algate fare amis" (893–94). One hears the apocalyptic voice of the "John" of *Vox Clamantis* as Gower proclaims that the decadent image will soon fall.

But a note of hope asserts itself at the end of the Prologue. In a manner typical of his structuring techniques Gower sets against the figure of degenerate time in Nebuchadnezzar's dream a contrasting image—the figure of Arion the harper, whose talents as a musician and master of form provide an antidote against time's corruption. This concluding passage thus recalls the Prologue's opening discussion of books and poetry and rounds off the overall argument of the Prologue with pleasing symmetry. The harper is a particularly resilient metaphor for Gower. In the *Mirour* he cites King David's playing the harp as one of the main signs of his being an exemplary king (22872) and elaborates for two stanzas (22897–920) on how the harper-king tunes his kingdom so that each estate is in harmony with the other, the high with the low and each with the middle, without conflict, in order that all may enjoy "la mesure" (22908). His discussion concludes:

> Rois q'ensi fait la concordance   [*The king who thus makes concorde*
> Bien porra du fine attemprance   *Is well able, through his fine tuning,*
> La harpe au bonne note trere.   *To draw forth good notes from*
>   *the harp.*]
>   (22918–20)

In the *Confessio*, Arion is such a king; with his art he redeems time and restores harmony. He is the epitome of the poet which Gower emulates in his effort to revive a sense of common good by means of his poem. With his harp Arion knew such "good mesure" that he reclaimed the peaceable kingdom. He made wild beasts tame and mild so that hind dwelt happily with lion, wolf with sheep, and hare with hound. But more important, he brought men into "good accord" so that "the comun with the lord, / And lord with the comun also, / He sette in love tuo / And putte awey malencolie" (1066–69). He made peace where hate held sway, and all for the common good of men. It is noteworthy that Gower's source for the story of Arion, Ovid's *Fasti* II.79 ff., speaks of the wild animals bedding together when soothed by his notes but makes no mention of the music's harmonious effect on man's governance. That, along with the feudal metaphor of harmonious estates, is Gower's addition to the tale. And it contains his main point. In the fallen world, common profit is an art which men must learn to value. The kingly man knows how to play well.

We see, then, that the Prologue to the *Confessio Amantis* offers a detailed statement of the need for common profit. In so doing it establishes the central theme of the poem and sets up the dimensions of the basic plot, that is, the movement from confinement and singular profit to a recognition of personal kingship and the recovery of domain. We shall meet Arion-types repeatedly in the progress of Amans' story, especially in the concluding tale of Apollonius, after which Amans himself will become a poet and sing the welfare of England.

PRÍÐE

THE LOVER'S CONFESSION is a mental journey, both a wandering and a way home. The conceptual model underlying Gower's plot is that of Boethius, whose mental itinerary in the *Consolation of Philosophy* became the basis of a whole genre of philosophic poetry in the later Middle Ages. The genre appears in poems as diverse as the Middle English *Sir Orfeo, Pearl, Piers Plowman*, Chaucer's dream visions, and Dante's *Divine Comedy*. Because of its concern with such philosophical issues as spiritual exile, faulty self-definition through misidentification of true possession (i.e., confusion of temporal goods with eternal), and the meaning and *locus* of personal, natural, and spiritual domain, the plot of the Boethian genre requires a pilgrimage of some sort. Experience and a sense of unfulfilled intent drive the viator toward adjustments in his perception of self and society, adjustments precipitated by encounters with events and consequences beyond his private scheme of reality which force redefinition of his understanding of causes and effects and a more subtle approach to perspective and personal disposition. The primary subject of such literature is the narrator's restless mind; the plot is his search for repose.

The skeletal structure of the Boethian plot normally follows four main steps:[1] *1*] There will be an opening description of the narrator's spiritual inertia and profound unhappiness. His psychological turmoil will be presented as an illness or unrest, usually in the form of a death wish of some sort. He will probably express a desire for help, but at the same time acknowledge that he does not know where to find it. *2*] The distracted narrator will perform a positive action which will precipitate a change of scene, whereupon new characters will appear who will be projections of different fragments of himself or his environment. The new setting will reflect the realm of the mind in which the quest is to take place. *3*] The argument of the poem will be conducted through dialogue between the narrator and the new characters. This is the most elastic part of the genre, and it is here and in the conclusion that the author will exercise the most originality as he chooses particular devices suitable to the intention of his poem. But regardless of the device, whether it be a descent into an underworld or a desert, a hart hunt or a walk beside a river coming from Paradise, a debate or a confession, the argument will most likely begin with questions of identity, such as "What are you?" or "What is the trouble with your soul?" It will then progress through a series of partial revelations which will be presented dramatically and will probably be reminiscent of Boethius' baring of his wound in order that Philosophy might apply the appropriate medicine. *4*] The analysis and therapy will end with a tense moment in which the disturbed persona will waver, then achieve a final revelation which will bring about his return, usually to or at least toward, home.

The *Confessio Amantis* is organized along the lines which I have outlined, though Gower will, as we shall see, exercise a great deal of ingenuity in working within them. His most radical change is the introduction and development of his complex social analogue between the state of England and the individual, a device which conjoins social criticism presented in a nonfictional mode with fiction. Often the connections are made by means of his motifs of kingship and common profit, though at times he will resort to direct commentary. Gower's persona thus must be capable of serving a double office, that of commentator and that of example. This Gower manages with remarkable alacrity and a self-conscious artistry about role playing which seems to characterize fourteenth-century English literary personae. Sometimes he uses Latin marginal glosses to remind the reader which perspective should occupy his attention. For example, opposite line 61 and following, Gower explains,

> Hic quasi in persona aliorum, quos amor alligat, fingens se auctor esse Amantem, varias eorum passiones variis huius libri distinccionibus per singula scribere proponit.[2]
> [*Here, as if in the mask of the others whom love binds, the author, pretending to be Amans, proposes to write separately of each of the various passions by means of the various divisions of his book.*]

Such glosses repeatedly clarify the distinction between authorial voice and "character," though the reader will seldom have difficulty differentiating authorial commentator from infatuated lover or in knowing when the poses are to be understood as foolish, ironic, or simply charming. But he should be aware that such shifts are allowable and likely within the limits of the poet's intention.

Gower casts his vagrant lover's itinerary in eight books, each of which is subdivided by Latin epigrams. The initial epigram of Book I defines the kind of love which the ensuing plot will explore. *Naturatus amor,* that sexual drive which makes earthly creatures wild, is typified by strife, contradiction, and the capriciousness of Fortune's Wheel. This first section of Book I forms a transition between the expository Prologue and the romance plot of the confession. In view of the epigram's straightforward assessment of natural love, Gower, returning to his English voice, carefully restricts his role as persona, delimiting the sphere of his moral responsibility more modestly than he had done in his Prologue.[3]

> I may noght strecche up to the hevene
> Min hand, ne setten al in evene
> This world, which evere is in balance:

> It stant noght in my sufficance
> So grete thinges to compasse.

(1–5)

In the *Confessio* he will not speak with the apocalyptic voice he attempted to embody in the *Vox Clamantis*. Rather, as an ordinary Englishman he will explain things which fall within his "compas." Precisely what is the reach of "min hand" or the boundary of "my sufficance?" The point is crucial to our motif of kingship and common profit. Without knowledge of the dimensions of his kingdom no man can rule himself adequately. Nor can he contribute to the larger community without such knowledge. He has neither place nor steadfastness.

The opening of Book I echoes Chaucer's poem "Truth: Balade de Bon Conseyl," where the reader is warned that the crock must not think to crush the wall or the hand to spurn an awl: "Gret reste stant in litel besinesse."[4] By "litel besinesse" Chaucer does not mean pettiness, but rather proper occupation in the "litel" world, that is, one's own microcosm or "compas," to use Gower's word. The persona of the *Confessio*, in attempting to define his own sense of suffisance, looks for just such "gret reste."

As Gower explains the operation of blind love in the world he proceeds to identify himself with it. He becomes Amans (61 ff.). What had begun as exposition evolves into dramatic monologue as the subjective persona of the poem takes shape. He says he will write to other lovers to explain point by point his circumstances in love so that "every man ensample take / Of wisdom which him is betake" (79–80). His point is not that we all become besotted like Amans, but rather that we take warning.

The second Latin epigram in Book I delimits the purview of the persona even further. Speaking in the first person, the poet, now in the role of lover, contrasts himself with Samson and Hercules in strength but, nonetheless, compares himself to them in love: he too has fallen. He then presents his role as that of a military patrol sent out by the captain who waits behind, secure from danger. So too the persona will act as a patrol for the reader. As lover he will scout the dangers which face the captain; that is, the poem (his confession) will be a patrol designed to help us as audience the better to command life's mission unscathed.

The romance plot of the *Confessio* begins as the narrator sets out walking one fresh May day.[5] But although he walks in an earthly paradise where birds sing and all seems vibrant and happy, he brings with him the "woful care," "wofull day," and "wofull chance" with which his willful desire afflicts him. He has become a solipsism. Unable to respond to the glorious creation around him (111) he throws himself prostrate on the ground, weeping and complaining to himself, ever wishing he were dead (120). Filled with self-pity, he conjures Venus and Cupid's support. Both suddenly appear before him. Cupid transfixes his "herte rote" (145) with the fiery love dart, then abandons him. Venus stays to question him further.

This opening description and event define the persona's dilemma and thus establish the main considerations of the plot. Though it seems to Amans that he is mightily under the sway of *naturatus amor,* he does not realize that he is behaving most unnaturally. His is, in truth, a monstrous crime against Nature. In his love fantasy he has overturned reason and set himself willfully apart from the mutual pleasures Nature commonly affords her creatures. He has no interest in creation around him; his singular concern is pampering his secretive emotions. Performing antics most strange to Nature's creatures, he is the epitome of alienation. The piercing of his heart by Cupid's dart clinches his loss of natural freedom. He is captive to his cupidity, and many lines will pass before he returns home from his spiritual exile. The patrol is in serious trouble; he is not even aware who the enemy is.

When Venus first addresses Amans, she asks him questions of identity: "What art thou, Sone?" (154, 160). Amans replies, "A Caitif that lith hiere: / What wolde ye, my Ladi diere?" (161–62). The question is reminiscent of Boethius' *Consolation,* where Philosophy asked, "What are you" of that distraught narrator. The right answer is, of course, "A man." But in his infatuation Amans has forgotten what a man should be. He asks to be cured of his affliction, but Venus says,

> Tell thi maladie:
> What is thi Sor of which thou pleignest?
> Ne hyd it noght, for if thou feignest,
> I can do the no medicine.
>
> (164–67)

Again her request reminds us of Philosophy's request that Boethius bare his wound by reiterating his illness. But Venus is no Lady Philosophy. Her intention is quite the opposite, her demands a parody of Philosophy's. Her motives are defensive and courtly, based on suspicion rather than mutuality. She has learned how to deal with "faitours." In her world nobody trusts anybody. Let Amans explain his intentions.

In a telling aside Amans lets us know that he is aware of her pretentiousness:

> And natheles sche wiste wel,
> Mi world stod on an other whiel
> Withouten eny faiterie.
>
> (177–79)

She knows well enough that he is no "faitour," but he remains obedient to her nonetheless. Perhaps the point is that Amans uses his reason as it pleases him. Though Reason is sufficiently present for him not to be fooled by Venus, he is sufficiently besotted by his own desire to fool himself. He goes along with her game because he wants to. He is a "faitour" only insofar as he deceives himself.

To develop the argument of his poem Gower uses the device of confession. It is a felicitous choice, as C. S. Lewis has observed,[6] because of the possibilities for variety and dramatic effects which it offers. But Gower did not choose the device for literary reasons alone. The idea of relating confession to Boethian psychology was not new to him; he had explored the idea as early as the *Mirour de l'Omme*. Confession, as he understood it, is a kind of psychoanalysis. It begins with a review of experience in an effort to find out why it is that one is the way he is, in order that he may ultimately reintegrate his mind and emotions. "You have forgotten what you are," Philosophy tells Boethius after he has confessed his troubles. Amans' problem is precisely the same. He is guilty of faulty self-definition. Having lost his natural orientation he is not only far from his heart's desire, but even uncertain of what that desire is. In the *Mirour* Gower introduced the subject of Boethian confession in his discussion of *Science,* the antidote for that form of *Accidie* called *Negligence* (14593–15096). *Science* is the art whereby man's Reason protects his soul from "oblivioun" (14691). It enables him to cope with forgetfulness caused by neglect and free himself from the captivity of illusions (cf. 14689–700). It enables him to use Memory effectively as defense against the confusing fragmentation of time. According to *Science,*

Du Reson est remembrançour,	[*It is to be remembered of Reason*
Que tout remeine en sa presence;	*That all remains in her presence;*
Du temps passé est recordour,	*She is recorder of time past*
Et le present voit tout entour,	*And she sees the present all around,*
Et le futur pourvoit et pense.	*And foresees and contemplates the*
	future.]

(14600–604)

When man becomes confused, confession becomes his means to open his confusions to the light of reason. Gower explains that "uns clercs Boece en sa leçoun" provides "la fourme de confessioun" (14833–34), which must be undertaken with the thoroughness of the priest's *quis, quid, ubi, perquos, quotiens, quomodo,* and *quando.*

Confessioun doit estre entiere,	[*Confession must be complete*
Qe riens y doit lesser derere:	*So that nothing be allowed to re-*
Pour ce l'escript du conscience	*main behind:*
Om doit parlire en tieu man-	*For the writing of conscience,*
iere,	*Man ought to speak in such a man-*
Sique l'acompte en soit plenere.	*ner*
Ce dist Boëce en sa science:	*That the account be made in full.*
"Cil q'est naufrez et garir pense,	*Thus says Boethius in his science:*

Devant le mire en sa presence,   *"If one is wounded and thinks to be*
Sicomme la plaie est large et   *healed,*
  fiere   *he must, without delay, in the physi-*
Descoverir doit sanz necli-   *cian's*
  gence;   *presence reveal how wide and severe*
Lors puet garir."   *the wound is. Then he may be*
                                                     healed."]

                                                                    (14893–903)

Gower goes on to note that no "emplastres" can heal the wound except "Contricioun . . . que toute en plour s'est remembree de ses pecches" (14911–13). Simply telling is no cure. The heart must become contrite, remembering each detail in tears.

In the *Confessio,* the forgetful Amans will have to search diligently his soul and speak out. Venus sends him to a confessor named Genius, who will become his attendant spirit. To Genius he appeals,

> I prai the let me noght mistime
> Mi schrifte, for I am destourbed
> In al myn herte, and so contourbed,
> That I ne may my wittes gete,
> So schal I moche thing foryete:
> Bot if thou wolt my schrifte oppose
> Fro point to point, thanne I suppose,
> Ther schal nothing be left behinde.
> Bot now my wittes ben so blinde,
> That I ne can miselven teche.
>
> (220–29)

There is a show of reasonableness in his request. He knows that in his cupidity his wits have been blinded, and he knows that in his "contourbed" witlessness (222) he is likely to be forgetful of what he should be remembering. Moreover, his intention is good, and that is no small matter. The confession will be thorough. Indeed, by the end of the poem there will be nothing left behind: Genius, "with his wordes debonaire" (231), will search out the circumstances of Amans' soul and through his questions redefine man in his natural and historical environments so that Amans may remember what he is and forget what he is not.

Appreciation of what goes on in the reeducation of a lover requires some background information on the confessor himself. Gower develops his character Genius from two well-known medieval counterparts, one in Alanus de Insulis' *De Planctu Naturae* and the other in Jean de Meun's *Roman de la Rose.* In these two antecedents Genius represents a combination of natural reason, ingenuity (what we would call "creativity"), and procreativity. He is subservient to Nature, and Nature, being vicar of God, is essentially good. That she is subject to time and mortality is not her fault, but rather man's, who, in sinning, acted "unnaturally." Genius looks after Nature's mortal creatures; he is pleased when each finds satisfaction proper to its created purpose, for then he himself, as creaturely inner nature, is properly satisfied as well. In some ways Genius is akin to Langland's "kynde knowing," that God-given faculty of man's higher nature which is so crucial to Will's search for his salvation in *Piers Plowman.* In Gower, Genius' primary means for judging behavior is to decide whether an act is natural or "unkynde." He is a felicitious choice for Gower's theme of man's crimes against Nature. It is to Genius that Amans must turn for penance, since in his idleness "genius" is what has been lost. Genius, with his "lust and lore," will help Amans to re-create a balanced view of himself and his surroundings.

Gower presents Genius as Venus' priest, but this does not make him necessarily subservient to her or entirely sympathetic with her motives. That relationship will depend upon who Venus is, or rather, upon how she is understood.[7] When she is exposed as Cupid's lascivious mother-lover he will scorn her; when she is understood to be man's natural longing for higher good he will honor her, that is, if he is serving his own office properly. Genius is not himself always farsighted, but he has a remarkably detailed understanding of Memory, Wit, and Will, and he values them highly as man's natural faculties. In Alanus, Venus helps Genius to fulfill his office of replenishing Nature (that is, the sexual urge for singular pleasure which Venus represents does help Nature reproduce her kind, even if only blindly). So too Gower's Genius enjoys assistance from Venus and the god of love. But he objects scornfully, as he did in the *Roman de la Rose,* to their selfish demands which turn natural love into unnatural fantasies or mutually exclusive, promiscuous, and unfruitful games. From the beginning of the poem it is clear that his interests are greater than those of the promiscuous Venus and that he will speak of more things than love, at least love as cupidinous Amans has come to define the term. In order to help Amans see beyond his infatuation, Genius will, as the poem progresses, ultimately instruct Amans in all the humanities.

Genius might perhaps be compared to that mental faculty which the Chartrian philosophers called *ingenium,* a faculty of perception neither wholly good nor wholly bad which is, according to John of Salisbury, "not only competent to comprehend the Arts, but may discover a straight and unhindered path to things which are, so to speak, naturally inaccessible."[8] Winthrop Wetherbee, summarizing the Chartrian view, suggests that *ingenium* "is a vital link in human consciousness, uniting the highest and the basest capacities of will and curiosity. It is closely related to imagination, the power of mind by which things absent are perceived, and thus to 'fantasies' of all sorts, from the wildest dream to the highest state of vision."[9] Gower's Genius certainly does have ambiguous qualities which, for good or ill, relate to the personal growth of Amans. Perhaps his most positive qualities are his desire to educate and his own educability. Although Genius' understanding of higher love is limited, he can appreciate it as history and experience have revealed it, just as Jean de Meun's Genius appreciates without fully understanding the *beau parc* of the good shepherd with its *fontaine de vie* toward the end of the *Roman de la Rose.* Most certainly he can see from his natural vantage point that the love of Cupid is inconstant and that that of Venus usually ends in mockery.

In short, we should understand Amans' confession to Genius as a reappraisal of his personal orientation within the confines of Nature. As such it involves a twofold process, both a turning outside himself to discover objectively man's use and misuse of his creative energies throughout history and a turning within himself to rediscover his own neglected creative ability. Genius is keeper of the past as well as the present. This feature of his office explains both his method of consoling Amans with examples from the past and his encouragement of Amans to be a good lover now. As keeper of the past he helps Amans sort out the entanglements of mankind's history so that Amans may be freed from his own confusion. To do this Genius questions, illustrates, and compares events of antiquity with events in Amans' personal life. His illustrations are not simply moral examples. They are the stories of mankind—the wisdom and error of the past since its beginning. Even as important as any inherent meaning they may hold is the reciprocal process of understanding which they provoke in their audience. Presented simply, essentially without commentary or explanation, they stand before Amans for the sake of "remembrance."

The tales, historical exempla, and wise sayings with which Genius catechizes Amans are organized according to the seven deadly sins. Use of so well established a traditional structure as the ranking of the vices imposes somewhat rigidly an external order on the *Confessio;* yet that very rigidity makes possible a looseness of application and byplay within the system which would not be possible if the system were not there. Genius can wander without getting lost, taking time out to discuss war, religion, or the history of labor without fear of his audience's losing its place in the overall format of his exorcism. In view of Gower's observations on Sin in the Prologue and his goal of assisting the people of England in their reconstitution of a healthy, undivided kingdom, the device fits well the intent. That it is an encyclopedic venture is necessary to the intent. That the pattern is well known suits the occasion well, for Genius speaks to benefit the whole community.

Gower had discussed the seven deadly sins in the *Mirour de l'Omme.* There he had given a genealogy of Sin *(Pecché),* her seven children incestuously conceived by Death *(Mort,* her son), and her thirty-five grandchildren, spawned as each of the seven begets five daughters through marriage to *Siécle* (time). For each of the seven and each of their five, Gower prescribes a remedy. The scheme may be outlined as follows:

SIN	REMEDY
I. Dame Orguil	Humilité
1. Ipocresie	Devocioun
2. Vaine gloire	Paour (fear)
3. Surquiderie (Presumpcioun)	Discrecioun
4. Avantance	Vergoigne (modesty)
5. Inobedience	Obedience
II. Dame Envye	Charité
1. Detraccioun	Loenge (praise)
2. Dolour d'autry Joye	Conjoye
3. Joye d'autry Mal	Compassion
4. Supplantacioun	Support
5. Fals Semblant	Bonne Entencioun
III. Ire	Patience
1. Malencolie	Modeste
2. Tencoun (Estrif et Contencioun)	Debonaireté
3. Hange (Haÿne: hatred)	Dileccioun
4. Contek	Concorde
5. Homicide	Pités
IV. Accidie (Sloth)	Prouesce
1. Sompnolence	Vigile
2. Peresce (laziness or cowardice)	Magnanimité
3. Lachesce (procrastination)	Constance
4. Oedivesce (idleness)	Sollicitude
5. Negligence	Science
V. Dame Avarice	Franchise
1. Covoitise	Justice
2. Ravyne	Almosne (almsgiving)
3. Usure	Liberalité
4. Simonie	Saint pourpos
5. Escharceté (niggardliness)	Largesce

VI.   Gloutenie (Gule)   Mesure
   1. Ingluvies (voracity)   Diete
   2. Delicacie   Abstinence
   3. Yveresce (drunkenness)   Sobreté
   4. Superfluité   Norreture (nourishment)
   5. Prodigalité   Moderacioun

VII. Leccherie (Luxure)   Chastité
   1. Fornicacioun   Bonnegarde
   2. Stupre (rape)   Virginité
   3. Avolterie   Matrimoine
   4. Incest   Continence
   5. Foldelit   Aspre (hard life)

(It should be noted that in discussing the daughters of the sins, Gower includes an entourage of attendants for each. The remedies are supplied by Resoun and Conscience after Resoun marries the Seven Virtues.)

Gower adheres strictly to the *Mirour*'s system of classification only in the first three books of the *Confessio*. But although the second half of his English poem abandons the fivefold division of sin as a structural device, the *Mirour*'s categories of both sins and remedies inform Gower's vocabulary and conceptualization of sin in the latter part of the *Confessio* as well.

Yet even when Genius is following the *Mirour*'s scheme meticulously, he does so with flexibility. The scheme helps him to define human behavior without confining his artistry. If he wishes to explain some "novellerie" (v.3955) which has no obvious connection with the exemplary point of his tale, he feels free to do so. Usually the confession moves through clusters of tales each of which will be assigned to subdivisions of a deadly sin but all of which will pertain to other subdivisions as well. In fact, sometimes tales assigned to a particular subdivision will exemplify the qualities of another vice better than the assigned tale does. For example, in Book v, the story of Jason's jilting of Medea exemplifies "Perjury"; Theseus' mistreatment of Ariadne exemplifies "Ingratitude." That Jason's story might just as well have demonstrated the evils of ingratitude does not bother Genius. Nor does it need to. One finds as he progresses through clusters of tales that they regularly enhance each other in this way. Their success as moral exempla is left to the reader's judgment. He is required to put his "remembrance" to work to see how tales and categories apply each to the other.

Within the confessional framework Gower uses various devices for introducing the tales. Sometimes an example will be offered to inform the ignorant Amans. Others will be offered as a corrective to his wayward behavior. Amans' puzzlement over his guilt or innocence adds subtlety and depth to his character. Sometimes he will think he is guiltless, all the while demonstrating a naïve blindness to the true character of the sin involved. For example, his predilection for his lady always qualifies his responses in amusing ways. The interplay of responses to the sins and their exempla enable Gower to develop Genius as a character as well. Often the confessor's predilections crop up as he expresses enthusiasm or disgust for an idea. Sometimes he will tell a story without even asking Amans about its pertinence to the lover's situation—he is just that eager to get on with it.

Genius begins the shrift by exorcising Amans' eyes and ears. If functioning properly, these windows of the mind help coordinate the little world with the greater so that a healthy response is possible. Amans' bizarre behavior in the wood has certainly demonstrated that he is not perceiving truly. So infatuated is he with his "lady" that he sees and hears only what he wants. Amans must become a more discerning critic before he can regain the balanced behavior which should characterize a man. Right use of eyes and ears demands the engagement of memory and reason as well as will. Many a man has fallen to grief as the result of "mislok," the seeing of what he should not see or of ignoring what he should meditate upon. The exempla Genius offers establish a motif of seeing and hearing. Repeatedly the tales will present men who, trapped by cupidity through misuse of their wits, struggle to learn again to see objectively through a more balanced perspective.

Genius tells two tales on looking and two on hearing. He explains that he will begin by exorcising the "yhe" because it is the wit "most principal of alle" (307).[10] After explaining how often people look to possess what does not belong to them, thus destroying themselves through false attachments and misidentifications, he compares mislooking to being wounded by Cupid's dart which enters the eye of the unwary and pierces the heart. Already then, Genius' comparison defines cupidity as sin. His first example of one who looks upon that which "ne toucheth" (313) him is Acteon. Having mislocated his proper purview by gazing lecherously on the chaste Diana, Acteon commits himself to an impropriety which transforms him into a beast. Though this Ovidian tale is well known, like most of Gower's stories, it is subtly altered from its source to suit Gower's particular point. For example, Gower omits Ovid's references to Acteon's hunting companions, concentrating exclusively on Acteon himself. He also omits the account of Diana's disrobing, the efforts of her attendant nymphs to hide her from the eyes of the intruder, their throwing of water on Acteon, the catalog of hounds, Acteon's efforts to speak, and the debate of the gods on the justice of Diana's revenge when Acteon is turned into a hart to be devoured by his own hounds. He emphasizes, on the other hand, Acteon's pride. (Pride will be the first of the seven sins discussed.) Ovid blames Acteon's tragedy on Fortune. Genius places the blame squarely on Acteon himself who might, had he wished to do so, have turned away his eyes. Instead "he his yhe awey ne swerveth" (366). Acteon incurs Diana's wrath for his unchaste act and is "forschop" (370). It is noteworthy that Gower also adds a conventional romance description of Acteon's entrance into the forest. The situation recalls Amans' own venture into the *hortus deliciarum* out of which he is unable to proceed once he is trapped by Cupid's dart. Acteon's punishment for his mislook is a transformation and death. Amans suffers a comparable transformation as he is changed from a rational man into a weeping "caitif" wishing death. Thanks to Genius' good instruction, he ultimately gets out of the wood. But only after Cupid's dart is removed.

The *Tale of Perseus and Medusa* underscores the same points made in the *Tale of Acteon,* this time by offering a positive rather than negative example. It too is a tale of transformation, as those who misuse their eyes by gazing upon the beautiful-horrible Medusa are turned to stone. Perseus is opposite to Acteon; he guards his eyes well. As in the other Ovidian tale, Gower again alters his source to stress Perseus' personal responsibility. Ovid explains that Perseus located Medusa by means of her reflection on his shield and that he slew her while she was sleeping. Gower omits the details of the reflection and Medusa's slumber. It is not her negligence but Perseus' diligence which concerns him. His Perseus is protected by "wisdom and prouesse" (429). He "covereth sauf his face" (432) with the "Schield of Pallas." That is to say, instead of his wayward eye controlling what he thinks, his wisdom guards his looking so that he maintains his manliness, and, rather than being monstrously transformed into stone, he destroys the monster. He slays, in fact, not only Medusa but her sisters Stellibon and Suriale as well, all with the sword of Mercury. Ovid makes no mention of the Psychopomp's sword, nor does he mention any sisters.[11] The sword as Gower uses it reminds us that the man who abides by wisdom acts with divine authority at his side. Gower adds the sisters to facilitate combining the story of the Gorgons with that of the Graeae. This combination is indeed a stroke of genius. His Medusa and her two sisters share only a single eye which they have to take turns using. But rather than suggesting common profit, the shared eye suggests greedy competition, thus accentuating the monsters' perverse, limited vision which contrasts with the breadth of wise Perseus' insight.

Amans gets the point of these beginning examples easily enough. When Genius asks him if he has his "yhen oght misthrowe" (549), he admits that he has. His lady is his Medusa. So attracted has he been to her that his heart has been turned to stone with "a priente of love grave" thereupon (555). Genius had also told him of Ulysses' guarding his ears against the Sirens, and here too Amans admits carelessness. He did not do as Ulysses did, but rather the voice of his lady has so befuddled him that his wit has "lost his Stiere" (560) and "I am topulled in my thoght" so that his "reson" is unable to show him how "I me mai defende" (565–67). Amans shows some signs of reasonableness by recognizing a likeness between his lady and Medusa and between himself and her victims. But there is a wide gap between recognizing that one is "astonied" and knowing what to do about it. Amans is very much in the clutches of willful fantasy, and though Genius will teach him much wisdom with which he might shield himself, it is a long journey to recovery once Cupid's arrow has already struck. But honest recognition that it has struck is a first step. So Genius begins his shrift in earnest, pacing Amans through the categories of sin to help his reason discover again its rightful place in Amans' personal governance.

Genius starts the confession with Pride and its five ministers, the first of which is Hypocrisy. Defined as "feigned conscience," Hypocrisy is a form of double-dealing whereby one takes advantage of his neighbor by deceiving him. It is thus a cardinal crime against community and to Gower's way of thinking one of the most fundamental ills of his time. The example Genius chooses is skillfully composed and merits careful attention.

The *Tale of Mundus and Paulina* illustrates superbly not only the threat to common profit posed by hypocrisy but also the ability of a healthy community to repair itself despite the threat. Paulina is the wife of a worthy Roman. She is also the fairest woman to man's sight in the city. Duke Mundus does not guard his eyes well. He falls in love with her and tries to win his suit, but to no avail. She is a chaste woman. So he bribes two priests of Isis, "godesse of childinge," who help him deceive the good woman. The priests call Paulina to the temple and tell her that the god Anubus has chosen her as his bride. After consulting her husband, who agrees that they must trust their priests and gods, Paulina goes obediently to the temple where Mundus, disguised as Anubus, seduces her. Next day, as Paulina returns home, Mundus meets her in the street and taunts her, claiming he was Anubus' "lieutenant." Chagrined at her gullibility and his hypocrisy, Paulina goes to her husband. They consult with their friends, then take the matter to the king. He passes judgment: the priests are executed, the temple cleansed, and Mundus banished.

What is of interest in this tale is not simply Mundus' hypocrisy or the final judgment. Mundus, as his name implies, behaves predictably enough. We might hope that *Mundus,* as a highly respected duke, would be *pure* (cf. *mundus,* the adjectival form of Latin *mundare,* to purify). But instead he behaves hypocritically like *mundus,* the world; he operates under the guise of purity to deceive the innocent.[12] Of greater interest, however, is the behavior of Paulina. Apart from her gullibility, she is a model wife in all her relationships. In her obedience to her husband she defines the strength of the community and the virtue of common profit. Though she is threatened by the episode, she is in no way hurt.

But what of her gullibility when the priests approach her with their fantastic scheme? To what extent is she guilty in the crime? The answer is "not at all." In some ways, her naïveté is even a virtue. A true community depends upon trust. She is completely obedient in her trust to the god who defines her primary marriage. In that obedience she trusts the god's agents, the priests. Their proposal is admittedly fantastic, and she perhaps lets her fantasy reach too high, at least so she feels after experience with the world has chastened her. But we must keep in mind that she is a pagan in a tradition where the gods frequently consort with men. Nor can Christians themselves be too scornful on this point.[13] Thus, when the priests make the request we are told,

> Glad was hire innocence tho
> Of suche wordes as sche herde,
> With humble chiere and thus answerde,
> And seide that the goddes wille
> Sche was al redy to fulfille.
>
> (852–56)

Recall that in the *Mirour de l'Omme* the antidote to *Ypocrisie* is *Devocioun.* There Gower cited King David as his authority, who said,

Soiez soubgit	*Be subject*
Au dieu sanz point delacioun,	*To God without hesitation,*
Si fai ta supplication.	*And make your supplication.*
	(10239–41)

The passage referred to is Psalm 36.7, which in the Vulgate reads "Subditus esto Domino, et ora eum." The "sanz point delacioun" is Gower's addition and is indeed the point to be considered. Paulina, "al redy" in her devotion, acts devoutly and without delay. Before condemning her gullibility, think of the consequences to a society if its members distrust its spiritual leaders. In a true society, as Gower's friend Chaucer reminds us, "mannes word was obligacioun."[14] The truth of man's word is no guarantee that it will always be understood correctly, however; thus one should seek good counsel to confirm one's interpretation, which is precisely what the prudent Paulina does. Notice that Paulina does not rush hastily into the priest's chamber saying "al redy." Rather she goes "to hire sovereign" (862), her husband, and tells him of the request. Her action is not a challenging of the priest's word, but rather an act of obedience within the framework of proper allegiances. Like a good husband he hears the case and judges according to what seems to be God's will. She then follows her husband's guidance. Though on the surface of things they are both being deceived, in fact they are confirming right order and the very strength of their community. In doing so they place themselves beyond deceit's harm. Their human marriage is strengthened as they both show obedience to their divine marriage. There will, in truth, be no cuckolding here, despite Mundus' hypocrisy.

As Paulina goes to church the priests play upon her naïveté, acting as if they were really in the presence of a goddess. As she devoutly asks for their guidance she perhaps seems again to be foolish. But that reflects only our jaundiced perspective of the world. It is the priests and Mundus who are the fools. The more they play upon her innocence, the more they commit themselves to fraud and isolate themselves from the community and their own office.

After the crime is committed the true community, which is beyond worldly deceits, repairs itself. On first learning of the deception, Paulina does not become frantic. Rather, she "bar it stille" (952) and returns home to her chamber to think it over. Naturally enough she weeps and cries out against "derke ypocrisie," but she does not try to commit suicide or lament forever as other literary heroines usually do in similar situations. Contrast her response, for example, with that of Lucrece, whose moral predicament St. Augustine so skillfully analyzed in *City of God*.[15] Though Lucrece was coerced, Augustine explains, she was a guiltless and chaste woman, at least until she committed suicide. Then she fell into sin indeed, for she murdered an innocent person. Augustine suggests that Lucrece's death reflects false pride and a distrust that her community would speculate pruriently about the rape. Fear of public opinion and lascivious glances mattered more than true virtue. But Paulina contemplates no such dark crimes against herself. Neither does she fear for her reputation. She knows and can trust her community.

An even better contrast with Paulina may be seen in Dorigen, the heroine of Chaucer's *Franklin's Tale*. Dorigen, upon threat of infidelity, weeps and wails and complains for two days, contemplating suicide. When her husband finally finds out, he threatens to kill her if she lets anyone else know. Paulina, on the other hand, though embarrassingly offended, seeks her husband's advice. We can now appreciate her going to him in the first place, for he has been as much offended as she. His response is very different from that of Arveragus. Instead of trying to hide the situation and act as if it did not exist, they face it rationally together. Paulina's husband's first concern is to reassure Paulina; that is the immediate need. It is also an action which reconfirms their marriage, making clear that it has in no way been tainted. He observes that she acted in ignorance but with good intent. There has been no infidelity nor cuckoldry. If anything, the event has strengthened their personal marriage. Next the husband calls his friends who come to advise him on what next to do. They agree that first the wife should be set "in reste" and that the matter should go to the king. They cheer poor Paulina "til that sche was somdiel amended" (1003), then on the third day they seek higher judgment. In behaving this way, they confirm and strengthen all communal relationships—the married couple to the society, and the society to the king. The voice of the people in this instance does indeed arrive at truth through mutual effort.

The priests, when confronted by the king, try to wiggle out. They place the blame on Mundus. But the wise king will have none of that logic. If anyone should know the harm of passing off guilt onto others it should be the priestly confessors. To fail to accept one's responsibilities is to lose one's domain; irresponsible behavior denies the validity of the community to which they were theoretically committed. The priests' offense is doubly great, the king says, for "thei ben tuo, / And tuo han more wit then on" (1020–21). Moreover, they abused not only Paulina and themselves as members of the community, but they abused their office as well. Paulina and her husband, on the other hand, found counsel in each other and in the community. They upheld their offices of husband, wife, and citizen. They should have had true counsel from the priests as well. So should Mundus. When he went to the priests they should have advised him against his crime. Instead their only counsel was complicity in betrayal. They are executed, for theirs has been the greatest crime. They were the most to have been trusted and were thus the greatest hypocrites.[16]

The priorities of common profit permeate the conclusion of the tale. After the avaricious priests are disposed of, the next act is to cleanse the temple so that the people's place of worship might be restored and the three estates function properly. Then the king turns to Mundus whose love sickness was the occasion for the disturbance. Because of man's frailty in love, the Duke is acquitted of the death penalty, but he is exiled. He may not remain a part of the community because he cannot be trusted. (Cf. Amans' fate as he lies exiled in the woods.) Genius observes at the end of the story that men should not believe all they hear, but his moral points more to the shame of society's fallen institutions than to Paulina's credulity. In such a world where there is no trust, we must learn to steer most carefully.

Gower follows the *Tale of Mundus and Paulina* with an account of the Trojan horse, another example of hypocrisy, one in which hypocrisy this time destroys the city. Genius' normal procedure is to give two examples, sometimes more, for each vice he explicates. But since the motif of kingship and common profit is more prominent in some tales than others, I shall concentrate on those which seem to me to enlarge the motif in significant ways. Let us move next to the *Tale of Florent*, a tale told to exemplify the rewards of obedience over such forms of Pride as Murmur, Complaint, and Inobedience.

Like the *Tale of Mundus and Paulina*, the *Tale of Florent* is a simple story simply told. The crux of the former tale centered upon Paulina's trust in the priests' word and her belief that man's word was "obligacioun." Gower continues to explore the idea in the *Tale of Florent*. Florent's truth to his word holds the key to his tale. And as in the *Tale of Mundus and Paulina,* such trust becomes the foundation of a stable community. The *Tale of Florent* is Gower's best-known story because of its analogue in Chaucer's *Wife of Bath's Tale,* with which it is usually unfavorably compared. The effect of Gower's poem is indeed different from the skillfully elaborated story in Chaucer, though it is not, therefore, necessarily inferior. Genius' reason for telling the story shares nothing in common with the rationale of Alisoun. In Gower's poem, Florent, nephew to the emperor, goes out to seek his fortune. By accident, he slays Branchus, son of the captain of a neighboring march. The captain and his wife vow vengeance but fear Florent's uncle, who is more powerful than they. Then Branchus' ancient "grantdame" proposes a solution. Mindful of Florent's integrity, she will get him to agree to answer a question he cannot answer, with the penalty agreed upon being the forfeiture of his life. Certain that there is no chance of Florent's finding the answer, the wicked old lady figures her plan must succeed. Florent's execution cannot be avenged, for it will have taken place with Florent's full consent, and consent precludes reprisal. For the old lady, who is the embodiment of Murmur and Complaint, the plot is strictly a matter of revenge. But the plan will backfire. Instead of her destroying Florent by his integrity, his integrity will establish a new community.

The question? "What is it that women most desire?" Florent, to whom word is obligation, would rather "dye / Than breke his trowthe and forto lye / In place ther as he was swore" (1511–13). After a year of searching unsuccessfully to find the answer to the perplexing question, Florent prepares to meet his doom; it would seem that he has failed. He reminds his friends of the details of his covenant and asks them not to interfere. The ordeal is his own; he has given his word. The old grandame's scheme might have worked, except for another old hag even more loathsome than herself whom Florent meets in the woods while returning to keep his word. Like the first hag, the second too would win Florent's life by his own consent. She also makes her plan hinge upon Florent's integrity. Her intent is opposite to the grandame's, however. Instead of wanting Florent's life in order to slay it, the old hag would have it in order to redeem her own and his too. She works for mutual gain so that both might enjoy their proper heritage. Unlike the grandame, who hypocritically "feigneth compaignie," the old hag lets her ugliness all hang out. Florent will have to take her just as she is, without any reassuring illusions.

Gower's treatment of the encounter with the loathly hag differs markedly from the Wife of Bath's. The contrast helps point up Gower's purpose. Gower emphasizes Florent's reluctance to become involved with the woman. She tells Florent outright what the price of the information will be—marriage. (The Wife of Bath's hag hides her intent until after the knight speaks at court.) Florent offers land, rents, and parks, instead of marriage, knowing that to the true man such possessions are really nothing. The Wife of Bath's surrogate hag would have been sorely tempted by such offers. But Florent's hag wants his "trouthe," nothing less. She knows that Truth is the foundation of a free estate (which is what she seeks), not land. Unlike the Wife of Bath's hag, who trails her prey right into Arthur's court in order to trap him, Gower's loathly woman remains in the woods. Florent proceeds to the scene of judgment alone. The hag knows she can count on his return, for she has his word. If he were not to return, he would be of no use to her anyway. He would be an oathbreaker, with whom no true community is possible. Poor Florent. Having escaped the "olde Mone," he gets the "foule grete Coise." Yet he obediently returns to the spot where he left her. How different this romance world, with its golden idealism, from our own. Like *Mundus and Paulina,* the *Tale of Florent* exemplifies an innocence which Gower found to be profoundly lacking in real society.

Gower skillfully saves his description of the old "vecke" until Florent's return to claim her. When we see what he sees, we laugh. We are not the ones to marry her! She was the loathliest hag man ever cast his eye upon.

Hire Nase bass, hire browes hyhe,
Hire yhen smale and depe set,
Hire chekes ben with teres wet,
And rivelen as an emty skyn
Hangende doun unto the chin,
Hire Lippes schrunken ben for age,
Ther was no grace in the visage,
Hir front was nargh, hir lockes hore,
Sche loketh forth as doth a More,
Hire Necke is schort, hir schuldres courbe,
That myhte a mannes lust destourbe,
Hire body gret and nothing smal,
And schortly to descrive hire al,
Sche hath no lith withoute a lak;
Bot lich unto the wollesak
Sche proferth hire unto this knyht.

                                   (1678–93)

(Needless to say, the Wife of Bath omits so unflattering a description from her tale.) Such a sight does indeed curb the young man's lust. This will be no willful marriage provoked by sweet fantasy. Florent takes the bitter with the sweet. After all, he gave his word. One might wonder why Florent is not more generous with the hag, the way Gawain is with Ragnell in *Sir Gawain and Dame Ragnell*. There are several reasons. Florent's commitment is a strictly private one; Gawain's is a public matter, an act of chivalry on behalf of his lord Arthur. In Gower, there is never any question but what Florent will fulfill his word. It would be unnatural, however, for him not to find her revolting. She appears to be very ugly. Gower has fun describing Florent's reluctance. There was nothing in the agreement that said he had to be enthusiastic. He travels as an owl by night, and would have a most secret wedding, if possible, then hide her away on some island until she dies.

But the old hag has other ideas. She holds Florent to the letter of their bargain. Gower delightfully juxtaposes her gleefulness with Florent's glumness (1764–66) as she drags poor Florent off to bed. He

knows that this bed business is part of the marriage bargain, so, duti-
fully obedient, he turns to the task. This turning is the climax to his
trials. He has been true to his word down to the last detail. Thus Truth
breaks enchantment, and he sees the woman as she truly is, a glorious
eighteen-year-old girl. Now his body, which had been so reluctant at
first, is put to the test it missed during the engagement: though Florent
demonstrated that his discipline was strong enough to cope with ugliness, can it show restraint in the face of naked beauty? The girl poses
her final question: Will Florent have her beautiful by night or by day?
Unable to decide he leaves the choice to her. After all, it is her beauty
that is in question. Florent's allowing her her rights of sovereignty over
her own domain enables her to pass permanently from beneath the
curse of her stepmother. The former princess is restored, and a marriage based on trust is achieved. So, of course, they live happily ever
after.

Gower's conclusion differs significantly from the conclusion of the
Wife of Bath not only in the antithetical treatment of the enchantment
motif but also in the introduction of the woman's lineage and the
reclaiming of sovereignty. The addition gives us a dramatic statement
of the rejuvenescence of kingship despite the machinations of evil
people. Obedience to truth redefines the community which seemed
threatened by hatred. The hateful Sicilian stepmother, like Branchus'
old grandame, thought to shape destruction of virtue; but in the end,
both only show how misshapen they themselves are in their evil. Stead-
fast obedience and trust, on the other hand, restore a beauty "that
nevere hierafter schal be lassed" (1836). Only then, Gower seems to say,
as Florent and the princess meet on even terms, is the mutual respect of
true community possible.

The *Trump of Death* (2021–2257) is the next extended tale to explore
the motif of common profit. The *Tale of Florent* dealt with the motif in
terms of personal integrity; this next tale works on more broad terms,
exploring the threefold interrelationship of one's personal community
with the community of mankind, the community of nature, and the
community of God. Gower introduces this wide range of topics by
means of a Mayday "pilgrimage" out of the city into the bosom of

spring. On the way, an event transpires which challenges the very meaning of the pilgrim-king's civilization. The event exposes and breaks down social artificialities which sometimes get in the way of true brotherhood. The meaning of the event is explained after the company returns to its city and contemplates the next day what happened. It is in their reflection that they put the various senses of community coherently together.

The tale begins with the king of Hungary leading his whole city out into the meadows to go a-maying. On the way he meets two decrepit pilgrims, sun-dried and wrinkled by age and weather. The king stops his procession, bows before the ancient pilgrims, kisses their hands and feet, and gives them gifts. Certain members of his courtly entourage are embarrassed by this show of brotherhood, however, especially the king's blood brother, who feels the king has been indiscreet and besmirched his royalty. He murmurs and complains behind the king's back about the debasement. But the king, unperturbed, proceeds with his festivities, for he sees that on this day all nature conspires to celebrate the blessed arrival of May.

> The day was merie and fair ynowh
> Echon with othre pleide and lowh,
> And fellen into tales newe,
> How that the freisshe floures grewe,
> And how the grene leves spronge,
> And how that love among the yonge
> Began the hertes thanne awake,
> And every bridd hath chose hire make.
>   (2081–88)

The king's celebration clearly defines his right relationship with nature and his people. The complaining brother, on the other hand, is blind to the rights of nature and the sanctity of the common good. That evening, when the king returns home, the prudish brother attempts to chastise him for humiliating the court before the vile rabble. The king agrees that an error has been committed and that amends should be made, but he holds his peace until after supper, not wanting to mar the public festivities. But the error and the amends he has in mind are not what the brother anticipates.

The king, thinking his brother's priggish counsel unhealthy (2122), devises a punishment to remedy his faulty perspective. The brother must learn to see better. There is a law in the land that when a man has been sentenced to death a certain trumpet is sounded before the door of his house. The king sends the trumpet to his brother's door. When the brother hears the horn, he knows he has been condemned to death by law. In a panic, he rouses his wife and children, dons garbs of penance and humiliation ("al naked bot of smok and scherte . . . al naked bot here schortes one" [2171, 2179]), and, with hair hanging about their ears, they all parade through the city to the palace, in hopes that their "sory teres" might win pardon from the king. At his approach the king asks the brother why he goes about so ill-dressed "in sihte of alle men aboute" (2221). The brother explains that the trumpet sounded at his door. The king then brings the point home. What the brother has forgotten is that all men are condemned to death by their very mortality; that is the law of nature beyond even the laws of men. No petition can change the fact.

> For al schal deie and al schal passe,
> Als wel a Leoun as an asse,
> Als wel a beggere as a lord,
> Towardes deth in on acord
> Thei schullen stonde.
>
> (2247–51)

Death humbles all living things. That is its virtue. It reminds man of his common nature with mortal creatures. It even helps keep him in touch with God. While celebrating May's rejuvenation of Nature, the king had recognized this basic truth when he saw the two pilgrims with their frailty so evident about them.

> In hem that were of so gret age
> Min oghne deth [I saw] thurgh here ymage,
> Which god hath set be lawe of kynde.
>
> (2229–31)

The king and his brother are thus reconciled. Death as well as joy binds men together with a sense of common humanity. Pride leads men to affectations and pretense, the forgetting of common ties. Death humiliates the proud, proving a necessary antidote for restoring a healthy perspective on life.[17]

Genius appropriately follows the *Trump of Death* with the *Tale of Narcissus*. In his presumptuous setting of self apart from common nature, Narcissus embodies a deadly form of Pride. Like the Hungarian king's brother in the previous tale, Narcissus denies his common humanity. Gower reshapes Ovid's story to heighten this idea of surquidry (presumption) as crime against common profit. He deletes Tiresias' prophecy, which had provided Ovid the context for relating the story, excises the account of Echo (he will use her story in another context), ignores the curse pronounced by Nemesis, and cuts out Narcissus' long death speech. He uses the hunt scene during which Ovid's Echo had encountered Narcissus as the occasion for Narcissus' coming upon the pool. Genius' Narcissus rides far ahead of the other hunters, thus exemplifying how in his pride he presumes to be superior to them all. Unlike Ovid's Narcissus, when Genius' Narcissus sees his reflection, he does not even recognize it as his own image. Instead, he thinks he sees some adoring sea nymph. Perhaps Gower's implication is that in Narcissism, there is only fantasy, not self-recognition. He alters Ovid further, having Narcissus commit suicide by smiting himself against a stone. The suicide suggests the destructive futility of self-indulgent love. In Ovid, Echo and the other adoring nymphs who see Narcissus pining away, look for him as he dies but find only the yellow flower. In Gower, the nymphs find the corpse and bury it. The effect perhaps suggests the regrouping of the community despite Narcissus' secretive actions. Even in the metamorphosis, as Gower presents it, the moral of common profit is enunciated. The flower which rises is an "unnatural flower," doomed to bloom apart from other flowers when it is still winter. Its fruit is thus a reminder to all men of Narcissus' surquidry.

The *Tale of Narcissus* occurs at the center of Book I. It is well placed, for it epitomizes the effect of pride on its protagonist in each of the tales distributed on either side. All the prideful are narcissistic, setting themselves above common nature or apart from the laws of community as they attempt to make God's order conform to their private desires. So it is with egotistical Mundus, the self-centered old "grantdame," and the aggressive brother of the king of Hungary, in those tales which went before. So too with Albinus, Nebuchadnezzar, and Don Petro in the tales that follow.

The *Tale of Albinus and Rosemund,* which exemplifies "Avantance" (boasting) as a form of Pride, is the bleakest tale in the first book, a tale in which the various characters turn upon one another and all end up dead. The tale relates to the motif of common profit through antithesis. Like the other stories we have explored, this tale examines interrelationships of family and community structures as well as individual psychic structures. King Albinus is a tyrant, the political manifestation of an egotist. He conquers nations to feed his pride by humiliating others. He defeats Gurmond and, cutting off his head, has his goldsmith make a cup of the skull. Among the prisoners he spies Gurmond's daughter Rosemund. Love and nature temporarily subdue him, and he marries Rosemund. For a time they live "in reste" and "love ech other wonder wel" (2489). But soon Albinus' tyrannical pride reasserts itself, and he plans his ultimate ego trip: a great feast "for his wyves sake" (2500). After tournaments and banquet, he has his cup brought:

> "Drink with thi fader, Dame," he seide.
> And sche to his biddinge obeide.
>
> (2551–52)

The king then announces to all that Rosemund has just drunk from her father's skull and boasts with what prowess he subdued not only Gurmond but also his daughter.

What is so bleak about the conclusion of this tale is the inevitability of the ensuing destruction as, almost machinelike, the parts of the corrupted community turn against each other with evil intent, once the king has abdicated kingliness. Rosemund remains silent after the boast, then quietly withdraws, feigning illness. In her chamber she and her maid Glodeside plot revenge. Helmege, the king's butler, loves Glodeside. She now encourages him and yields to his pleasure. But on "the nyht secounde," the queen, instead of Glodeside, waits in the dark bed. By means of such blackmail, the trapped butler necessarily does what the queen commands, that is, murder Albinus by some "wyle." The women's plot is ingenious in that it maliciously engages the victim (i.e., Helmege) by playing to his desires. But such plots seldom turn out as planned. Fortune sees to that. Just as Fortune turned Albinus' plot askew, so she upsets Rosemund's. The difference is that to Albinus such a reversal is tragic: he falls from his lofty estate. To Rosemund it is relief: the infection has at last run its course. After murdering Albinus, the Queen, Glodeside, and Helmege flee to Ravenna. But when the Duke of Ravenna learns of the murder he secretly poisons them. The ending is as quiet as Albinus' boasting was loud. It is an appropriate conclusion, however, albeit stark, for once Albinus' poisonous pride has infected the most intimate areas of his trust (i.e., his personal marriage itself), his once loving wife becomes as venomous as he. Poison takes them all.

Albinus' boasting leads Genius and Amans into discussion of the last form of Pride, namely, Vain Glory, which Genius exemplifies with the biblical story of Nebuchadnezzar's punishment for failing to heed common profit. In his pride Nebuchadnezzar became king of all kings. But God warned him of vain glory in a dream of a high tree which had large leaves and was full of fruit and birds. In the shelter of this tree all kinds of beasts fed. Then a voice sounded from heaven to cut down the tree so that only the root remained, which must eat grass like an ox until heaven washed it seven times. The king asked Daniel to interpret the dream, which he did: the tree is the king holding sway over all peoples as provider and protector. But because of Vain Glory, he shall be hewn down by God, his reign overthrown, and he himself transformed into an ox to feed on grass for seven years unless he change his ways. But the king ignores Daniel's explication and lets the counsel "passe out of his mynde" (2951). Suddenly, the prophecy comes true. The king is transported to a wild forest and transformed to an ox. Metaphors of wilderness and bestiality delineate for Nebuchadnezzar what bestial action delineated in the previous tale. In either case the king behaves not as he should, and the whole community suffers by his unnaturalness. But unlike Albinus, Nebuchadnezzar ultimately sees his deformity and prays to the Creator:

> O mihti godd, that al hast wroght
> And al myht bringe ayein to noght,
> Now knowe I wel, bot al of thee,
> This world hath no prosperite:
> In thin aspect ben alle liche,
> The povere man and ek the riche.
>
> (3005–10)

Because of his humble recognition of the common nature of mankind, his kingship is restored. With that personal orientation, in the "twinklinge of a lok," he regains man's form and, as king, reforms his reign. Now it is Pride that passes "evere afterward out of memoire" (3038). This positive example, after the bleak conclusion of Albinus, stands as a particularly apt model for the fallen Amans to consider, for like Nebuchadnezzar, he has lost his kingship and, as he lies tethered by Cupid's dart on his "swote grene pleine" (113), has forgotten who he is. In the end of his venture, after the passage of seven books, Amans too will remember man's form, let cupidity pass out of his mind, and, in the twinkling of a look into himself, reclaim his kingship.

Gower concludes the first book with his *Tale of Three Questions,* a story which pulls together the principal motifs which preceded it into a pleasing knot. No source is known for the story, and so well does it accomplish its nodal function that one wonders if Gower might not have varied his practice of always working from a traditional story and supplied one of his own. Whatever the case, the tale reads like an old inherited tale and seems in keeping with his moral purpose of reincorporating ancient lore into the consciousness of his audience. So even though Genius may have invented the whole story, we should not consider that a blemish. Its appropriateness seems ample justification.

The main argument of the first book of the *Confessio Amantis* has dealt with the deleterious effects of Pride upon the hierarchy of man's soul and upon the soul's analogous hierarchical forms with the family and society. Through this concluding tale Gower now poses a riddle, the answering of which restores an individual, his family, and a court. It also leads to marriage, thus creating a new family for the benefit of both court and kingdom.

In the *Tale of Three Questions* we meet a young king who, though he is wise, is very academic in his love of "depe ymaginaciouns / And strange interpretaciouns" (3069–70). Although his love of the abstract will yield to a most fleshly reality by the end of his story, at the beginning so pleased is the young king with his wisdom and skill in answering questions that he is in danger of becoming vainglorious, boastful, and begrudging. When one of his knights presumes to challenge him, his ego is threatened. He falls into "an Envie" and decides to destroy the presumptuous knight by putting to him a riddle he cannot answer; the penalty for a false answer will be death. Should his spiteful plan unfold as he enviously schemes, he would indeed end up being an evil king and, despite his "wisdom," become a tyrant who used his potentially excellent wit no better than the old grandame and her riddle in the *Tale of Florent*. But in the workings of the event, workings to which he must respond as he goes, there is another fate in store for him.

The riddle he poses is threefold. Though its answers are designed to humiliate the presumptuous knight, they comment upon the king as well. The first question is, "What is it in the world which men need least but devote themselves to most?" The second, "What is of greatest worth yet of least cost?" The third, "What is of greatest cost but of least worth?" When confronted with the riddle and its penalty the knight sees his grievous error in presuming against the king, but there seems no hope. His fourteen-year-old daughter notices his state of depression and asks its cause. When told the reason she asks if she might answer in his place, allowing that there are some things a woman might win that a man cannot. Since the knight has no hope anyway, he agrees to her request. Fortunately for him, he, like Apollonius in Book VIII, has a well-trained daughter. She has learned to use her wits and memory as well as her will and, at the appointed time, answers the three points by way of "reason": What the world needs least but men devote themselves to most is Earth, which though it gets on well without man's labor, is nonetheless that which men labor most to help. Second, that which costs least but is worth most is Humility, witness the gift from the Father bestowed upon the humble Mary. Finally, that which is most worthless but which costs most is Pride, for though it costs man his place in heaven, it returns only woe. She concludes with a humble appeal on behalf of her father, a perfect answer to the real demand against his arrogance.

What the father could not gain alone, the father and daughter gain together. The king is indeed pleased with her answer and releases the father. In fact, he is so pleased that he allows that if she were of more noble birth he would marry her. Since she is not, however, he offers a gift of her choice. (Perhaps he has overheard the *Tale of Florent* and knows that such allowances to women bring unexpected rewards!) To his surprise she chooses not for herself but that her father be made an earl. How commendable that the daughter should so love and honor her father that his concern would be her own. The king is pleased with her lack of selfishness and grants the request. She then reminds him of his previous observation on marriage, allowing that he is still a bachelor, that she is now an earl's daughter, and that the king's word is akin to truth itself.[18] The king, delighted now as much by her wit as her beauty, marries her.

Part of our delight in the *Tale of the Three Questions* lies in its ingenious logic, a logic most appropriate to the topic of wisdom which so concerns the king. The king, having established a syllogism, is pleased when the daughter supplies the middle term which makes her an earl's daughter. As in the instance with her father, where the two together did what the one could not do alone, so again the bride and groom arrive at a marriage through their mutual contributions. It is charming to think that beauty, innocence, and wit might win for a change. But that is

Gower's version of an ideal community. Each wins by serving the other.

Though the potentiality for self-destruction is always present in Gower's world (at any number of points the *Tale of Three Questions* might have turned into a plot like that of Albinus and Rosemund, the Trump of Death, or Mundus and Paulina—the threat of Narcissism is never far off), right reason, proper remembrance, and a willingness to play with good intent are sufficient for man to maintain his kingdoms (whether great or small) in good stead. The people of the *Tale of Three Questions* arrive at a flexible friendship instead of proud and arrogant boasting, vainglory, and so on. Reason tempers their judgments, and in the end each assumes a sort of equality through his common humanity and good use of his God-given wits. Not only does each achieve a new title at the end of the story, Gower now gives them all personal names—King Alphonse, Don Petro, and wise Peronelle. The effect of reserving their names until the end is like Gower's reserving the name of his persona until the end of the eighth book. The true personal identity comes only after selfish love has been put aside and an adult sense of common profit is realized. Each then has a place and the wherewithal to be himself without jeopardizing others.

The *Tale of Three Questions* leaves us with an image of three witty adults growing old together, swapping their stories and riddles to the end of their days in order to maintain proper definitions of themselves. The effect is a perfect conclusion to Book I and to the Prologue as well. Its charming resolution engages us as audience through its delight; it challenges our memory and wit with its riddle; and it pleases us courteously with its moral. The tale thus accomplishes in its telling that restorative which Gower so believed traditional fiction could achieve. One feels not only refreshed at the end of the tale but indeed wedded to Gower's community of peoples and good intentions. And that is moral Gower's primary goal.

envy

LIKE PRIDE, Envy—the desire to build oneself up at another's expense—is a crime against community. Here, as before, Genius follows the five subdivisions of the sin which Gower had outlined in the *Mirour de l'Omme:* Detraction, Dolour d'autry Joye, Joye d'autry Mal, Supplantacioun, and Fals Semblant. He reorders them, however, according to degree of social involvement. Beginning with Sorrow over another's joy and Joy over another's sorrow, he then proceeds to Detraction, and ends with False-Seeming and Supplantation. That is, in the *Confessio,* where welfare of community comprises Gower's central concern, those sins having greatest political implications, especially Supplantation, are dealt with last as if in climax.[1] In fact, when he gets to Supplantation, Genius exceeds his usual quota of two exemplary tales for each vice and adds a third.

Book II has fewer long tales than the first book (only four exceed two hundred lines), though the *Tale of Constance* is one of the longest in the

whole of the *Confessio*. The book contains many short examples of the
vice, however, some dealt with in a couple of lines. Perhaps because of
the social qualities of Envy, examples taken from history predominate.
(Cf. the tales of Constance, Demetrius and Perseus, Popes Boniface
and Celestin, Achitophel, and Constantine and Sylvester.) Moreover,
throughout this book, one is struck by the consistency with which
characters are rewarded precisely according to their deserts. Dramatic
irony has been a prominent feature of Gower's rhetoric; it lies also at
the heart of his conception of history. We have already noted in our
discussion of the Prologue Gower's firm insistence that evil is the result
and punishment of man's perversity. Man reaps what he sows. Gower's
keen sense of justice pervades all of the *Confessio*, but it is especially
pronounced in his historical exempla, where often he uses the occasion
to move outside the immediate fiction of Amans and Genius to attack
the ominous ills of his time. Dramatic irony forms an important feature
of his notion of common profit. When one like Constantine is piteous,
he receives pity in return. When he behaves as a true king, his kingdom
behaves as true vassal. On the other hand, when one like Pope Boniface
acts selfishly, his crimes revisit him, often in unexpected forms,
though, in retrospect, always in just forms.

   But before entering into discussion of the historical tales of Book II, I
would like to consider briefly two others, the *Tale of the Travellers and the
Angel*, which occurs at the beginning of the book, and the *Tale of
Deianira and Nessus*, which occurs toward the end. Both concentrate on
the self-destructive effects of Envy. Though neither is a historical tale,
both afford excellent examples of dramatic irony as it teaches common
profit.

   In the *Tale of the Travellers and the Angel* two "friends," one covetous
and the other envious, encounter an angel whom Jupiter has sent to
earth to get a report on the ills of the world. After talking with the two
men for a time the angel learns all he needs to know. In appreciation of
their exemplary "cooperation," the angel offers to reward them each
with a gift. To one he offers whatever that one wishes; to the other he
will give double what the first asks for. The first traveller, being covetous and not wanting his fellow to have twice what he has, defers from

choosing in hopes of winning double gain. The second, unable to abide the thought that his friend should outstrip him twofold, wishes that one of his eyes be put out. Thus his friend is made totally blind. The tale illustrates with admirable brevity the first two of Envy's children, Sorrow over another's joy and Joy over another's sorrow. The punishment accentuates the importance of guarding well one's eyes, a point Genius had emphasized at the outset of the confession. Each vice so blinds the afflicted that he literally becomes blind, and what is worse, each according to his own wish. The ironic profits of each choice are as profound as they are just.

The self-destructive nature of Envy is explored more subtly in the *Tale of Deianira and Nessus,* a tale exemplifying False-Seeming. The story is well known: Hercules and his lover Deianira travel with the centaur Nessus until they come to a stream. Nessus helps Deianira across while guilefully directing Hercules into a deep part. He then tries to elope with Deianira while Hercules flounders, but Hercules shoots him from afar with a poisoned arrow. While dying, Nessus gives Deianira his blood-soaked shirt, telling her that it will win back her husband's affections for her should they ever wane; she should, however, keep the gift a secret. Years later, when Hercules abandons Deianira to love Eolen, Deianira gives him the shirt. But Nessus has tricked them. The shirt burns Hercules with such fire that he builds a funeral pyre in his rage and cremates himself.

This tale of False-Seeming is organized around a series of deceits which Gower heightens with some skill. All three of the main characters are deceivers in one way or another, and all suffer punishments appropriate to their deceit. The initial deception by Nessus is obvious enough. He tricks Hercules at the waterway and is slain. His subsequent deception, contrived as he dies, is more subtle in that it is perpetrated long after he is dead, and depends upon the deceits of others, if it is to succeed. The gift of the shirt seems at first to be an act of generosity. Its subtlety lies in Nessus' knowledge that Deianira is so attached to Hercules that she will take it gladly in order to maintain the love of her friend. She, of course, will unwittingly destroy her lover even as she tries to keep him for herself. But Nessus' second deceit would have harmed no one had they not themselves been involved in deceit. Even Deianira is not entirely guiltless of False-Seeming. The stipulation that she keep the gift a secret implicates her as well as Hercules, Eolen, and Nessus in the web of intrigue. When Hercules deceives Deianira by stepping out with Eolen, the stage is set for the denouement. Gower skillfully sets off the irony of the climax through clothing metaphors, as each must wear what he chooses. How well Hercules gets on with his new flame! As they meet at each other's houses

> Sche [Eolen] made Hercules so nyce
> Upon hir Love and so assote
> That he him clotheth in hire cote,
> And sche in his was clothed ofte.
>   (2268–71)

It was on one of these occasions, of course, that the cloth he clothes himself with is that prepared by Nessus, a garb long destined for Hercules, not only by the design of Nessus but by Deianira as well and even Hercules himself, for on that earlier occasion when he shot the arrow his intent was to slay anyone who would dare to separate him from his Deianira. Earlier in the tale Gower had stressed the fact that the venom in the centaur's shirt came from Hercules' poisoned arrow (2237). Thus Hercules is literally tormented by his own brew. In the *Tale of Deianira and Nessus,* as each manipulates others in order to possess what he desires, each loses what he loves. Hercules' suicide, whereby he makes his own pyre, "with strengthe al of his oghne myght" (2299), seems a fitting conclusion for the ironic intrigues of False-Seeming against common profit.

The three principal tales of Book II—the *Tale of Constance,* the *Tale of Celestine and Boniface,* and the *Tale of Constantine and Silvestris*—concern what were held by the fourteenth century to be historical personages. The first, the *Tale of Constance,* exemplifies the destructive possibilities of Detraction, though it provides insight into other forms of Envy as well. Unlike the protagonists of other exemplary tales on the children of Envy, the protagonist of this tale exemplifies a virtue—Constancy. The heroine's name links her story with the second longest tale in Book II, the *Tale of Constantine and Sylvester,* which Genius appends to the end of his discussion of Envy to illustrate that vice's antidote, namely Charity. Both tales concern the discovery and maintenance of man's true estate: The *Tale of Constance* explains how England became a Christian nation; the *Tale of Constantine* explains how the Roman Empire became Christian. Maintenance of the Christian estate might, indeed, be taken as the definition of Constancy, and for that matter, Envy's antidote, Charity.

The complex plot of the *Tale of Constance* is essentially the same as it is in Trivet's *Chronique* or Chaucer's *Man of Law's Tale,* with which it inevitably suffers by comparison since it lacks the sentimental and agitated persona that keeps Chaucer's tale lively despite itself. Yet given the function for which it is intended, Gower's version serves very well. Even though she may not know what Fortune holds in store for her, Gower's Constance is one who knows where her true estate lies: she is constant in her relationship with God. Fortune takes her from one end of the world to the other—from Rome at the middle of the world's map to the sultan of Asia in the Far East, and then from there to the opposite end of the world, Northumbria (about as far west and north as you could go without falling off). Yet, regardless of where she is physically placed, her spiritual estate is always true. Christ is her center.

Perhaps because of the security of her spiritual center, Constance's personal estate is capable of growing. Unlike the two travellers in the preceding tale who met with the angel and found satisfaction only at each other's expense, Constance is able to enjoy the close friendship of Hermyngeld without feeling threatened. She shares her world with her friend. She is able also to be a good wife to Alla, and, with the birth of her child, she is a good mother. She is a good judge of people and trusts those whose intentions are good. For example, even though Alla seems in the letter forged by Domilde to behave tyrannically, Constance does not condemn him hastily. As she explains to the Roman Senator who found her ship adrift,

I hadde a lord, and thus he bad,
That I forth with my litel Sone
Upon the wawes scholden wone,
Bot why the cause was, I not:
Bot he which alle thinges wot
Yit hath, I thonke him, of his miht
Mi child and me so kept upriht
That we be save both tuo.

(1150–58)

Constance keeps her sense of hierarchy in order. She sees macrocosmic harmony despite her trials, and she does not question or challenge the decisions of her microcosmic lord. She simply does not know why he has acted as he did. He perhaps has his reasons even though she does not know them.

This is not to say that in her trust of mankind Constance is a fool. Though she keeps open the avenues of reconciliation with Alla, she understands enough of the world to take care of herself when the occasion demands. Unlike Chaucer's totally docile Custance, who leaves everything up to the Lord, Gower's Constance uses her wits to combat evil. When the wicked steward Theloüs spots her ship adrift off the coast of Spain and thinks he will "demene hire at his oghne wille" (1101), he fails to reckon with her shrewdness. He boards the ship and tells her he will take "of hire his lust" (1109) or kill her in the trying. When she sees no escape, she "seide he scholde hire wel conforte" (1113), providing he first look out at the port to make sure no one is nearby who might discover him. As Theloüs peers overboard to check, Constance prays to God, and "sodeinliche he was out throwe" (1121) and drowned. The point is not that Constance resorts to false-seeming; she in fact has told the truth. Theloüs might indeed have enjoyed her had not God been standing by to watch over and protect her. The villain is undone by his own selfishness. When he saw Constance's helpless "astat" (1094), he tyrannically thought to add to his personal estate by taking her. But as he starts guarding what is not his to guard, he is overthrown. Misgovernance ends in self-destruction.

Antithetical to the God-centered Constance are the two wicked mothers-in-law—the Sarazine and Domilde. They define their estates selfishly. They detract from others because they fear others will detract from them. Lacking the divine center which holds Constance's community intact despite Fortune's adversity, they see people as opponents rather than companions. Because of their envious dispositions neither the Sarazine nor Domilde is capable of developing a mature sense of community which would enable their lives to grow to fruition. Their efforts to protect themselves thus lead to self-diminishment. The Sarazine, for example, would "destourb" the forthcoming marriage of her son because if it should occur, she thinks, "Than have I lost my joies hiere, / For myn astat schal so be lassed" (648–49). Because of her Envy, she is incapable of realizing that the marriage would enhance and glorify her estate. Because of her perverted notion of estate she loses everything—son, heritage, and life. So, too, with Domilde, whose personal notion of domain is challenged by her son Alla's marriage. Like the Sarazine, she is too rigid to enlarge her concept of domain to include a growing and mutually profitable community with daughter-in-law and grandchild. She ends up being executed for treason—for a crime against the state.

In his telling of the *Tale of Constance* Gower repeatedly heightens the political implications of the story to enhance his analysis of the conflict between common and singular profit as it affects the fruition of individuals and communities. For example, Elda, the king's chamberlain, "a knyhtly man after his lawe"(727), is converted to Christianity by the miraculous cure of a blind man, a cure which revealed to him the power of Christ through the ministry of Constance and his wife Hermyngeld. His response to the miracle is a profound desire to share it with his king. He plans a meeting between Alla and Constance in hope that a marriage might ensue. His motivation is a generous sign of common profit. At this point, Gower's alterations of his source bear careful attention. His Elda sends a trusted knight to prepare for Alla's arrival. In Trivet the knight, named "Sessoun" (Gower leaves him nameless— perhaps he is too false a man to claim specific identity),[2] is simply keeper of the castle during Elda's absence, who, having made a pass at

Constance, fears her reporting his misconduct and thus tries to discredit her. But Gower adds the commission to make preparation for the lord's visit. His knight has the opportunity to participate in a glorious community event.

But the "false knyht" lacks Elda's sense of common profit. He fails to see the meaning of the conversions and impending marriages. Ignoring the interest of his lord and master he is more near-sighted than the "bysne man" [nearsighted man] by the shore whose vision God restored. He tries to claim Constance for himself, thus betraying both his political and personal attachments. When Constance refuses him, his love turns to hate, and he plots revenge. Here again Gower embellishes his source. The false knight guilefully announces the planned visit of the king. Unlike the treasonous knight, however, Constance and Hermyngeld respond charitably to the new responsibily. They spend the "long dai" setting "thinges in arrai / That al was as it scholde be / Of every thing in his degree" (818–20). Their efforts at preparation seem thwarted, however, for after they retire exhausted to bed, the false knight murders Hermyngeld in her sleep and places the "rasour knif" (and thus presumably the blame) beside the sleeping Constance. Next day he accuses her of the deed, but his selfish efforts bring him neither joy nor reward. Elda is not fooled. He calls for a Bible on which the knight might swear, whereupon a voice from heaven proclaims the deceit and smites the knight's eyes out, a fit punishment for his blind behavior. Gower then adds a confession prior to the knight's death. In death, the whole deceit is laid bare.

The king, who in Gower's version does not witness the event, arrives the next day. As he listens to the strange events he "tok it into remembrance" and "thoghte more than he seide" (894–95). He accepts baptism and Christ's faith, and despite the murder, the marriage takes place after "asseured ech til other is" (902). After the consummation Constance is immediately with child, a sign that "the hihe makere of nature / Hire hath visited in a throwe" (916–17). In short, what is of interest here is the way Gower expands the account of the false knight in terms of a series of individual responsibilities and consequences. The seeker after singular profit loses all—first his sense of attachment, then his eyes, then his life. The fruit of his near-sighted efforts is murder of his feudal mistress and then his own death. The seekers of common profit, though sorely tried by the selfishness of false men in their midst, have powers of recuperation which lead to increase and fruition of the community to the benefit of all. Alla's reflections upon divine events within human patterns as opposed to the knight's heedless selfishness show the proper mode of behavior, a behavior mindful of one's political as well as personal being.

Each of Constance's selfish antagonists—the Sarazine, the slayer of Hermyngeld, Domilde, and Theloüs—has false notions of estate. Each would add to himself by taking from others. It is easy to see in their lives why Envy is a sin. A virtue enhances a community's domain; a vice destroys community, if only for the vicious man. The wicked women of the tale offer good examples of how the children of Envy reflect each other in their selfishness as they get bogged down in the age-old patterns of vice. For example, though Domilde's behavior ostensibly exemplifies Detraction, it defines the other forms of Envy as well. Domilde grieves over Constance's fecund nuptial joy and takes pleasure over her sorrow; moreoever, as she forges the letters, she anticipates the vices of False-Seeming and Supplantation which Genius will soon be explaining. As a mirror which Genius holds up to Amans, the *Tale of Constance* invites the mind to recall all the characteristics of the vice as they reflect each other. That exercise in discernment is necessary if the mind hopes to reclaim or maintain the larger boundaries of its domain.

Gower's manipulation of the conclusion of the *Tale of Constance* effectively sets off his idea of personal freedom and communal fulfillment. As in Chaucer and Trivet's versions of the story, Gower's King Alla rediscovers Constance while on pilgrimage to Rome seeking absolution for his soul's sake from the pope. But unlike Chaucer or Trivet, Gower places the encounter with Constance on the return trip. His Alla gets all the way to Rome, goes to the pope who carefully searches his conscience, and then sets out for home. This plot alteration adds a characteristic touch for Gower. His Alla must first be personally cleansed as preparation for whatever other reconciliations there are to be. The king sets his life in hierarchal order so that other reorderings may follow. Gower then adds a second original touch. After Alla's confession, we learn that he "thoghte in reverence / Of his astat, er that he wente, / To make a feste" (1358–60). It is during his meditation upon his estate that he discovers his son Morris. As he looks at the boy, natural love and remembrance of Constance's countenance set in motion the sequence of events which restores the reconstructed family. That reconstruction comes through a reclaiming of feudal allegiances, as the public and private events grow each through the auspices of the other.

Gower makes much of the role of Morris in the restitution of Alla's estate. We have seen elsewhere in the *Confessio* instances of children helping to restore their parents. With Peronelle in the *Tale of the Three Questions* and Thais in the *Tale of Apollonius* it is the seed of instruction implanted by the wise parents which returns fruitfully to save them in bewildering circumstances. In the *Tale of Constance* the child is simply an extension of the parent through the good grace of nature which has clothed child and parent "of a suite bothe" (1378). Alla knows and loves the child "kyndely," even though he does not understand the "cause why" (1382). The effect is like that of the "comun vois, which mai noght lie" (Prol. 124), a shared voice which men know by their common nature, as we saw in the populace in the *Tale of Paulina and Mundus* and in the *Trump of Death*. Alla is of such a humble disposition as to be open to Nature's generous responses. As in the story of Apollonius, the child provokes remembrance, whereby the father reclaims, through his constancy, his wife.

A further small addition Gower makes is the riddle on Constance's name, a riddle so transparent that the modern reader is likely to smile at its naïveté, as Alla does himself. Yet the riddle is part of an important pattern in the *Confessio*, a pattern crucial to the theme of common profit and well-governed estate. It is part of the ever-present need to see things as they are and to call things by their right names. We have already noted in our discussion of the *Tale of the Three Questions* which concludes Book I that the names of King Alphonse, Dame Peronelle, and Don Petro are withheld until each person is restored to his proper social context, a context which allows each his full moral dimensions.

So, too, in the larger pattern of the persona's journey from "caityf" to "John Gower." One of the curious features of Constance's various journeys is the secrecy with which she maintains her identity. She is sufficiently whole to maintain her "privité." She does not tell Alla who she really is, nor does she identify herself to uncle Arcenius after he has rescued her. They must find out on their own. Her true identity cannot be something bestowed upon her like a title or identification badge. Even after she is reunited with Alla she keeps her secret. He reads well enough the riddle which pertains to him: "Couste" is Constance's Saxon name. That is the name he knew and that is, along with his son Morris, his initial access in reclaiming her. But her true "astat" she still keeps hidden until the great feast in honor of the emperor. Only when she reclaims her larger family does she become truly known.

In this final revelation Morris is again sent as envoy, this time to the emperor. The emperor will discover his heir. Gower adds a grand processional to the story he found in Trivet; his Constance comes riding "upon a Mule whyt amblaunt" (1506). The point of the procession, along with the emphasis on the date as the twelfth year since Morris' birth, is perhaps to heighten the apocalyptic overtones of the conclusion. As all secrets and mysteries are uncovered Gower's audience is perhaps reminded that for the true Christian, full realization of his community, and thus of his own estate, will be known only in that great apocalyptic feast toward which every man is progressing. To the emperor, the reclaiming of the daughter is like a resurrection—he might have had no more wonder, Genius tells us, had his mother come "fro deth to lyve out of the grave" (1525). Indeed, this final revelation enables Morris, Constance, Alla, and the emperor to enter into and enjoy their full familial ties. Kings now know kings, husbands their wives, children their fathers and grandparents, and grandparents and fathers their children, and in the discovery all perceive the mysterious workings of God. Clear definitions of others help each to define himself. In short, as Constance reveals of her own "astat the trowthe plein" (1452), the rest all come to know theirs. And that, Gower implies, is how it will be at the ultimate unveiling, when all is made known to the one and only communion.

Gower concludes Book II with another historical tale, the *Tale of*

Constantine and Sylvester, which likewise demonstrates the reclaiming of true estate through constancy, natural inclination, self-discovery, and remembrance of common profit. But before examining that tale closely, I wish to note briefly the sequence on Supplantation which precedes it. We have already observed that Gower alters the order of species of Envy from the *Mirour de l'Omme* to save Supplantation—that most politically significant of Envy's children—for the last. This particular species of Envy has been well prepared for in the previous tales. By the time we come to the last of Envy's brood we have encountered supplanters aplenty: the wicked steward of Elda in the *Tale of Constance,* who would have supplanted King Alla by taking Constance for himself; Perseus, who supplanted his brother Demetrius and in so doing destroyed his family heritage; Nessus, who would have supplanted Hercules through his false-seeming; and numerous brief examples like Diomede, who supplanted Troilus in the competition for Criseyde (2451–55). Not only does Genius then devote three more tales to the vice, he adds an unusually long introduction as well. Of particular interest here are his attacks on capitalists like the Lombards—men who make gain without real labor, or as Genius so quaintly puts it, those who take the bird to market while others beat the bushes. Such men trade chalk for cheese to reap large profits for themselves. The attack reflects Gower's profound distrust of the new economics based on "Lombard" values, for which he never has a good word. The mercantile definition of "profit" is antithetical to "common profit." It seeks "gain" rather than "benefit." Earlier in his discussion of False-Seeming, Genius had singled the Lombards out as enemies of the commonweal by explaining that their craft is "Fa Crere," a sort of make-believe to cheat men of the profits from their own land (2100 ff.). Gower sees a metaphysical connection between Lombard economics and lovers' fantasies. Both deny common profit. Each uses its "respectable" craft *Fa Crere* to win something for nothing, thus usurping another's rights.

Genius' first extended example of Supplantation, the *Tale of Geta and Amphitrion,* explains Supplantation as a form of cupidity. Geta loves the "lusti faire Almeene"; but he is so slow in making his love known that his friend Amphitrion moves in and, by disguising his voice as Geta's, wins Almeene's bed before Geta gets there. Genius shows disgust for such action, despite the fact that bedding takes place, on grounds that the love was won through "sleyhte of love" and enchantment. The ship of love is rudderless "so that he can no reson stiere" (2495). Amphitrion seems to share that craft of the Lombards, "Fa Crere," to rob his friend and companion, all in the name of love.

The second example of Supplantation, the *Tale of the False Bachelor,* though still a romance, is of greater moral weight. Here a Roman prince defies his father by ignoring the father's refusal to grant the son permission to seek adventure in distant lands. At night the prince sneaks out anyway, taking only a steward with him. He wins great honors fighting for the sultan of Persia against the caliph of Egypt. In the final battle the sultan explains that if he should be slain he will bestow his daughter's ring upon the one most worthy of marrying her and of succeeding to the throne. The prince wins the ring and confides the good news to his steward. That night the steward steals the ring and claims the girl and throne for himself. The supplanted prince dies of lovesickness after sending a letter of reconciliation to his father. In coming to fetch his dead son's body the Roman emperor exposes the supplantation. So shocked are the Saracens that they turn the steward over to the Romans, who exact justice. There is a certain irony in the fact that the son, in supplanting the judgment of his father in order to fulfill his romantic notions, set the example by which his own fate is determined; the rebel against his father is undone by a supplanter in his own service. That supplanter, however, ends up being judged by the law he sought to circumvent.

The third example of Supplantation, the *Tale of Celestine and Boniface,* is the most important, however. Moving from romance to history, Genius uses the story to impress Amans with the farthest reaches of Envy as it infects real men, even men in highest places.[3] After the death of Pope Nicholas, he explains, the cardinals elected Celestine, "an holy clerk reclus" (2817), to be pope. But one cardinal was envious.

> He feigneth love, he feigneth pes,
> Outward he doth the reverence,
> Bot al withinne his conscience

> Thurgh fals ymaginacioun
> He thoghte Supplantacioun.
>
> (2842–46)

This "fals ymaginacioun" causes the envious cardinal to resort to his own make believe; he hires a clerk to whisper at night through a trumpet so that Pope Celestine might think it the voice of God advising him to resign. When Celestine is fooled and resigns, the envious cardinal, who directed the whole procedure, is named pope in his place. Ironically this man with the sneaking countenance takes the name of Pope Boniface. After gaining the papacy he combines Pride with Envy and openly boasts of his deceit. "Lowyz the King of France" opposes his impiety; Boniface retailiates by excommunicating the king. So the king sends "Sire Guilliam de Langharet," who captures the pope and imprisons him in a tower. There, "he for hunger bothe hise hondes / Eet of and deide, god wot how" (3028–59).

The legend of Boniface's pride grows historically out of his strong stand against the growing national powers, especially France. In his bull *Unam Sanctam*, Pope Boniface VIII claimed that there is only one final authoritative power on earth and that is the pope. The bull virtually insists that both swords, the temporal as well as the spiritual, belong to the pope. No doctrine was more offensive to Gower; it epitomized the church's scramble for power. After Boniface's capture the papacy was for seventy years resident at Avignon, thus bringing about the schism which Gower found to be so abhorrent and so damaging to the church as an institution. Recall his juxtaposition in the Prologue of the simple virtues taught by Christ with the disputes over worldly control led by the papacy.

> If men behielden the vertus
> That Crist in Erthe taghte here,
> Thei scholden noght in such manere,
> Among hem that ben holden wise,
> The Papacie so desguise
> Upon diverse eleccioun,

Which stant after thaffeccioun
Of sondry londes al aboute:
Bot whan god wole, it schal were oute,
For trowthe mot stonde ate laste.
Bot yet thei argumenten faste
Upon the Pope and his astat,
Wherof thei falle in gret debat;
This clerk seith yee, that other nay,
And thus thei dryve forth the day,
And ech of hem himself amendeth
Of worldes good, bot non entendeth
To that which comun profit were.

(Prol. 360–77)

The pope's estate should without question rest in Christ. Boniface's whoring after worldly power was to Gower's way of thinking tantamount to Judas' betrayal.

Gower's rendition of the ascent and fall of Boniface contains a number of historical inaccuracies (e.g., the French king who opposed Boniface was not "Lowys" but Philip IV).[4] In several instances, however, his alterations of details (or perhaps he found them already altered in his source), add significant touches to his theme. For example, Boniface was not captured at Avignon, as Gower states (3001); but for Gower the detail is important, for he wishes to link Boniface as fully as possible with the origins of the schism. Nor is it likely that Boniface ate his own hands. In truth, he deliberately refused food, thus starving himself. But the image of the envious man devouring himself is the most important detail in the story. The church destroys itself when its officials supplant Christ and, with Envy and Avarice, devour their own members. Such robbing of the people is a form of cannibalism.

Perhaps what counts most for Gower in the rhetoric of the story is its aura of history. The account of Boniface leads Genius into a discussion reminiscent of the Prologue. He attacks the evils of simony and mercenary chapmen who, like the priests, are supplanters trying to dispossess their fellowmen of what is rightfully theirs. The historicity of the tale effectively enables Gower to break directly into the lives of his audience without jeopardizing the framework of his fiction. It enables him to tie up observations on Envy and to introduce its antidote, Charity, by way of yet another historical tale, that of *Constantine and Silvester*. Envy is "Moder of malice" (3076); Charity is "Moder of Pite" (3174). In Book II's summary tale, pity leads Constantine to realize his common ties with all humanity. His charity in turn leads to his discovery of God and his own true empire. In terms of the motif of kingship and common profit his tale ties the knot for Book II.

The *Tale of Constantine and Sylvester* proceeds as follows: Constantine is emperor of Rome, but in his youth he contracted leprosy "in his visage" so that he is forced to stay in his chamber to hide his deformity. His physicians recommend that he might remedy his disease by bathing in the blood of children under seven years of age. So mothers and children are called. They arrive at night with their babes "soukende on the Tete" (3228). The wailing of mothers and children awakens Constantine. But their cry provokes a spiritual awakening as well. He sees what a false king he would be to feed on his people rather than succoring them as he should. (Contrast Boniface's grim cannibalism.) Almost as in a vision he realizes that his subjects have as much right to life as he himself. Thus rather than robbing what is near at hand, he sees more deeply and cries out,

> O thou divine pourveance,
> Which every man in the balance
> Of kinde hast formed to be liche,
> The povere is bore as is the riche
> And deieth in the same wise,
> Upon the fol, upon the wise
> Siknesse and hele entrecomune;
>
> . . . .
>
> And ek of Soule resonable
> The povere child is bore als able
> To vertu as the kinges Sone;

For every man his oghne wone
After the lust of his assay
The vice or vertu chese may.
Thus stonden alle men franchised.

(3243–63)

As Constantine begins to hear and see with a vision wider than his personal concern, "divine pourveance" enlarges his concept of himself. Despite his ugly face, his fate becomes opposite to that of the spiritually depraved Boniface. In recognizing the franchise of all men, his own franchise increases. His bonny insight comes to him as a "remembrance" (3274), a knowing again of

How he that made lawe of kinde
Wolde every man to lawe binde,
And bad a man, such as he wolde
Toward himself, riht such he scholde
Toward an other don also.

(3275–79)

Instead of murdering the babes, Constantine feeds them, clothes them, and sees that they are escorted home safely. Let God be his physician. He who would be master must be "servant to pite" (3300).

The effect of Constantine's charity is miraculous. The community now prays for its leader, and God has pity on the pitying. In a vision the next night, God sends Constantine in the names of St. Peter and St. Paul to Pope Sylvester on "Mont Celion." Sylvester instructs the emperor in the history of man, explaining the Fall, Advent, Nativity, Crucifixion, Resurrection, Ascension, and Judgment, emphasizing that in the end, every man—the plowman as well as the knight, and "lewd men" as well as the great clerk—"schal stonde upon his oghne werk" (3424) and be judged accordingly. The cup which was designed by Constantine's earthly counselors to bathe the leper in baby's blood is now used to baptize him. With his new life and light the old blind malady falls away like scales (3456 ff.). The whole city is christened and Constantine founds two churches, St. Peter's and St. Paul's.

Constantine's leprosy in his "visage" is an obvious sign of man's deformity without God's grace. Through baptism he is made whole. But more is involved than the simple sacramental act. Constantine has it within his God-given nature to discover God. So does every man. That potentiality is part of Gower's notion of the "lawe of kinde." Accompanying his theory of the equality of man in the truly essential matters of life (i.e., death, judgment, and the potential recipience of God's grace) is an oft asserted confidence in mankind's common understanding of charity. Such assertions are not just an aspect of Genius' character (or, if they are, then they abide in the genius of every man). Too often we encounter tales in the *Confessio* where the protagonist, through remembrance of the needs of mankind and the laws of nature, discovers the "golden rule" and proclaims, whether he be Christian or pagan, the virtue of "divine pourveance." As Genius later explains, Christ bought *all* men and made them free in token of perfect charity (III.2494 ff).

Constantine's kingship is realized through his charitable behavior. That, rather than the accident of his birth into high political office, is what gives him true royalty and true subjects. With his baptism into the history of salvation he becomes a city builder rather than a baby destroyer. The *Mirour de l'Omme* names five children of Charité: Loenge (praise), Conjoye, Compassion, Support, and Bonne Entencioun. Constantine's actions embody all five virtues, beginning with his compassion and good entente toward the children (rather than joy in another's sorrow), then his offering them support (rather than supplantation and false-seeming), and finally, joining with the people of his kingdom in joy and praise of God (rather than grief at another's joy or detraction). The tale is thus most apt as a conclusion to Genius' discussion of Envy. Like the *Tale of Three Questions,* with which Gower ended the first book,[5] and like the first historical tale in Book II, the *Tale of Constance* with which this tale is paired almost as a frame, the *Tale of Constantine* offers a positive answer, a remedy against the ills discussed elsewhere in the book.

But unlike the *Tale of the Three Questions,* this tale does not end on a positive note. Gower uses the contrast to drive home forcefully his scathing attack on ecclesiastical corruption. With his charitable establishment of the two churches in Rome, Constantine also unwittingly gave worldly franchise to the pope. Though Gower's (or at least Genius') faith in the "lawe of kinde" seems boundless, his confidence in human institutions, especially political institutions, is small. Constantine may have been right in establishing the pope as public head of an earthly institution, but Genius warns that the action spells doom to the welfare of Christendom, a doom which the preceding *Tale of Boniface* has painfully brought home. There can be no doubt where Gower stood on the current disputes of his day on the legal and political rights of the church in the secular domain.[6] With the enfranchisement of the pope a voice was heard on high to proclaim: "To day is venym schad / In holi cherche of temporal, / Which medleth with the spiritual" (3490–92). Elaboration of the point shall await until the fifth book of the *Confessio* which deals with Avarice, but then it will be given the most lengthy treatment of any single historical topic in the poem. Avarice is closer kin to Envy than any other vice and in its greed for singular advancement destroys man's common good just as surely as Pride or Envy. Constantine indeed provides an appropriate concluding exemplum. But beyond his pious discovery of true kingship hangs the pall of Supplantation as a covetous papacy which culminates in Boniface, and the Schism is enfranchised.[7]

wrath
and sloth

BOOKS III AND IV deal less directly with common profit than the first
two books did, partly because Gower chooses to develop here the frame
plot centered in his characterization of Amans. The exempla in these
two books pertain more often to individual caricature than to the
common good. On the other hand, the motif of kingship is con-
siderably enlarged here, especially through negative example. Neither
book contains notably compelling narratives except, perhaps, for the
Tale of Diogenes in Book III and the *Tale of Rosiphelee* in Book IV. But the
character of Amans as courtier is most charmingly developed in the
best tradition of the French *dit amoreux.* His tender infatuation defines
his preoccupations and frustrations, infatuations he will ultimately
abandon at the end of the poem when he puts Venus aside. His
confusion reminds one repeatedly of the problems of misgovernance
which fantasy imposes on the fantasizer. Though Gower does not talk
directly about kingship in these books, he does explore man's mental

trinity more fully than before, especially the confusion wrought when Will usurps the rights and jurisdiction of Reason.

Gower's presentation of his infatuated lover in these books reminds one of Chaucer or Jean de Meun in its lively dialogue. The tone of Gower's narrative is less satiric than that of either of the other poets, however, partly because of the easygoing pace of his narrative and partly because his persona, as we encounter him in the dramatic context of his confession, is so eager to improve his moral character. Amans can be amazingly candid and at the same time amazingly blind about his preoccupations. Rather than biting satire we more often get sentimental comedy. We should not be deceived, however, by the friendly disposition and harmless indulgences of Amans. Gower made clear in *Vox Clamantis* the corruptive effects which Venus' service has upon a knight.[1] Though Amans' lover's antics are in their way amusing, Gower never lets us forget their inanity. The tone and mood of the *Confessio,* more tolerant than the scathing attacks of *Vox Clamantis,* are designed to tease one from his fatuities.

Another aspect of Books III and IV which adds to their liveliness is Gower's management of Genius. In these books Gower combines with Amans' vigorous cupidity his fullest characterization of Genius as guardian of "kynde." "Kynde," her rights and demands, constitutes a principal subtopic of these two books. Gower allows Genius his moment in the dramatic interplay with Amans and gives him more latitude as a personification than he enjoys elsewhere in the poem.

J. A. Burrow has observed that though the *Confessio Amantis* lacks subtly portrayed characters in its exemplary narratives, one character, Amans himself, is given full treatment.[2] Burrow's observation is particularly apt here in Books III and IV, where Amans' full range of youthful impetuosity and melancholy adds a loquacious zest to his confessions. In some of the liveliest verse of the poem Amans explains how he burns with impatience for being so clumsy in love. So angry he becomes with himself that he even dreams while waking. His intractable mistress' "nay" sounds in his ears a thousand times a day as he broods and counts his years of wasted effort. But if he goes home, he is so upset by her absence that he abuses his servants. So he returns.

Then, so "overgladed" is his thought (III.106), he forgets all earlier resolves. Yet, if she looks elsewhere when they are together—and inevitably she does—then his melancholic anger returns, and he is "with al so mat" that everything seems evil.

> And thus myn hand ayein the pricke
> I hurte and have do many day,
> And go so forth as I go may,
> Fulofte bitinge on my lippe,
> And make unto miself a whippe,
> With which in many a chele and hete
> Mi wofull herte is so tobete,
> That all my wittes ben unsofte
> And I am wroth, I not how ofte.
>
> (III.116–24)

Such passages carry Amans far beyond the figure of conventional lover, though nearly every element of the description is conventional. It is a tribute to Gower's artistry that he is able to surpass the literary mold he has chosen for his persona. Amans is no ordinary fire and ice courtier. His uniqueness lies in his gentle candor; his impatience with himself almost reaches dimensions of self-satire, certainly of dramatic self-parody. As he explains in his impetuous recognition of his comical deformity, he bears forth his "angri snoute / Ful manye times in a yer" (III.128–29).

When Genius comments on the evil and unnaturalness of Wrath, Amans readily agrees. He even asserts, "Let every man love as he wile." How generous of him—except for the qualifier which inevitably follows: "So it be noght my ladi" (III.399). Genius gets correspondingly lively responses from Amans in his discussion of Cheste, Hate, Contek, and Homicide. Amans becomes so shrewd an analyst of his situation that he makes fine academic distinctions. For example, he does not "hate" his lady; he loves her. But he "hates" her words—those thousands of "nays" which stand between him and happiness. He also hates anyone who maligns her or hinders his friendship. As he pouts, it is evident that he has plenty of smoldering hate. Indeed, Amans is so lively in his confession of "hate" that Genius is disturbed by his intensity of feelings (III. 933 ff.). In his account of frustration in love's war (III.1148) Amans offers candid appraisal of the conflict between wit and reason in contention with will. Will always demands his "oghne rewle" and leaves Amans caught between hope and the frustrations of fantasy. One of the most amusing passages in this section occurs when we meet that burly old acquaintance from the people of the *Roman de la Rose*, Danger (III.1537 ff.). Amans, like his French predecessor, hates Danger so much that he would gladly murder him, regardless of Genius' preaching against homicide.

Throughout these books of the *Confessio* Gower manages effectively to keep an immediacy of response and passion about Amans which is disarming in its blend of naïveté and candor. Amans readily—almost indulgently—admits to guilt of the many forms of Sloth and Anger. The discrepancy between his notion of business and productive behavior is ironic, however. He insists that he has not been guilty of negligence; on the contrary, he has been most diligent searching (albeit unsuccessfully) for ways to fathom love's craft. Nor has he been idle in his attempts to effect love: he follows his lady about, always trying to be of service should the occasion arise. Especially delicious for him is the reward for his diligence at mass in the chapel where sometimes he even manages to touch her.

> Somdiel I mai the betre fare,
> Whan I, that mai noght fiele hir bare,
> Mai lede hire clothed in myn arm.
>   (IV.1139–41)

Such industry! From the perspective of reason, of course, his busy infatuation is the essence of idleness in its neglect of rational behavior. Only blind will could see merit in such bustle. When will is made sovereign at the expense of memory and reason, that tyranny inevitably yields chaos. Amans' willful self-indulgence backfires; he gets misery where he sought joy. Instead of offering fulfillment, the games of his fantasy remind him that in truth he is *not* touching her "bare" as he desires; moreover, they set off a most painful "collacioun" as his "imagynacioun" titillates then frustrates him:

> Ha lord, hou sche is softe,
> How sche is round, hou sche is smal!
> Now wolde god I hadde hire al
> Withoute danger at mi wille!
>
> (IV.1146–49)

Since "mi wille" is never satisfied, and since Danger is always there, all his "besi thoght" gets "torned ydel into noght" (IV.1152), despite his dogged endeavor. Genius does not help Amans much here. He exhorts him to more lively activity in his comical *Tale of Rosiphelee,* as if Amans would choose to be left holding love's halters anyway. But the joke is that the more he tries to be busy in love's idle service, the more haltered he becomes.

The role of Genius in this section, so different from his premises in the conclusion of the poem where he exhorts Amans to forego Venus, may at first be puzzling. Yet he is as amusing as Amans because of the persistence of his particularly limited point of view. Here more than elsewhere his perspective is defined by one aspect of "kynde," that is, by Nature's desire and need to keep herself regenerate and plenitudinous. Sloth is especially odious to Genius since, when provoked by Sloth, he would have all creatures bending their sturdy backs in love. This particular aspect of his character, an aspect which Gower takes from the *Roman de la Rose,*[3] accounts not only for his moralizing but also for his selection of tales. As he explains,

> Love is an occupation,
> Which forto kepe hise lustes save
> Scholde every gentil herte have.
>
> (IV.1452–54)

From this perspective, Amans' diligence in love's service is perhaps not entirely idle. Only his games of the imagination seem slothful to Genius. Should he be able to get Amans well bedded he would be pleased. This eagerness to reproduce enables Genius to praise Venus, despite his scorn for some aspects of her behavior later in Book v. She does at least keep paramours, and that may be good, despite the jangling and unrest. Best love, as far as Genius is concerned, however, is that which "set is upon mariage" (IV.1477), since ease increases the likelihood of engendering and offers greatest security to the children. Genius uses the biblical example of Jephthah's daughter to lend support to his theory of the importance of engendering. Engendering involves more than a few moments in bed; the behavior of lovers before and after is part of the process. Thus Genius places high value on Gentilesse, which makes men most worthy as lovers. Its value surpasses earthly goods, which tend to detract from a love relationship rather than enhance it. Rightly understood, Gentilesse should lead hardy men to consummate their love. That is Nature's way.

Genius' attitude toward love blends reason and obedience. It causes him almost to excuse the incest of Canacee and Machaire: "Nature tok hem into lore and tawht hem so" (III.175 ff.). The brother and sister simply followed where their eyes led them, so that will reigned "where witt hath lore his remembrance" (III.188). Their crime was not so much the physical act as the twisting of right order in the mind. Nor was it as grievous as the wrath of the father, which destroys Canacee and her baby. Later, when Amans explains how powerful his own will is, Genius makes some allowance for headstrong persistence in the struggle against reason, since its drive often leads to coupling. As far as Genius is concerned, incest is bad simply because it tends to be nearsighted and ultimately self-destructive, as is any fantasy. Thus at the end of the *Confessio* he will single incest out for his final judgment before releasing Amans. Yet here in the middle of the poem he is willing to make allowances and would not have us judge eager young lovers too harshly. They follow their passions, and such impulse may have some merit to it, especially if they are young. His defense of passion leads him into a discussion of Tiresias, who affronted nature by striking a pair of snakes which were coupling. For so unnatural a response to Nature's process, Tiresias was turned into a woman. What a fate! We all must indeed learn to respect Nature's ways.

In Genius' eyes the sexual urge almost excuses many a crime. Recall the punishment bestowed upon the crow for telling on Cornide (III.783–817), or Jupiter's punishment of the nymph Laar for informing on his promiscuity (III.818–42). Even at the beginning of the *Confessio* in the *Tale of Mundus and Paulina*, physical passion had been the extenuating circumstance which saved Mundus' life. Perhaps that is the point; such passions and delicacies keep the world going. So committed to hardiness in love is Genius in this section of the *Confessio* that he even allows Nature powers of transformation in her efforts to attain her ends. We have noted how Genius had earlier explained the way Tiresias got turned to a woman as punishment for his affront to sexual promise; now he describes positive transformations as well. Pygmalion's idol becomes real as a result of his diligence and produces him a baby (IV.371–445), and Alcyone is turned into a bird-mothering Halcyon for her diligence in love, which reaches even beyond the watery grave (IV.2927–3126); the princess Iphis, who was disguised as a boy since her parents wanted a prince, is turned into a real boy when married to Iante so that he might lead a merrier life and produce children (IV.446–515). Though such transformations may not make much sense to reason, they do to Genius, who has complete confidence in the powers of sex to create. And indeed, many a man's fantasy has led him into conjunctions with idols which produce real babies. Thus the *Tale of Rosiphelee* and its accompanying tale of Jephthah's daughter who lamented about dying a virgin are well placed and exemplify Genius' own ruling disposition. But before making any final judgment on Genius' propensities we must keep in mind the context of his exonerations of sexual potency. He is explaining the physically debilitating effects of Sloth. Were he using these examples in his examination of some other vice, his assessment would probably be less tolerant. We should also bear in mind the distinction between sexual urge as a biological phenomenon in contrast to fantasy, which, like masturbation, serves no good end. Genius approves the one passionately, but scorns the other.

It is in these passages where we judge both Amans and Genius in terms of particular willful perspectives that the tone of the *Confessio* becomes most complex. Judicious appraisal is complicated by the fact that in the next book Genius will assume an almost antithetical posture to the one he maintains in his discussion of Sloth. In Book v he will scold Amans for trying to steal a kiss and will strongly endorse virginity, so strongly, in fact, that Amans has to speak up on behalf of multiplication. We need to keep the poem's larger structures in mind in order not to be confused by Genius' personally biased and not altogether predictable pronouncements and to appreciate the subtle interplay of attitudes as Gower juxtaposes premises and situations. Often he will advance his idea through oppositions and debate. The device of argumentation was not limited to the philosophers of Gower's day but constituted a favorite procedure for men of letters as well. Notice that Genius usually relates the passionate sexual drive, which he so readily ennobles even though it leads men astray, with youth. Canacee, Cornide, Thisbe, Phyllis, Laar, and Rosiphelee are all very young, without experience to help them acquire the balanced perspective necessary for countering will effectively with wit and reason. Each, for whatever reason, is in danger of being tyrannized by will. Those who end their lives violently are like Canacee's child, rolled out from "the moder barm" to bask briefly in their mother's blood because it is "hot and warm" (iii.312 ff.). The image offers a fit emblem of Youth following that nature which he "mot obeie."

But in addition to providing an abundance of young heroines who naïvely follow blind will, these two books also offer counterbalancing examples of wise old men like Socrates, Diogenes, Tiresias, Nestor, and Solomon. Perhaps Gower got his idea of juxtaposing Youth and Age from Jean de Meun, where Reason instructs the Amant (with little success) in the virtue of mature wisdom over willful passion.[4] But as in the *Roman de la Rose,* Gower's many wise old men, though admirably presented by Genius, speak scarcely at all to the preoccupied Amans, who will hear what he wants to hear, nothing more. When Genius suggests that Amans might learn to discipline his will were he to study Ovid, Amans simply refuses. He will not tolerate counsel against his passion, except in the exigency of extreme frustration, and even then his reasoning is more akin to ratiocination than rationality. His domain remains persistently under the rule of a "boy-king."

Amans does, however, ask for a remedy against willfulness, after becoming disturbed by his propensity for melancholy. In response Genius tells him the *Tale of Diogenes and Alexander*. This tale is paired with a second Alexandrian tale at Book III's conclusion. More importantly, it constitutes an early discussion of the disciplining of the will, a topic which will become more prominent toward the end of the *Confessio*. Diogenes, Genius explains, has so studied the world and its circumstances that he comes to live completely according to wit and reason. When challenged by Alexander, he remains seated in his tub in the sun, feeling no compulsion to bow and scrape before the monarch. When asked why, he informs his majesty that the emperor is slave to Diogenes' servant. When asked to explain further, Diogenes observes that he (Diogenes) has become master of his will, while Alexander is mastered by his. The king compulsively wages wars under the illusion of power in hope of conquering faraway lands; Diogenes enjoys the sun at home in his tub, a sun far beyond the emperor's grasp. The tale makes clear that Diogenes, not Alexander, is the true king.

The *Tale of Diogenes* prepares the way for the *Tale of Alexander and the Pirate*, which Genius uses at the end of Book III to exemplify the folly of war and the emptiness of the tyrant's glory. Alexander's great exploits are compared with the petty thefts of a pirate; the only difference is that the emperor's robberies are conducted on a larger scale. Gower follows through on his story to describe Alexander's violent death by poison, far away from his homeland. The moral is self-evident: "Thus was he slain that whilom slowh" (III.2461). A true king is one like wise old Diogenes or patient Socrates who so knows his domain that he cannot be routed. Tyrants, like Alexander, in truth conquer nothing; in extending their territory where they have no right, they only offend people by imposing their wills upon them and die in alienation. The same fate holds true for all who are tyrannized by their wills.

Gower's connecting Alexander with willfulness and inept kingship raises an important issue in the *Confessio,* an issue he will return to at the end of Book VI when Genius uses Alexander's sorcerous teacher Nectanabus to introduce the extended analysis of kingship in Book VII. It might seem to the casual observer of history that Alexander's death by poison was a mere trick of chance. But for Gower, "fate" connects directly to the behavior of will. For some, proper use of will leads to the fulfilling of their natures, the achieving of a proper identity; for others who abuse the balance of the natural faculties and become slaves to their desires, the end will be self-destruction. In *Vox Clamantis* Gower observed,

> Set sibi quisque suam sortem facit, et sibi casum
> Vt libet incurrit, et sibi fata creat;
> Atque voluntatis mens libera quod facit actum
> Pro variis meritis nomine sortis habet.
> Debet enim semper sors esse pedisseca mentis,
> Ex qua sortitur quod sibi nomen erit.
>
> (II.iv.203–8)

[*Yet each man shapes for himself his own destiny, incurs his own lot according to his desire, and creates his own fate* (fata).
In fact, a free mind voluntarily claims what it does for its various deserts in the name of fate (sortis). *In truth, fate* (sors) *ought always to be handmaiden to the mind, from which the name itself which will be its own is chosen.*]

(Recall Gower's procedure of allowing his people to win their names at the end of their stories.) In the Alexandrian tales of Book III of the *Confessio* Diogenes is not merely a free man; he is free because he has so fated it through discreet use of his mind. He sits at the center of his own circle. The willful man commits himself to a war which has no boundaries and over which he has no control. He wanders in pursuit of an unpredictable enemy. Well might he heed the advice of the celestial voice at the beginning of the *Vox Clamantis* which, addressing that wandering persona in his political exile, had admonished:

Si tibi guerra foris pateat, tamen interiori
Pace, iuuante deo, te pacienter habe.
(I.xx.2027–28)

*[If war spreads out all around you, maintain yourself, with God's help
through an interior peace]*

Because of the interconnectedness of will and fate, one might paradox-
ically define the tyrant as one who is tyrannized. His fate is kin to his
fantasy; or, to anticipate the point made at the end of Book VI, his *sors*
results from his sorcery, a *sors* to which he is blind because of his blind
willfulness.

Genius follows his discussion of Alexander and the pirate with his
discourse on war. In his anathema on war, Genius even condemns the
Crusades. Christ's death bought life for men, not further pursuit of
death. Gower uses the occasion to attack once again the worldly policies
of the church. The church has become so perverse in coveting the
world's goods that it seeks bloodshed and manslaughter rather than
peace. Such acts are not only against Christ's law of charity but against
natural law as well (2581 ff.). In no uncertain terms Gower cuts
through the rhetoric of "causes" and takes a strongly pacifistic stand,
much stronger, in fact, than that which he had taken in *Vox Clamantis*.[5]
Alexander exemplifies war, which is simply an extension to a grand
scale of willful behavior against the common good. From such a perspective, Amans' self-indulgent aggressions seem less charming.

In each of the Alexander stories Genius places strong emphasis on
Alexander's lack of wit: he "set al his entente" on conquests so that

Reson mihte him non governe,
Bot of his will he was so sterne,
That al the world he overran.
(III.2443–45)

Yet, for all his aggressions, he was self-deceived and died with "strong
puison envenimed."

> And as he hath the world mistimed
> Noght as he scholde with his wit,
> Noght as he wolde it was aquit.
>
> (III.2457–60)

Despite his great scheme, the world followed its own calendar. The only significant consequence of his willful attempt to regulate the world according to his desire was his own untimely death. Alexander did not know his own place and thus "mistimed" the world.

We have noted in our discussion of Gower's notion of history how important to an individual's psychological health a just sense of time and place must be. Here, further in the progression of Amans' shrift, Genius has used tales of the tyrant Alexander to move our consciousness toward reassessment of right governance and good rule.[6] The last tale in Book III, the *Tale of Telephus and Teucer,* shows how to end war; it stands in opposition to the Alexander stories and returns our attention to the larger motif of common profit. Teucer was once gracious to Achilles' son Telephus. Later, when Achilles had overthrown Teucer at Troy, Telephus interceded on Teucer's behalf, winning mercy for mercy. In the end, after peace was restored, Teucer made Telephus his heir. Pity and patience thus displace the children of Wrath. The moral derived from the story may be projected back through the whole of the third book.

> Lo, this ensample is mad therfore,
> That thou miht take remembrance,
> Mi Sone; and whan thou sest a chaunce,
> Of other mannes passioun
> Tak pite and compassioun,
> And let nothing to thee be lief,
> Which to an other man is grief.
>
> (III.2718–24)

The moral recasts neatly Amans' small willful aggressions in a wider moral perspective and succinctly emphasizes common profit as a feature of good rule for both states and individuals.

The lively characterization of Amans and Genius continues in Book IV, though this book lacks the positive conclusion of Book III. Instead of ending with a general example of an antidotal kind, as he did in the first three books of the *Confessio*, Gower ends Book IV on a note of despair. The book manifests careful structuring to set up this unexpected climax to the first half of the poem. In Book IV Gower moves away from the pattern of fivefold subdivision of the vices which he followed in the first three books. Focusing on Amans' vacillation between hope and despair, Gower incorporates effectively wit and sobriety as Amans shows through his behavior that he understands the tales better than he admits. The beginning of Book IV is symmetrically yoked with its conclusion as the opening *Tale of Dido and Aeneas* reechoes in the concluding *Tale of Iphis and Araxarathen*. The topic of both is suicide resulting from a lover's inability to find a proper balance between willful desire and reason. Araxarathon, like Aeneas, is hard and too slow; Iphis, like Dido, is soft and too quick. Genius, sensing such an imbalance in the depairing Amans, tells the tale in an effort to reestablish in Amans' mind Aristotle's golden mean. Thus common profit is still a pertinent topic at the conclusion of Book IV, but it is arrived at in a different way.

Book IV begins as the first three had begun, proceeding from one child of Sloth to another in regular order. But after discussing the fifth child, Idleness, Genius and Amans fall into debate. Genius exhorts Amans to be a powerful knight in arms, thereby winning his lady's praise and perhaps more. Amans responds by applying the lore against war he had learned in Book III. Christ said that no man should slay another. This is true, he says, even when applied to heathen and enemies of the faith.

> A Sarazin if I sle schal,
> I sle the Soule forth withal,
> And that was nevere Cristes lore.
> (IV.1679–81)

The tone of their "debat" is light as Amans takes the offensive and comes up with examples of his own, some of which are even bookish, to refute Genius' position. We might almost conclude that he has made some real advance through his instruction, except that he has his private reasons as well as his moral ones, and they carry the greater weight. Although his learned examples provide matter for sober reflection, they are interlarded with assertions which reveal his same old blind spots. One reason not to go to war in foreign crusades is that Christ put no blessing on such aggression. Another is that Amans is not about to wander off to foreign lands leaving his lady behind.

> What scholde I winne over the Se
> If I mi ladi loste at hom?
>
> (iv.1664–65)

Besides, he argues, did not Achilles quit the Trojan war for the sake of Polixene? The truth of the matter is, of course, that his "ladi" *is* the foreign land to which his will has exiled him anyway, at least as far as reason is concerned, and he has been for years at war with Fortune and Danger and their troops. Thus, instead of exemplifying peaceful industry in his challenging of Genius, Amans' special pleading provides one further instance of Sloth.

This interplay between Amans' reason and his will provides light satire on the courtly knight of heroic tradition. Amans is anything but heroic. As with the Lombard chapmen, the economics of the situation rather than its moral profundity make best sense to him.

> It were a schort beyete
> To winne chaf and lese whete.
>
> (iv.1709–10)

Nor is he simply too lazy to face the hardship of travel; if his lady were to say he should "travaile" for her love, then,

> me thenkth trewely
> I mihte fle thurghout the Sky,

And go thurghout the depe Se,
For al ne sette I at a stre
What thonk that I mihte elles gete.
                                    (iv.1713–17)

One might anticipate that Amans' blend of moral truth and private
interest would leave Genius at a loss to reply, but with characteristic
resilience he comes up with a counter example, the story of Nauplus
and Ulysses, which demonstrates that there may be times when one has
to go to war, regardless of personal interests. He then supplies three
further examples of laudable prowess as well. The effect is somewhat
like Chauntecleer's overwhelming reply to Pertelote's scrap of wisdom
from Cato in Chaucer's *Nun's Priest's Tale.* When Genius then offers still
further examples whereby prowess leads to success in love, Amans is
more than placated—"Mi fader, therof hiere I wolde" (iv.2028)—and
the confession proceeds amicably apace. But a gap between Amans'
words and his intent has been exposed, regardless of Genius' argument, a gap which will widen toward disenchantment by the end of
Book iv.

Genius' defense of prowess leads him into the first of three learned
digressions, each of which pertains to one of the three estates which
Gower had discussed in the Prologue. Though such exemplary matter
seems gratuitous and at best only loosely related to the vice under
consideration, each discussion is tied into the poem through the motif
of common profit and bears directly upon the plot of Amans' education. This first expository section pertains to the history of labor and
thus is appropriately placed in the book written against Sloth. It is
designed to instruct Amans in the proper industry of the third estate.
Genius explains that men now living need such knowledge "als wel in
Scole as elleswhere" (iv.2348), since if each generation were required to
discover all the inventions for itself, men would not advance very far,
especially since men of former times were more wise and hardy than
men of these later days.

> Here lyves thanne were longe,
> Here wittes grete, here mihtes stronge,
> Here hertes ful of besinesse.
>
> (IV.2353–55)

If Amans is to grow beyond his infatuation, he must learn from others and "drawe into memoire" (2359) their names and the history of their virtuous deeds.

But though Amans is well instructed in the virtue of laboring to advance mankind's common good, the instruction has little effect upon him. Genius concludes by discussing the masters of the craft of poetry, Ovid in particular, whom he suggests Amans might read if he wishes to get a true insight into his love troubles. But Amans is not about to be taken in.

> My fader, if thei mihte spede
> Mi love, I wolde his bokes rede;
> And if thei techen to restreigne
> Mi love, it were an ydel peine
> To lerne a thing which mai noght be.
>
> (IV.2675–79)

Clearly Amans has his own private definition of idleness. As we shall see in our discussion of Book VIII, Genius' sermon will ultimately have a more positive effect. But here Amans is still too much "the greene tree" (IV.2680) whose root feeds on an illusion of his lady to consider anything other than the nourishment of his fantasy.

As Book IV progresses we see then that its structure is markedly different from that of the first three books. Instead of withholding the main didactic thrust of the argument for the end of the book, Gower places it in the middle. He then adds two further children of Sloth—Somnolence and Tristesce. The variation is pleasing to the reader and enables Gower to dramatize Amans' headstrong infatuation even beyond that of the lively third book. Instead of considering soberly the usefulness of labor for man's common good, Amans explains his waking and sleeping dreams. Genius had introduced "Somnolence" as one of Sloth's progeny who goes to bed early when there is revelry to be had and in fitting consequence is punished with dreams of

> Hou that he stiketh in the Myr
> And hou he sitteth be the fyr
> And claweth on his bare schanckes,
> And hou he clymbeth up the banckes
> And falleth into Slades depe.
>
> (IV.2723–27)

But should he dream a "lusti swevene," such a somnolent thinks he is in heaven and in possession of the whole world. Amans quickly asserts that he is no such "slepi snoute." If there were a chance for revelry with his lady, even a touch of her hand, he would be there, dancing, skipping, touching the ground no more than "the Ro, which renneth on the Mor" (IV.2786). He would rather his eyes were torn from his head, or worse, that Atropos had slain him in his mother's womb, than such "Sompnolence have used" (IV.2770). Such a response is sexually aggressive and healthy, albeit somewhat misdirected. It seems less healthy, however, when we see the degree to which it is perverted to fantasy, as Amans explains all his devices for being with her—dancing, games like dice, debating of love questions, reading aloud *Troilus*, all the while imagining what he would really like to be doing. Clearly, Amans is lovesick. When she tries to take leave of him and says, "have good day" (IV.2814), he invents excuses for tarrying and has a dozen rituals for parting, from chatter to kneeling to kissing. When finally she gets him to the door he recalls the ring he lost, or something else, which he must look for, and thus enjoys the parting ritual all over again. When finally he does go home to bed he curses night and wishes day would hasten. But when he sleeps and dreams of her, then no lock or wall can close out his heart which consummates its wedding.

> Thus is he with hire overall,
> That be hire lief, or be hire loth,

> Into hire bedd myn herte goth,
> And softly takth hire in his arm
> And fieleth hou that sche is warm,
> And wissheth that his body were
> To fiele that he fieleth there.
>   (IV.2882–88)

Danger is left behind and in sleep he finds such joy as never he found awake. Then he regrets to awaken, but wishes instead

> To meten evere of such a swevene,
> For thanne I hadde a slepi hevene.
>   (IV.2915–16)

Poor Amans does not seem to realize that he has just confirmed Genius' definition of Sloth's progeny Somnolence. Neither does Genius, however. Instead, he is so moved by the bedtime fantasy and the delectable fruition of its "slepi hevene" that he tells the *Tale of Ceix and Alceone* to console Amans with the thought that maybe, sometime, his dream might come true. So Ovid speaks to Amans after all, though without his moral gloss. There is no need for that, for the dramatic action of what follows supplies the lack. A reader knowledgeable of the literature of Gower's contemporaries will recall Chaucer's ending of the story of Seys and Alcyone which more closely parallels the moralization of a glossator like that of the Old French *Ovide Moralisé*.[7] Alcyone's indulgence in her fantasy is the essence of idleness and leads to despondency and ultimately death. In the *Confessio Amantis* the dramatic effect is similar. Amans' diligent somnolence leaves him on the verge of despair.

Gower's addition of Despair as a seventh child of Envy is a master stroke. It provides fitting conclusion to the first half of the *Confessio* as well as a vivid portrayal of the vacillating lover. Amans shares more than he would like to see with Dido and Phyllis, those lovers strung up between hope and suicide. This last child of Sloth is one Amans readily enough recognizes: "I am in Tristesce al amidde / And fulfild of De-

sesperance" (iv.3498–99). Genius ends the book with the tale of Iphis'
suicide outside the gate of his would-be mistress, Araxarathen, who
refuses to recognize him. It is a fit emblem of the lover of fantasy's fate.
Though Genius may not have a very full understanding of the moral
implications of this tale of self-destruction through indulgence of willful fantasy, his example at least shows Amans the futility of despondency. That is in itself some consolation.

BOOK V

avaRice

AS GOWER EMBARKS upon the second half of his poem he returns to the voice of the Prologue. For fifty-seven lines he reviews the larger history of mankind to reassert the primal virtue of common profit: When God first created man, "al was set to the comune" (5); it was the "kinde of man" (2) to ignore winning and losing; nor was man preoccupied with "gret encress" (3) or making his fortune. Then Avarice introduced the notion of private property and competition for goods. Peace fled,

> And werre cam on every side
> Which alle love leide aside
> And of comun his propre made,
> So that in stede of schovele and spade
> The scharpe swerd was take on honde.
>   (13–17)

With the loss of "comun," Isaiah's golden age vanishes and weapons of aggression replace farm tools.

Gower looked on Avarice as the most eminent and destructive vice of his day.[1] In *Vox Clamantis* he expatiated on the evils of Avarice beyond all other vices, and in the *Confessio* it not only is the subject of the longest book but it permeates all other parts of the poem as well. We have already noted how the Prologue to the *Confessio* singled out Avarice as the worst of crimes, corrupting especially the church. Shepherds (i.e., the priesthood) use "the scharpe pricke in stede of salve" (Prol. 396) and tear wool from any sheep "whil ther is eny thing to pile" (Prol. 401). The introduction to Book v explains how avaricious man's primary concern ceases to be the discriminating understanding of his fellow-man and the common good but rather becomes the maintaining of walls around his gold (19 ff.). Economic values replace moral values, and the self gets misdefined by goods. Though the avaricious man often has more than enough material goods, he always thinks he is poor. And poor he is in commonweal. Misreading the uneasiness caused by his spiritual poverty, he thinks he can make up for his dissatisfaction by further increase of worldly goods. Thus he ever feels thwarted by a lack of self-sufficiency which he interprets as a need to acquire more and more (40 ff.). Rather than lord, he becomes "thrall" to his goods, "and as soubgit thus serveth he, / Wher that he scholde maister be" (55–56). With such insane accumulation of goods he loses proper kingship as well as his common property.

The church, which should be man's guide (pastor), is of little help in restoring a just perspective because it is so preoccupied with worldly gain. Its guiding examples, men like Pope Boniface (end of Book ii), encourage vicious contention for worldly prizes. Probably the reason for Gower's introduction of the long digression on world religions in Book v is the second estate's propensity for avaricious behavior. Gower introduces the discussion in a curious way. After the diatribe against the corruptive effects of Avarice against the common good, Genius links the social with the personal by comparing jealousy in love to Avarice. Jealousy is a political concept—the protection of one's possessions. It could be a positive idea such as the proper protection of one's true estate. But usually, in cupidinous behavior, it manifests itself through Avarice's minions, that is, the holding of what does not rightly belong to one. To Gower's way of thinking, this is precisely the problem of the church. Christians may believe in a jealous God, but in their own jealousy they share little of that divine sense of possession. The church has set its heart on earthly treasure. When Genius tells the story of Venus' infidelity with Mars as an example of the dangers of jealousy, Amans asks about the curious ethics of the Roman gods. Genius replies by outlining the history of the five main world religions—Chaldean, Egyptian, Greek, Jewish, and Christian. Though Christianity forms the quincunx of his argument, and thus quite evidently should reflect the true fulfillment of mankind's religious aspirations, in recounting the history of the Christian church Gower uses the occasion to expose further the church's sacrilegious "misentente." It is not easy to recognize which religion is more pagan—that of the ancients or that of modern Christians.

Although Gower supports the institutional position of the church in its attack on "Anticristes lollardie" (1807), his diatribe turns with Wyclifite fervor on the institution's worldliness. Genius relates the story of the corrupt Trojan priest Thoas who was supposed to guard the Palladion under lock and key. Thoas was jealous in the wrong way. He sold the key to Antenor for money, thus allowing the Palladion to be stolen, foredooming the whole city. Thoas excused himself to his conscience by turning his back on the theft so that he would not actually see what happened. Genius says the situation is the same now, as prelates, knowing that faith is decreasing and that the moral virtues which they are supposed to be guarding have ceased to have meaning, ignore spiritual needs to concentrate on worldly gain (1850 ff.). Though they are "the wardes of the cherche keie," through "mishand-linge" they "ben myswreynt" (1868–69) and have left Peter's ship to flounder. They have sown "cokkel" where Christ sowed "goode Grein" (1880 ff.). Though their hand is slack upon the plow, they are swift enough in their rush toward "the worldes Avarice." Theirs is an idolatrous sacrifice rather than the redeeming sacrifice of Christ they were ordained to perform (1949 ff.). Largess is the remedy for Avarice, but the only "largesse" they know is largeness of Avarice. It is no accident, then, that Gower places his discussion of Christianity and its avaricious priesthood at the center of his overall poem.

Partly because of the lengthy discussion of religions, and partly because it begins the last half of the *Confessio,* Book v is constructed quite differently from the first four. Not only does it open with a demi-prologue; Gower changes the entire format for presenting his exemplary material. Unlike the first books where we encountered five "ministers," "progeny," or "fellows," each modeled on classifications in the *Mirour de l'Omme,* Genius now depicts a whole court and "Scole" run by Avarice, replete with servants, spies, counselors, princes, high justices, thieves, and so on, there being ten main figures in all:[2] Coveitise, a servant and "principal Outward" to Avarice (i.e., head of central intelligence); False-witness and Perjury, both counselors; Usury, who sits on the high bench; Skarsnesse, another counselor, this time to blind Coveitise, whose lineage he shares; Ingratitude, a fellow to Avarice; Ravine, a visiting prince; Robbery, a poor man's Coveitise who lurks outside the court; Stealth and his peacocklike companion Michery, who both pose as servants; and finally Sacrilege, a stealthy thief who robs holy church.

Nor does Genius begin with discussion of individuals in the vice's entourage as he did in the first half of the poem. After the introductory fifty-seven lines on Avarice's corruption of common profit, Genius tells two general tales about Avarice, the story of Midas and the story of Tantalus. He then picks up the lover's personal redefinition of the vice as Jealousy, the Avarice of a lover's heart. His example, the *Tale of Vulcan and Venus,* leads to discussion of the history of religion, as we have seen. The anatomy of Avarice's court does not begin until after that sin's effects upon holy church have been fully detailed. Thereafter, the account of Avarice's court is straightforward, except for Genius' defense of Virginity, which occurs after his discourse on Robbery. It is noteworthy, however, that he concludes his description of the court with Sacrilege. In view of the history of religion with which Genius introduced the court of Avarice, a history which had ended with observations on Avarice as a form of idolatry, the placement of

Sacrilege in the ultimate position is abundantly justified. Thoas' sacrilege led to the fall of Troy; the present churchman's avarice threatens the New Troy. Significantly, Genius uses the story of Paris and Helen, which begins with the fall of the first Troy and anticipates the destruction of the next, to exemplify Sacrilege. The Troy matter functions in this book as the Alexandrian matter did in Book IV, to bind together beginning and end. The analogy between London and New Troy was a favorite with Gower. He used it elaborately at the end of Book I of *Vox Clamantis,* where he described the Peasants' Revolt as a fall of Troy.[3] In the *Confessio* the comparison is especially poignant, as we have seen, in the 1390 recension, where Richard II's London is called "the toun of newe Troye" (Prol. 37*). Though a Troy may be newly rebuilt, it may just as surely fall, as Priam's story indicates. Let England beware.

Book V is thus more intricately conceived than the others. In fact, Gower gives it not only its own prologue but a resumé as well. After the account of Troy's sacrilegious doom, Genius reviews all ten members of Avarice's court (7617–23) and concludes by juxtaposing Avarice and Prodigality, two extremes, with Largess as the virtue in the middle. This discussion of an Aristotelian mean moves us a step closer to the full-fledged analysis of Aristotle on the education of the king to occur in Book VII. The new structure of Book V, with its prologue, new development, resumé, and transitional link, turns the plot toward its conclusion, even as the second half of the poem gets underway. This new impetus is reflected also in an interesting shift in the development of Genius. Although Book V ends on a comical note with Genius consoling Amans for having had no opportunities to be large with his lady, after the discussion of religion Genius is never quite the same. The earthy priest we had known from Books III and IV becomes more reflective. In the earlier books Genius had been most eager to defend natural passion and seemed intent upon extolling the aggressive prowess of male lovers. The same mentality, which provokes entertaining repartee with Amans, continues into the beginning of Book V, where Genius criticizes Vulcan for prying into his wife's love affairs, suggesting that the cuckold feign ignorance rather than complain. Well might we expect Amans to rebel against his confessor's example, for what man as jealous as Amans could feign ignorance if he saw what Vulcan saw? It is that example which causes Amans to question the credibility of the pagan gods, however, a question which induces the turning point of the poem.

The issue which provokes this reversal in the *Confessio* is, then, cuckoldry. As Genius outlines the history of the gods, he himself is embarrassed by them. He cries out comically against Jupiter, that castrator who sets himself up as king (what lewdness), and finally against Venus too, whose priest he is. Knowing Genius' sentiments on fruitfulness in love, one can readily appreciate his chagrin at Jupiter's dastardly behavior. There goes the golden age! His embarrassment with Venus stems from different grounds, however. She is too lascivious. Amans has to press hard to get Genius to tell all her promiscuity. Following the humiliation, Genius is less expansive about the virtue of sexual activity. Clearly, married love is preferable to lascivious love; it is more natural and more fruitful. After recounting the story of Echo, Genius advises Amans that if he should marry he should be true to his wife. One love is sufficient; a man should not ask for more. Book v is filled with marriage breakers—the nameless steward who sells his wife to the king; Jason who betrays the sympathetically portrayed Medea; Theseus who abandons Ariadne; Tereus who betrays his wife and rapes his sister-in-law; Agamemnon who rapes Crises' daughter, thus prolonging the war; and Paris who runs off with Helen. For each Genius shows utter scorn. Even more impressive is his defense of Virginity. Gower capitalizes on this new comic incongruity as Amans has to defend "multiplicacioun" to Genius; Genius responds with rousing praise of the sanctity of maidenhead. It would seem that nature's confessor is becoming mindful of the generative obligations of the soul.

One reminder we must set for ourselves as readers of the *Confessio* is, to be sure, that Genius always responds to given contexts which obviate the need for a systematic philosophy. For example, his defense of Canacee's natural passion occurs as part of his protest against the outrageous tyranny of her father's unnatural anger. His defense of prowess in love, which leads him into the dispute on crusades and war, grows out of his eagerness to denigrate Sloth. Here in Book v, his

defense of chastity comes in response to the violent denial of a woman's
will by Ravine and Robbery. Being an act outside the laws of ordinance
(6431), it irritates Genius' love of orderly progression. Genius is ever
mindful of Aristotle's mean, and what at first seems inconsistency in his
character usually ends up being, in truth, an attempt to mediate extreme positions through debate and juxtaposition of examples. If the
lover swings off balance in one way, Genius will swing the other.
Nevertheless, after his explanation of the gods and his humiliation at
being in the service of Venus, Genius becomes a more sober confessor.
Though still occasionally sympathetic toward cupidity, he is no longer
guilty of encouraging it. His emphasis falls on the virtuous mean and
reasonable behavior. In Book VI he swiftly moves to the exposing of
false wisdom, then devotes all of VII to the pursuit of true wisdom. In
VIII he gives up his role as Venus' priest entirely and simply advises
Amans as a personal friend to stop trying to be Venus' knight.

It would be a mistake to view Genius as an entirely consistent or
psychologically developed character. (In fact, the same is true for
Amans, whose Boethian journey from love's captive to enlightened
Englishman is plotted only in broad terms.) Genius has no "psychology" at all, despite the numerous vivid scenes in which he opposes
Amans' fatuities with his questions. He is primarily a structural device.
Yet Gower allows him his dramatic moments. As Genius encourages
Amans to explain his love difficulties and sympathizes with Amans'
turmoil, offering hope of summer after winter, the effect is comical. It
allows the reader an easy way into understanding the essential vanity of
nurturing one's fantasies for the sake of illusory emotional refresh-
ment. Such a presentation of Love's Priest is indeed a "middel weie";
Genius is not a good Christian priest, but neither is he some pagan
demon. He falls in between to the satisfaction of the reader's own
hungry wit. Nothing more is necessary.

As Genius draws Amans out of his impassioned captivity, Amans
becomes living proof of his own limitations. Indeed, we even discover
that in some ways Amans is an admirable fellow. He has no major
vices—he could never really murder, rape, or steal. Gentle soul that he
is, he is shocked at the very thought of such violence. His errors are

essentially harmless, afflicting none other than himself, and there the harm carries an ever-present penance, namely his comically predictable frustration which instructs us as readers pleasingly enough with its blend of "lust and lore." That it is a blended revelation makes it the more entertaining a challenge to our own moral sensibilities, and that is Gower's goal. The golden mean announced in the Prologue as Gower's rhetorical principal now in Book v emerges as Genius' moral principal as well.

Kingship and common profit are prominent motifs in individual tales of the fifth book as well as in its structure and expository sections. I shall restrict my discussion to four tales: The *Tale of Virgil's Mirror* (2031–2237), the *Tale of Medea and Jason* (3247–4229), the *Tale of Adrian and Bardus* (4923–5162), and the *Tale of Paris and Helen* (7225–7590).

Gower begins his exemplification of the "Scole" of Avarice with the *Tale of Virgil's Mirror,* a tale designed to show how covetousness undermines whole community, for there is "no worse thing / Than Covoitise aboute a king" (2229–30). The motif of common profit is developed in two ways, first through the destruction of the community due to the corrupt king, and second, through the restoration of justice by the people as they retaliate against the king. Gower takes the story from the Old French prose *Roman de Sept Sages,* though he manipulates his source in several ways to set off his theme. The tale begins with an account of a marvelous mirror constructed by the wise clerk Virgil when Rome was in its "noble plit." Placed in a tower so that it might scan the countryside for thirty miles around and forewarn the Romans of any approaching enemy, the mirror kept the city secure from harm. Genius refers to it as "the tounes ÿe" (2034). The tower, with its mirror and distinguished architect, functions as an emblem of wisdom, recalling Genius' admonition to Amans in Book i: "thin yhe forto kepe and warde, / So that it passe noght his warde" (331-32). It seems the Roman emperor did not heed the genial advice much better than Amans, for in turning his eyes covetously toward gold he ignores the keeping of his city's eye and tumbles from power.

Gower names his foolish emperor "Crassus" (he is simply called "Le

Roy de Romme" in the Old French source).⁴ Whether or not he has in
mind the popular story of the rich Lydian king Croesus or some
account of the historical Roman emperor Gracchus, who lived some
years prior to Virgil (thus posing the problem of anachronism), is
beside the point. More germane is the pun on the fourteenth-century
Latin usage of *crassus,* meaning "dense or stupid." For the Emperor
Crassus is indeed unwise, and woe to the kingdom ruled by an unwise
king. Genius tells how Hannibal of Carthage (another "addition" not
found in the source) devises a plan for pillaging the proud Romans.
Hannibal is foil to the dim-witted Crassus; he is a "worthi and wise"
king (2058), a man capable of keeping his own counsel (2059) rather
than mindlessly following whims or false counselors in hope of indulging his will.

But stupid Crassus lacks such wisdom. Hannibal sends to Rome three
"philosophers" who claim they have powers of discovering the location
of gold in their dreams. That appeals to Crassus, since he spends his
time "evere desirous of gold to gete" (2070–71). The first philosopher,
having hid a coffer of gold in the city the night before, tells the emperor
he has dreamed of such a treasure in that very place. Foolish Crassus
calls his "Mynours" and hastens to draw up the "tresor redi" (2124). Of
course it is found, and who could be happier than Crassus? The second
philosopher dreams of another such well-placed treasure. It too is
retrieved. The third then tells Crassus, "riht in his Ere" (2145), which
he guards no better than the "tounes ÿe," of the greatest treasure of all,
hidden, alas, beneath the mirror. So the greedy king undermines
Virgil's work of wisdom which so long guarded the city, replacing the
foundations of the tower with wooden timbers in order to excavate the
imaginary treasure. The philosophers sneak in by night, cover the
timbers with pitch, sulphur, and rosin, ignite the mess, then slip away to
watch the tower collapse.

The philosophers pronounce the tale's moral: "Lo, what
coveitise / Mai do with hem that be noght wise" (2187–88). The significant undermining in the story was not that of the tower, but rather that
of the dull Crassus' ill-founded wisdom. By failing to keep proper vigil,
Crassus, like Thoas, threw away the key to his own Palladion. The

foundationless tower was simply the external manifestation of his own stupidity. The consequences of his folly are predictable: Hannibal sweeps in with his army and slaughters so many Romans that their bodies form a bridge across the Tiber. Thus all Rome suffers from the folly of an unwise king.

One other detail in the conclusion is noteworthy. We are told that in his pillaging, Hannibal collects from dead Roman gentlemen's hands three bushels of gold rings. Those three bushels recall Crassus' hopes of obtaining three coffers of gold by means of the false philosophers' flattery. On a simple level Hannibal's collection reflects poetic justice as his cleverness yields more than his original investment—three bushels for two coffers. But it has further resonance. All of those gold rings belonged metaphorically to Crassus insofar as he as king is defined by his subjects and their possessions. But Crassus was a literalist, the sort of tyrant who would rather possess literally the rings of his people behind the walls of his treasury than dispense his wealth among his people as a true king should. As Gower explains in *O Deus Immense,* a king should compute his treasure as the hearts of his people, not their gold.[5] In ignoring the tower and the people's welfare to seek for his treasure gold, rather than love and fidelity, he denied the true nature of kingship. He is too blind to see that all the wealth of his kingdom is already his own so long as his kingdom possesses its own wealth. His perverse literalism in wanting all the gold for his personal coffer is unhappily carried through in the story's conclusion. The people, in one final act of ritual homage, set Crassus in his royal chair and satisfy his thirst for gold by melting it and pouring it down his throat. Their act is a parody of feudal gift giving, just as Crassus' false kingship was a parody of true. Perhaps their matching literalism left him more mindful of the "comun vois, which mai noght lie" (Prol. 124).

Gower's theory of a secure state, whether psychological or political, resides in his notion of feudal marriage. Each estate is married to the other, and its members to the society at large. For the community to succeed, all parties in the marriage must behave toward each other with trust and largess. If one party refuses to cooperate, whether he be king or steward, the marriage is spoiled. It is interesting that Gower would choose as his tale exemplifying perjury not some spy story or account of a traitor such as Antenor, but rather a story about marriage. His choice demonstrates the importance of the marriage metaphor in his conceptualization of community and right governance.

Yet even in granting the notion that in a feudal society marriage-breaking constitutes perjury, Gower's choice of *Jason and Medea* as his example remains peculiar. The lovers' marriage is secretive, without sanction of the system at large. But it is this very peculiarity which suits the tale so well to Gower's intent as he molds the well-known story in unique ways. He wants a story which focuses on personal commitment, yet which does so within the larger context of feudal commitments as well. He also wants a tale which relates to the Troy legend. The result is a fascinating manipulation of perspective as Genius draws our sentiments toward Medea in order to outrage us at Jason's selfish perjury, only to have the story turn upon us in its conclusion as we, cursing the man who thinks only of himself and wishing for feudal responsibility, recall Medea's own selfish treatment of her father, a feudal marriage she had ignored in her eagerness for personal consummations.

Gower's *Jason and Medea* is based on two principal sources, Benoit's *Roman de Troye* and Ovid's *Metamorphoses*. He makes numerous alterations, however, to point the tale toward his peculiar ends. Readers have often noted how sympathetically Medea is presented in Gower's version. To set off more effectively his marriage theme and to place the villainy of perjury the more solidly on Jason's shoulders, Gower makes Medea into a heroine rather than a mere witch. His Medea is a devout wife up until the very end when Jason destroys the match, a point which Gower emphasizes again and again.

Gower omits the beginning of Benoit's account which relates Peleus' *mal porpens* to exterminate Jason by sending him on the suicidal quest for the fleece.[6] The omission denies Jason an excuse for his pragmatic relationship with Medea and diverts our sympathy as well. Gower's Jason undertakes the adventure to please his fancy, not because of contingent pressures. Thus he has no valid grounds for nullifying the marriage after he returns to Greece and becomes king. Gower also omits the visit to the *porz de Troie* (Benoit, 981) and the discourteous affronts by Lamedon, since that too might draw our sympathy toward the offended guest. That part of Jason's story will, of course, come up later in Book v as part of the *Tale of Paris and Helen*. Instead, Gower sends Jason swiftly to Colchis, to Medea, and to his primary concern. He adds to Benoit's story a conversation between Oetes (Medea's father) and Jason in which Jason is exhorted not to attempt to take the fleece. The effect is to emphasize Jason's willfulness in pursuing his course. His is no desperate commitment, as in the traditional versions. The responsibility for what ensues rests strictly upon Jason's choices. He is not so keen on obtaining the fleece that he has no time for Medea, however, once he has seen her.

In describing the courtship Gower alters Benoit's story with subtle care. Oetes calls his daughter to entertain Jason. Benoit notes that she is Oetes' only child and heir (Benoit, 1215). Gower omits the detail, perhaps on grounds that it draws sympathy to the father. Jason's behavior is managed differently too. In Gower's version Jason's avarice is immediately apparent as he quickly looks Medea over and, seeing the possibility of gain, "ayein hire goth" (3371). Her response is initially cautious—he is not unbecoming to her (3272), so she welcomes him courteously, takes him "softe" by the hand, and seats him. Gower omits at this point Benoit's elaborate description of Medea's hair, eyes, broad forehead, arms, chin, good speech, and manners (Benoit, 1265–90), to concentrate on her feelings instead. She seems less a temptress, more a sensitive girl. Gower would have us respond to her youthful vulnerability and to Jason's aggression. Jason is not trapped by the magical prowess of some dragon-mastering sex queen. Gower also eliminates Benoit's several hundred lines of dialogue between the young couple. Instead, he tells swiftly how Medea has heard of Jason's great fame and worthiness; she is prepared to like him, and as she studiously beholds him, falls quickly in love. The two do not speak; rather, "here hertes bothe of on acord / Ben set to love" (3390–91), apparently by the magnetic attraction of desire alone. In place of the elaborate Old French dialogue, Gower offers one simple detail.

> Forthi sche gan hir yhe impresse
> Upon his face and his stature,

> And thoghte hou nevere creature
> Was so wel farende as was he.
>   (3378–81)

Like so many of Genius' lovers, Medea fails to guard well her "yhe." It is a small fault, but it will prove sufficient to her undoing.

That night Jason ponders his future. Should he seek the fleece or seek love? After many "yeas" and "nays" he decides to let the fleece wait and pursue more lively game. Next day, as Medea is worrying how to protect so noble a person as Jason from inevitable destruction, Jason is worrying about how to capture tender Medea. When they are seated together the following evening, Jason "besoughte hir grace" (3440). She expresses concern for his safety and says she will grant his boon and more besides—that is, she will tell him how to save his life, providing he will promise to remain true to his vows of love.

> If thou wolt holde covenant
> To love, of al the remenant/
> I schal thi lif and honour save.
>   (3449–51)

The point here is not that Medea drives a hard bargain. Rather her reply is notable for its largess. She will be obedient to his will providing his will remains true. She will save his life as well. Jason thanks her and presses for immediate access to her chamber. That night, Medea sends her maid to Jason to lead the way. Genius stresses Medea's modesty when Jason arrives—"sche with simple chiere and meke, / Whan sche him sih, wax al aschamed" (3480–81)—and also the care with which she secures the approval of the gods for "sikernesse of Mariage" (3483).

> Sche fette forth a riche ymage,
> Which was figure of Jupiter,
> And Jason swor and seide ther,
> That also wiss god scholde him helpe,
> That if Medea dede him helpe,
> That he his pourpos myhte winne,

> Thei scholde nevere parte atwinne,
> Bot evere whil him lasteth lif,
> He wolde hire holde for his wif.
>   (3484–92)

What had been largess on Medea's part, Jason turns into part of the "bargain." Even so, he takes his oath on it, and Medea places her trust in his hands. The charge of perjury is clinched against Jason should he subsequently abandon her. The contrasting dispositions of the lovers accentuate Jason's avaricious desire to win both Medea and the fleece for the sake of personal rather than mutual gain. Because of his selfishness there is little sense of common profit in the marriage; thus there will be small hope for what Genius later calls "the fruit of rihtwisnesse" (7627).

Gower portrays the wedding night with consummate skill as "thei hadden bothe what thei wolde" (3499) and then talk the rest of the night about strategy for winning the fleece. He alters his source by having Medea, thoughtful girl that she is, note the swift passage of time (in Benoit, Jason keeps watch). It is she who urges Jason to arise before being discovered.

> Bot, Sire, for it is nyh day,
> Ariseth up, so that I may
> Delivere you what thing I have,
> That mai youre lif and honour save.
>   (3547–50)

As she puts it, her concern is not her reputation but rather Jason's safety. She needs time to give Jason the ring, ointment, and ox glue. She is already an obedient wife looking after her husband.

Gower also adds to his source an elaborate parting (3634–59) in which Medea tenderly weeps, swoons, and reiterates her trust and joy in her new husband. The passage is nicely modulated by the paired speeches of the two lovers (3642–45 and 3652–59). Their nuptial vows are pointedly reconfirmed as she prays that the gods help Jason, "mi trust, mi lust, mi lif, min hele" (3643), and he swears "be my trouthe" to return with "such tidinge, / The which schal make ous bothe game" (3658–59).

During the conquest of the golden fleece Genius repeatedly reminds the reader of Jason's debt to Medea. He would have got nowhere without her advice. Jason remembers well enough the details of her instructions on sowing the dragon's teeth, repeating the charms, making the right prayers, and so on. Too bad his recollection of his wedding vow was not so strong.

The reunion of the lovers is masterfully presented, again through alteration of the source. After Jason has captured the fleece, Gower shifts the point of view to Medea, who waits and prays "upon a Tour alofte" for "the kniht which hath mi maidenhiede" (3736 ff.). As she looks out to sea she sees the fleece glitter in the sun and knows Jason's success. Then the perspective shifts to that of the waiting Greeks, who are less certain. The effect is to personalize Medea further and restress her trust, faith, and pleasure in her husband. This careful manipulation of perspective continues as Gower juxtaposes the raucous reception for the returning hero, as everyone praises Jason for his godlike heroism, with Medea's shy happiness as she whispers while he passes, "Welcome, O worthi kniht Jason" (3788), yet fears kissing him for shame. Later she sends her maid to inquire after Jason (another unique detail in Gower's version)[7] and has a bath prepared for him. Gower again juxtaposes Medea's shy, unassuming response with that of the mob at the evening banquet. Never once does she desire to take credit where in fact credit is due. Nor is Jason wont to give credit. Instead, as they are once again seated together, they speak "as thei dorste" (3842). Unlike Benoit, Gower has his couple set sail immediately that night for Greece, rather than having them wait a month to get underway. His Jason is not one to wait around.

As Gower moves into that part of the tale told by Ovid, he continues to make alterations which heighten one's affection for Medea and delineate qualities of an obedient wife. He stresses immediately Medea's giving birth to two sons and adds a comment about the great joy they bring to Jason's father, old Eson, who is thrilled at "thencress of

his lignage" (3941). Gower includes the episode in which Medea restores Eson's youth, but again makes important changes. In Ovid,
Jason offers to have years taken off his life in order that they might be
added to his father's. Gower deletes the offer, perhaps because it
suggests that Jason is capable of an unselfish thought. Also in Ovid,
Medea, when confronted with Jason's selfless offer toward his father,
thinks about her own father Oetes whom she so disappointed; she
marvels somewhat enviously at Jason's family loyalty. This detail
Gower also omits, again because it would detract from our sympathy
for Medea. Her abrupt treatment of her father is a blemish Gower
glosses over. Once she is married to Jason she puts away father and
mother and is obedient to her husband alone. Gower's Medea performs the miraculous restoration of Eson strictly out of loyalty to Jason.
She would be "toward him trewe" (3950).

Though the lengthy description of the rejuvenation ritual has little
bearing on the moral function of Gower's tale, Genius includes a
condensed version "for the novellerie" (3955), and indeed it does make
entertaining reading. In Ovid, after Medea gets the necessary potions
and returns to apply them to Eson she specifically sends Jason away. In
the *Confessio*, however, "sche bad alle othre go" (4060). Gower thus
avoids the problem of having the wife order the husband around,
which would not be in keeping with the marriage relationship as he
wants it defined. He also adds tender touches to Medea's care for Eson,
undoubtedly to show her consideration. In Ovid she casts a spell over
Eson before going to work on him. In Gower she says her charms, but
then, like a loving mother, "tok Eson in bothe hire armes / And made
him forto slepe faste" (4068–69). Ovid offers a grisly account of her
cutting Eson's throat in order to change his blood. In Gower she makes
"a wounde upon his side" (4157) through which the tired old blood
slides out. Once Eson has been restored, Genius leaves no doubt about
Medea's glorious achievement.

> Lo, what mihte eny man devise,
> A womman schewe in eny wise

> Mor hertly love in every stede,
> Than Medea to Jason dede?
>   (4175–78)

What largess. What an obedient, self-sacrificing wife. How fortunate a marriage.

That is, if Jason had upheld his part of the covenant. The denouement in Gower's version is swift. King Peleus dies and Jason becomes king. In Ovid, Medea is responsible for Peleus' death, since she persuaded his daughters to murder him while thinking they were going to restore his youth by letting out his old blood as she did Eson's; her treachery is in some measure a repayment for Peleus' intended treachery against Jason when he sent him to seek the golden fleece. But Gower omits both details. His Jason is simply made king, whereupon he leaves Medea and takes "a newe." Once the marriage is ruined, Medea is changed. Jason's perjury has denied her very definition of herself. She becomes now her opposite and takes revenge most viciously, burning up Creusa with a mantel she sends as a gift and slaughtering Jason's children right "before his yhe" (4216). That is a sight his wayward glance did not anticipate. So the marriage produced no good fruit at all. Eson's proud heritage comes to nothing. But that is because of Jason's perjury which broke the sacred bonds between them. A community is nothing without the loyalty of its members.

Gower's conclusion to Medea's story carries an additional irony. Perhaps her trust in Jason was nearsighted from the beginning. Despite the sincerity of her lover's commitment she was not mindful of her other larger communal ties, the ties of family. Though her youth in some ways excused her, she should have seen better. Despite her remarkable powers of sorcery she did not act wisely in following her desire. If anything, her sorcery kept her from facing up to the situation earlier. In the end, even more appalling than Medea's revenge is the emptiness with which her story concludes. "Lo, this schal be thi forfeture" (4214), Medea says to Jason as she slaughters the children. Though she takes refuge with Pallas, the generations of Oetes and Eson have ceased to be.

The *Tale of Adrian and Bardus* is designed with simple ingenuity to exemplify "unkindeschipe." We have seen Gower begin Book v with an account of man's fall from a primeval state of commonweal through the corruptive usurpations of Avarice. To help Amans understand the dilemma of man trapped in a world distorted by willful aggression, Genius drew extensively on stories illustrative of decrepit civilizations which collapse through their societies' inability to relate actions to responsibilities—stories like the fall of Rome in the *Tale of Virgil's Mirror,* the ruin of a family in *Jason and Medea,* or the destruction of Troy in the various Troy stories in Book v. The *Tale of Adrian and Bardus* approaches the problem from a different perspective. Rather than describing the effects of Avarice on social structures which are consequently destroyed, here Gower explores the problem within the philosophical parameters of Fortune and Nature. Avarice divides man from his true nature; the avaricious man thus behaves unnaturally. "Unkindeschipe" is more than ingratitude; it is a denial or perversion of man's innate sense of his common nature. In his résumé of the ten members of Avarice's court at the end of Book v, Genius lists "unkin-deschipe" in the middle, glossing it with an extra line as that "which nevere drouh to felaschipe" (7620). Gower approaches the com-plexities of "unkindeschipe" through two contrasting figures, Adrian and Bardus. The main difference between the two is that one man is rich, the other poor. They are in some ways similar, however. Both are subject to Fortune, and both are subject to Avarice, though the degree of Avarice's influence on each differs. Bardus' poverty has been for him a protection. Need has forced him to keep in touch with the world outside himself. Necessity keeps him mindful of his interdependence with nature.

Riches, on the other hand, enable Adrian to assume an indepen-dence of his fellow creatures. Or at least so it seems. He is a "gret lord" of Rome. But although Fortune has placed him socially above others, he is morally deficient. Love of goods has made him incapable of acknowledging human fellowship. Fortune is the first to educe the deficiency of this "unkinde man." As he rides "per cas" out hunting, "it hapneth at a soudein wente" (4942) that, "thurgh happ, the which noman eschuieth" (4944), his horse stumbles, and he is thrown into a deep pit. Fortune also arranges that none of Adrian's servants are in the vicinity of his fall. Thus he is abandoned, "clepende and criende al the day / For socour and deliverance" (4952–53). The pit implies the plight into which his avarice has led him. He has long been spiritually isolated from his fellowmen. To get out of the pit he will feign largess, though it will take the action of the emperor to impose right order upon this benighted man.

Juxtaposed to the rich Adrian is Bardus, a poor woodcutter whose only "liflode" is what he can "lode" on his ass's back (4961). His affairs also lie in Fortune's hands; he sells his sticks, "grene" or "drie," depending on what he finds, to "who that wolde hem beie" (4960). Quite by chance, "as it fell him forto tarie" (4964), he stops near the pit "that ilke time" to truss up his load. To his surprise he hears a dim noise come from the earth which, when he places his ear to the pit, says, "Ha, help hier Adrian, / And I wol yiven half mi good" (4970–71). At the prospect of such wealth, Bardus overcomes his fear, untrusses his load, ties his staff to his trussline, and drops it into the hole to pull out the rich man. His action is perhaps a parody of the familiar icon of Christ the fisherman with his staff (cross) tied to a line drawing men's souls from the pit.[8] Here, however, though men help each other in a tight spot, their motives are indeed questionable. Adrian offers a generous reward, but he has no intention of paying, and Bardus, though he helps the rich man get out, does so because he would "gladly winne" (4973). The emphasis Gower places on the covenant established by word of mouth and oath between the two is noteworthy (4975–85; 5014–15; 5032). As Bardus repeatedly asks for guarantees of payment, one wonders if he would have helped Adrian had he not taken his oath. Later, after he has obtained the magic jewel from the serpent, Bardus shows no concern for the jewelers to whom he sells the disappearing gem. Not that they require sympathy. Their motives in buying it are no purer than Bardus'. When offered the stone they rush to buy it without "delaiement." The implication seems to be that all men are afflicted with an avaricious blight.

But despite his morally deficient perspective, Bardus discovers something he had not expected as he begins to help Adrian. To his astonishment, as he fishes in the hole he finds a creature of nature. An ape and a serpent as well have fallen "per chance" (4993) into the same pit. This, it seems, must be the very pit of fallen nature. Bardus pulls out each animal respectively, convinced that he is victim of some "fantosme." Only Adrian's insistent cajoling, oath-swearing, and promises of reward convince him to lower the rope a third time. When Adrian grabs the staff he crosses himself and orders Bardus to haul away. Adrian's hypocritical blessing of himself says in effect, "You God, Bardus, and Ass, help me, though I do not plan to help any but myself in return." For as soon as he is out of the pit his blessing turns to curses. Experience has taught him nothing of common profit, and he is, alas, too perverse to learn. Without even so much as "grant merci" (5028) he sets straight out for his private palace. When poor Bardus reminds him of their "covenant" he gets a threat of murder in place of reward.

But although Avarice has completely perverted Adrian's nature, "kindeschipe" has not disappeared from the world at large. Something positive in nature did come from that hole. Next day, when Bardus goes again to collect wood, a strange thing happens. Fortune, it seems, and Avarice are not the only influences on his life. Nature asserts herself with a kingly justice which both astonishes and instructs the poor man. The ape he had unwittingly helped is waiting with a great "route" of sticks he has gathered in return for Bardus' kindness. A few days later, a second strange thing happens. "The grete gastli serpent" (5062) glides up and gives Bardus a gem from its mouth. This gem has magical properties, for when Bardus sells it, it always returns to his purse along with the money the jeweler paid for it. The larger implication is, perhaps, that kindness, no matter how often spent, is never diminished; rather, it grows with use. One would gather that this kindness dwells in the very animal souls of creation. Creatures with rational souls have perversely abused it, however, the price being, as we have seen, the obscuring of common profit and loss of the peaceful repose of a golden age.

There is, however, in addition to the working of nature, a second positive force in the story—the Emperor Justinian. Like the emperors in the *Gesta Romanorum* (tales with which *Adrian and Bardus* has strong affinities), which are almost always glossed as the Creator or Orderer and Judge of creation, Justinian represents a power of right order and justice beyond the capers of willful men or Fortune. When the emperor hears Bardus' tale he is astonished, not at the magical gem, but at Adrian:

> the worm and ek the beste,
> Althogh thei maden no beheste,
> His travail hadden wel aquit;
> Bot he which hadde a mannes wit,
> And made his covenant be mouthe
> And swor therto al that he couthe
> To parte and yiven half his good
> Hath nou foryete hou that it stod,
> As he which wol no trouthe holde.
>
> (5131–39)

In stressing the covenant between Adrian and Bardus, Genius comments upon the discrepancy between man's ability to make covenants and his unwillingness to abide by his word. Adrian and his oath-breaking exemplifies perjury every bit as well as Jason did before him, and also "skarsnesse" as well as "unkindeschipenesse." Men with their words and wits can make covenants. Thus, presumably, they should be able to profit each other as the simpler beasts are not able to do. The ape and serpent could not get out of the pit alone. It took human wit, human language, and a human covenant to free them. But though men may have loftier powers than the simpler creatures of "kynde," they use their abilities perversely for singular profit, even to the point of Sacrilege, that ultimate form of Avarice, as exemplified by Adrian when he crosses himself to save his skin with no intent of fulfilling his vows. It takes Fortune and Nature to converge with simpler forms of life to remind man of the virtue of his rationality which, when rightly assessed and justly administered, is more potent than even the "vertu" of the serpent's stone.

The *Tale of Paris and Helen* is the last of the tales exemplifying subdivisions of Avarice. It is a good concluding tale since it ties together a nexus of Trojan materials, bad marriages, and stories of crumbling societies prominent in Book v. In the *Tale of Paris and Helen* we see three civilizations, two Trojan and one Greek, grow in strength only to lose their achievements through selfish pride, greed, and intolerance of others. In each instance Gower emphasizes opportunities for peace and good will which each kingdom selfishly ignores. First he tells of Lamedon, who refuses hospitality to Jason and Hercules on their way to win the golden fleece. For Lamedon's "unkindeschipe" the Greeks return and destroy his city. But that victory is not enough. As a final indignity they take Lamedon's daughter Esiona and give her to Thelamon. Lamedon's son Priam then rebuilds the city. Once more a tower is "sett upon a roche" (7242) and the city seems impregnable. Within the city, however, Priam's thoughts turn jealously to revenge. He calls a council, but instead of war the parliament takes a moderate line and advises "accord and pes" (7270). The state thus seems to be operating as it should, according to Gower's standard, with the king seeking counsel and the people offering mature judgment directed toward the common good. (Cf. Prol. 157–58: "Althogh a man be wys himselve, / Yit is the wisdom more of tuelve.") Instead of making war the Trojans send Antenor to ask for the return of Esiona. Now the Greeks seal their own doom: Thelamon refuses to let Esiona go. The price of his greed will be loss of the Greek queen and, ultimately, after Troy's demise, their own kingdoms.

The Trojans call a second parliament. Hector advises again for peace:

> Betre is to leve, than beginne
> Thing which as mai noght ben achieved;
> He is noght wys that fint him grieved,
> And doth so that his grief be more.
>   (7346–49)

But Paris, his ego galled, objects:

> Strong thing it is to soffre wrong,
> And suffre schame is more strong.
>
> (7377–78)

He tells of his dream of the golden apple and proposes that they follow that dream in order to win the Greek lady and at the same time aggrieve "oure enemies." Despite Hector's wise words and the objections of Cassandra and Helenus, the Trojans decide to have their revenge. They will follow Paris' willful dream instead of their mature judgment. Pride, Avarice, and jealousy carry the day and the once impregnable tower is again in jeopardy as those inside behave unwisely.

Paris goes to the island where Helen dwells. She hears of his coming and goes eagerly to the Temple of Venus to see him. In his "freisshe mod" he "made hir chiere" with such success that he takes her heart with him "er that he wente away" (7518). Evidently Helen did not guard her looking and thinking well, for instead of seeing the danger, she remains at the temple "in contemplacion" until Paris returns that night to abduct her. All celebrate their arrival back in Troy except Helenus and Cassandra, who know

> That Paris out of holi place
> Be Stelthe hath take a mannes wif,
> Wherof that he schal lese his lif
> And many a worthi man therto,
> And al the Cite be fordo,
> Which nevere schal be mad ayein.
>
> (7572–77)

The robbery of the "holi place" prefigures the fall of the Palladion and stands figuratively as well for all forms of cuckoldry and misdefinition of rightful domain. Genius' forecast of the outcome of Trojan history (7576–77) that the city will fall, never again to be rebuilt, reminds us here that in Paris' action a whole community is at stake. The security of the tower, representing (as it did in the *Tale of Virgil's Mirror*) the city's strength, depends upon the wisdom of its maintenance. It can fall only if betrayed from within. Paris' sacrilege and covetousness, like that of Priest Thoas or stupid Crassus, spells the city's doom.

That the Greeks in their revenge upon Troy ultimately destroy themselves is explained elsewhere in the *Confessio*, but their immanent destruction hangs over the account here as well. None of the three societies, because of pride and avarice, is able to survive long. Rather, each blindly perpetrates the same offenses against the other. As Genius makes his résumé of Book v, his list of the divisions of Avarice (7610–27) seems a summary of the vices exhibited in the *Tale of Paris and Helen*. Besides Sacrilege we see there Coveitise, Fals Brocage, Stelthe, Ravine, Skarsnesse, Unkindschipe, and Robberie. Only Usure and Perjury were not dealt with, though Jason, who was Genius' example of Perjury is mentioned. Finally, by choosing a tale which depicts the loss of a whole kingdom to conclude his study of Avarice, Gower once again ties our attention to the motif of kingship and common profit both as social and personal virtues.

Book v ends with Genius stressing, as he did at the end of Book iv, the importance of controlling the will to arrive at the proper mean. The implication is that each man must protect the tower of his judgment by defining his possessions rightly. Avarice and prodigality are extremes between which lie liberality and suffisaunce. If man willfully chooses an extreme and in doing so obscures his true intent, Fortune and Nature upset his false schemes and help him to redefine the individual nature which his willful disposition led astray. Genius allows in his conclusion that the avaricious may seem to flower as they accumulate riches, but Avarice never bears fruit.

> It floureth, bot it schal noght greine
> Unto the fruit of rihtwisnesse.
> (7626–27)

Indeed, it is remarkable how consistently the avaricious, not only in the four tales we have considered but in all Genius' examples, end up with nothing. One recalls tales such as those of Echo, Tantalas, Midas, Tereus, Leucothoe, Calistona, and Cornix. The fruitlessness of each avaricious endeavor accounts for the emphasis Genius places on virginity and marriage in Book v. The latter represent proper saving and proper use. Both produce "fruit of rihtwisnesse" and stand as antitheses to Avarice's barren acts. The discovery of true marriages and the exposing of false, whether through adversity of Fortune, the justice of Nature, or right use of reason, will remain prominent considerations until the end of the *Confessio*. If he is to recover his true sense of kingship and proper domain, Amans must first discover where his true mistress lies.

BOOK VI

gluttony

BOOK VI CONTINUES to devolve new structural patterns in preparation for the seventh book of the *Confessio Amantis* on kingship. Since Book VII's purview is the governance of will by wit and reason, that book is, as we shall see, an antidote to all the sins discussed in the poem. The structural changes wrought in Book V, with its prologue, fulsome court of Avarice, résumé, and announcement of the golden mean, turn the plot in a new direction. Not only did that book make abundantly clear that Avarice lies at the center of man's present day problems, it also proved a climax to Genius' method of instructing through categorical exorcism. Though Genius, as confessor, continues his categorical method into the last book of the poem, it is only a shadow of its earlier usage. In the second half, the poem's concern shifts from categories of sin to the general psychology of willfulness.

At the outset of Book VI Genius announces that so numerous are the branches of Gluttony, the great original sin, that he will consider only two categories—Drunkenness and Delicacy. In the *Mirour* Gower had subdivided the sin into Ingluvies (voracity), Delicacie, Yveresce (drunkenness), Superfluitie and Prodigalitie. It is noteworthy that Genius had already begun discussing Superfluitie and Prodigalitie at the end of Book v. As he presents Drunkenness and Delicacy in Book vi, he regularly refers to the other manifestations of Gluttony mentioned in the *Mirour*, though he does not discuss them formally. Clearly he has not forgotten the categories; only his method has changed. Even the two categories he does formally announce get comparatively short shrift. Neither has an extended exemplary tale. Instead, our attention is turned to willful Amans' desires as he describes how besotted he is in love.

Amans admits to intoxication with love. One look at his lady's fair face makes him high and sets his lusty thoughts to work in hopes of having "mi wille."

> And thus thenkende I stonde stille
> Withoute blenchinge of myn yhe,
> Riht as me thoghte that I syhe
> Of Paradis the moste joie.
>   (204–7)

As he fails to guard his eye his temperature rises to that of fire; yet, so sweet and so soothing is the eye's draught that

> Me thenkth as thogh I were aslepe
> And that I were in goddes barm.
>   (227–28)

When she is not there to be looked upon or when his fantasy fades, he suffers from a miserable hangover, shivering with chill "so it coldeth at myn herte" (241).

That he is guilty of Delicacy is less certain, Amans thinks, since he has only "smale lustes" to feed on. Yet as he begins to discuss his fantasy life we discover that he has become a most rarified lover. In truth, Delicacy is the essence of his problem as he suffers from what Patrick Gallacher has wittily labeled "erotic malnutrition."[1] Amans explains how he feasts at the tables of three cooks—his Eye, his Ear, and his Thought. Each gives him such delectable feasts that he imagines himself in Paradise. The extended discussion on how he uses his eyes and ears to supply his fantasy hearkens once again back to that crucial passage at the beginning of the poem where Genius, in response to Amans' besotted condition (his original sin), had warned Amans of the need to guard well his eyes and ears. The seeing and hearing motif which Gower had developed throughout the poem reaches its climax here (688–950) as Amans explains how he feeds his heart with his lady's goodly looks, her fame, and the sound of her voice; such fodder gives his fantasy strength to project his lover's situation into the romances he reads or hears—romances like that of Ydoine and Amadas (879). Though it may be that the senses were given to man to help him understand reality aright, they do not function that way for Amans. He willfully makes them see what he wants to see. Indeed, his third cook, Thought, delineated in the marginal gloss as "Qualiter cogitatus impressiones leticie ymaginatiuas cordibus inserit amantum,"[2] is not rational thought, but rather a form of "ymaginacioun" (cf. vii.4270 ff.) which always cooks "with fantasie and with desir" (916). "Thoght" never serves plain food, but rather food "of woldes and of wisshes, / Therof have I my fulle disshes" (923–24). There is nothing real about such dishes, no actual feeling or taste, says Amans (942; cf. 925); his Thought, like the Plover, feeds on air (943), a delicate feast indeed.

Though Genius' response to Amans' account of his lover's feast is comic as he allows that Amans has fed on "delices wonder smale" (954), the overall effect is sobering. The essential wrong of any sin lies in its separation of the mind and its faculties from reality. Amans has not only dramatized his exile, he has demonstrated how uncreative his mind has become as it turns away from realities to spin fantasies. The discussion of Delicacy is well placed in the poem, for it represents the ultimate refinement of the whole process of sin which climaxes in decadent indulgence with style and sophistication to maintain (almost) and enjoy (almost) an illusion of Paradise. Genius initially answers Amans' Delicacy with two true stories (he will not chasten fantasy with "fable"), the story of Dives and Lazarus from the Bible and a story about Nero. The main answer to Amans' intoxication with his fantasy life comes later in the book, however, when Genius puts aside his categories of Gluttony and explains "Sorcery." Indeed, the Delicacy of Amans' cupidity is, as we shall see, a subtle form of Sorcery in which he ousts reason so that will might conjure what it desires without regard for Nature's laws. Sorcerous Delicacy allows the will to re-create events according to its special wishes and even perverts the senses so that they conspire.

Gower devotes the last half and more of Book VI to Sorcery, thereby focusing attention on the psychology of sin. The implication is that as a sinner becomes more experienced, he becomes more adept and artful at indulging his fantasy life; he learns refined ways of circumventing his common nature and Nature's common laws. It takes skill to advance one's private rule. Delicacy is a craftsman, a craftsman of fantasy.

But there is another side as well. Selfish love, what Gower glosses as "carnal concupiscence,"[3] insists on having its own way; it must continually reconstruct reality to protect itself. It always feels threatened and reacts assertively. Since it has rejected external reality, nothing in external reality supports it, except by chance. Will must become all things to itself—creator and creation, giver and receiver, stimulus and satisfaction. In so whimsical a circumstance the soul's other faculties become confused and inoperative.

> Wit can no reson understonde,
> Bot let the governance stonde
> To Will, which thanne wext so wylde,
> That he can noght himselve schylde
> Fro no peril.
>
> (1241–45)

As "he tempteth hevene and erthe and helle" (1259), the lover of fantasy puts God's laws aside (1256; 1278) to follow "the lawes of his heste" (1263), laws "withoute insyhte of his corage" (1275). The latter qualification is crucial, pointing up that schizophrenic aspect of fantasy which ignores inner "corage." Natural insight, man's chiefest defense (the eye in his tower), is blocked to allow will more license.

> He stant so ferforth out of reule,
> Ther is no wit that mai him reule.
> (1283–84)

Selfish love, Genius explains, though it may well dote upon the concoctions of ear and eye, is as dim in its perception of the heart's insights as the blind steed Bayard who falls "in the dich amidde" (1281).

Genius' example of Nero's delicacy illustrates admirably the blindness and vain flattery of self-indulgence. Nero invites three men to feast with him. We are told that they have done nothing to deserve such an honor (1176). As they flatter themselves with thoughts of their splendid fortune, they are, of course, guilty of Delicacy. After dinner, one of the men is given a fine horse to ride, the second a place to sleep, and the third a chamber to walk in. But afterward, "al thilke game / Was into wofull ernest torned" (1178–79). Nero has them slain and their stomachs cut open to see who digested his food best. Since the one who walked contained the food most digested, Nero thereafter walked after his meals. The story skillfully sets off the blindness of self-indulgence by describing how "wonder glad" the men are upon receipt of the emperor's gifts. As they "prike and prance aboute" (1191), or whatever, flattering themselves with their unearned grandeur, they say in effect, "Look at me! Aren't I fine?"—that is, until the game turns to earnest. Then they get a reward beyond their fondest expectations—death, which sets the balance right. Nero's squandering of their lives to indulge his fancy is, of course, the height of Delicacy, and his tyrannical game the greatest vanity of all. Having continuously indulged himself at the expense of his subjects, he destroys his kingdom and enjoys the same reward that the three men received. His miserable end by suicide doubly proves the uselessness of Delicacy.

It perhaps comes as a surprise to discover over half of Book VI is devoted to Genius' discussion of Sorcery. The only two extended tales in the book occur in this latter part. Their effect is to focus attention on will, which remains our primary consideration until the *Confessio* is over. We have seen already, especially in the third and fourth books, Amans comically indulging his fantasy, in some instances even with the encouragement of Genius. But now as Genius relates such indulgence to conjuring, its pernicious insinuations become more apparent. By the time Genius finishes discussing Sorcery (i.e., the manipulation of nature for self-gratification), Amans is ready to be exorcised on a full scale.

The two tales of sorcery, the *Tale of Telegonus and Ulysses* and the *Tale of Nectanabus,* share one common feature: in neither is the sorcerer able to foresee his own death. The point is important, for it is the nature of fantasy to end in a death beyond the powers of the fantasizer. The philosopher accommodates his understanding to death. The sorcerer, through his delicate revision of reality, obscures death. And with such obfuscation, he loses (as we will recall from the *Trump of Death* in Book I) essential insights into his natural limits and true possessions.

One might well expect to find an account of Ulysses' encounter with Circe in a medieval discussion of Gluttony. But Gower's use of the story in the *Tale of Ulysses and Telegonus* is subtle beyond our expectations. Traditionally Circe's victims, whose lust and greed turn them into animals, are glossed as gluttons. Ulysses is the moderate one who escapes Circe's design through control of his will. But in Gower's version Ulysses is the gluttonous one. Although he, unlike his men, escapes being turned into "foules, / To beres, tigres, Apes, oules, / Or elles be som other weie" (1449–51), he falls victim of a subtler form of gluttony—Sorcery, the delicate gluttony of attaining desire of will through illusion. Apart from this small fault he is an altogether successful king. Ulysses uses sorcery to outmaneuver the sorceresses Calypso and Circe: "He kepte him sobre and made hem wilde" (1462). Yet although he controls one form of indulgence, he flatters himself with another. He subdues Circe to his desire, with the result that a child is conceived unbeknownst to him. Circe raises the child Telegonus. She perpetuates an illusion which Ulysses himself created, namely, the illusion that Ulysses is a wondrous king. When Telegonus comes of age,

Circe happily sends him to his father. Her own fantasy is reflected in the "thousand" greetings she would have her son convey to Ulysses for her (1656).

By most standards Ulysses succeeds as a king. After he returns from Troy to Penelope we are told that so well does he rule, the people tax themselves to keep him supplied.

> The presens every day be newed,
> He was with yiftes al besnewed;
> The poeple was of him so glad.
>
> . . . .
>
> Thus have Uluxes what we wolde,
> His wif was such as sche be scholde,
> His poeple was to him sougit,
> Him lacketh nothing of delit.
>
> (1497–1508)

But Fortune turns on Ulysses at the height of his glory. As he sleeps one night, his "yhen fedde" (1522) upon a dream, a dream which prophesies his death. It is a dream he cannot comprehend. He envisions a beautiful youth who approaches him like an Angel. He embraces the youth and would embrace again, but the apparition steps back and warns him that the love between them now will be the death of one or the other. Ulysses asks for an explanation, but is shown instead a banner embroidered with three fishes which are said to be the sign of an empire. Then the youth vanishes.

In attempting to fathom the dream Ulysses recognizes a likeness between himself and the youth, but not knowing that he begot a child on Circe, he thinks the youth must represent Telemachus, whom he consequently confines. He also doubles his bodyguards. But the child he should fear, the child of his fantasy, approaches despite Ulysses' defenses. When Telegonus is stopped at the gate, he proclaims his lineage, only to be mocked by the guards. But being a king's son, he retaliates and slays five of the best. Upon hearing the ruckus Ulysses himself rushes to the defense, casting his spear at Telegonus. But he misses. The boy then drives his lance through Ulysses. Attached to the lance is the banner, a sign of Circe's domain. Circe thus overcomes the great king after all, though neither intended it so. Genius puts the moral this way:

> Lo, whereof Sorcerie serveth.
> Thurgh Sorcerie his lust he wan,
> Thurgh Sorcerie his wo began,
> Thurgh Sorcerie his love he ches,
> Thurgh Sorcerie his lif he les;
> The child was gete in Sorcerie,
> The which dede al this felonie:
> Thing which was ayein kynde wroght
> Unkindeliche it was aboght;
> The child his oghne fader slowh,
> That was unkindeschipe ynowh.
>
> (1768–78)

Fantasy produces children as if by magic, children which destroy their progenitors. Perhaps the sorcerer's child should be glossed as his "fate." (Cf. the pun on *sors* [fate] implicit in "sorcery," in *Vox Clamantis* II.iv.203–8, discussed above, "Books III and IV.") In view of Gower's introductory observations on will's ousting of reason and abusing the senses, it may be that Telegonus' attack on Ulysses' castle and his slaying of the five guards implies a modest allegory: Will's sorcerous progeny, the child of fantasy, assaults Reason in the king's stronghold (i.e., the tower being the soul's domain), first by overthrowing the otherwise reliable five senses, and then by striking down the king himself. Such, at least, is the pattern as Gower presents it in his discussion of will and fantasy, and although Genius does not explicate the allegory in such explicit terms, the explication fits nonetheless, both with the poem and the commonplace iconography of will and reason.

Genius' explanation of his tales is never very elaborate. That is because, being part of the plot, he has his own bias. Moreover, Gower's poetry, by its nature, is designed to suggest broad possibilities which the reader must explore himself. Genius does offer some important leads, however, even though he may not recognize their full import. The *Tale of Ulysses and Telegonus,* for example, scrutinizes the limitations of human knowledge. Ulysses was for the most part a good king. He was one of the wisest men in history. Yet even so, he was unable to understand clearly his own fate.

> Men sein, a man hath knowleching
> Save of himself of alle thing;
> His oghne chance noman knoweth,
> Bot as fortune it on him throweth:
> Was nevere yit so wys a clerk,
> Which mihte knowe al goddes werk,
> Ne the secret which god hath set
> Ayein a man mai noght be let.
>   (1567–74)

Genius' observation on the limits of man's vision raises several problems which must be faced if the plot of Amans, the willful "caitif," is to find a resolution.

   If man cannot know those things which pertain to his own fate, then how can it be said that he controls his fate? Of what value is human wisdom? How can he possibly defend his tower from fantasy and Fortune's assault? Will he not, as Genius so often implies, be Fortune's fool? If he "thenketh to ben a king," as we are led to believe each man should think (cf. VIII.2110), to what should he apply himself? In his own assessment of such questions Genius cannot fully appreciate true philosophy; it is beyond his powers to do so. As he explains:

> For wisdom, hou that evere it stonde,
> To him that can it understonde
> Doth gret profit in sondri wise;
> Bot touchende of so hih aprise,
> Which is noght unto Venus knowe,

> I mai it noght miselve knowe,
> Which of hir court am al forthdrawe
> And can nothing bot of hir lawe.
>
> (2421–28)

Genius works within the domain of Venus, whose court thrives on mutability. He has sufficient insight into Fortune not to trust her. He also has sufficient faith in Nature to admire her laws, regardless of Venus whom he serves. When her cupidinous caprice goes against the "law of kynde" he senses the injustice even though he may not be able to analyze why. Thus his ambivalence about fantasy, which we have noted. Though he may encourage Amans to hope for fulfillment in love, he rejects unnatural means of obtaining love. He is indeed shrewd to have perceived a relationship between fantasy and sorcery. Many of the answers to questions of Wisdom, the powers of Fortune, and the nature of stable kingship will unfold in Book VII on the education of the king and in Book VIII in the story of Apollonius. Even though Genius cannot understand philosophy fully, his cunning is sufficient to transmit what he has heard. As he puts it:

> For thogh I be noght al cunnynge
> Upon the forme of this [philosophical] wrytynge,
> Som part therof yit have I herd,
> In this matiere hou it hath ferd.
>
> (2437–40)

Though he cannot fully appreciate higher philosophy, he is shrewd enough to see that philosophy is worthy of serious human endeavor. Moreover, he perceives what kinds of behavior are foolish within Fortune's domain. (Cf. his attack on Fa Crere [make-believe], in II. 2100 ff., discussed above, "Book II.") The foolishness of fantasy is self-evident, as his second tale on sorcery makes abundantly clear.

The story of Nectanabus is a foil to good kingship and the art of proper governance. Next to the *Tale of Apollonius* in Book VIII, it is the most important tale in the *Confessio*. As an elaborate example of how not to be a king, it introduces the seventh book explicating the philosophy of true kingship. Being a negative example, it finds its opposite in the *Tale of Apollonius,* the tale which forms the other side of the frame around Book VII.

Genius begins the *Tale of Nectanabus* with praise of the "hihe creatour of thinges, / Which is the king of alle kinges" (1789–90). In contrast to such a wise king is "king Nectanabus" of Egypt who is a "creatour" only through his sorcery. But though the mysterious Creator of all things suffers the likes of Nectanabus to ply his magic, it becomes apparent by the end of the story that such activity is antithetical to the true creator's behavior, a parody which ends not with "fruit of rihtwissnesse" but rather vanity. The first example of Nectanabus' power is his magical discovery that Egypt is about to be attacked by "enemys." But what he does not realize is that enemies always surround and assault kingdoms, and that it is the responsibility of the good king to defend his true home. Instead, Nectanabus quickly flees incognito "out of his oghne lond" (1803) to safety in Greece. Thus it would seem that his "wicchecraft" has held him in good stead. In Greece he sees Queen Olimpia, King Philip's wife, while she is celebrating her birthday. As she rides on a white mule through the town, she is so beautiful that he "couthe noght withdrawe his lok" (1858). Though he may have celebrated powers of vision he has not learned to guard his looking well. Neither has Olimpia, for as she sees his strange stare she is in turn sufficiently attracted to inquire about the stranger. Like Mundus in Book I, Nectanabus is able to convince her that a god wishes to couple with her to create a child who will rule the world, and like Mundus, he plays "god's instrument" and performs the deed. Later he is even able to convince Philip by magic that the child is the consequence of Anubus' desire. The child born is, of course, Alexander who does succeed, as Nectanabus had forecast, in becoming conqueror of the world. So again it would seem that Nectanabus has been a wise man.

But the conclusion of the tale proves his ultimate folly. The sorcerer ends up beguiling himself. Like "wise" Ulysses, despite his "wisdom," he is unable to understand his own end. Perhaps that is because he has so ignored the law of kind and natural ends. His art has told him that he shall be slain by his own son, but he does not perceive how. Alexander, who is his pupil as well as his progeny, wonders about the prophecy and, being ignorant of his true lineage, decides to prove that the "olde dotard lieth" (2307). He pushes him off the palace wall, calling out,

> Ly doun there apart:
> Wherof nou serveth al thin art?
> Thou knewe alle othre mennes chance
> And of thiself hast ignorance:
> That thou hast seid amonges alle
> Of thi persone, is noght befalle.
>   (2311–16)

So the Oedipal prophecy comes true and with dramatic irony as well. Alexander is right in his pronouncement even though ostensibly proven wrong; Nectanabus has indeed spoken of himself in ignorance. His art, moreover, has served him poorly in the end. In its secrecy and private goals, his art leaves the wizard lying "apart." The child of fantasy has again isolated and slain its progenitor.

Genius is unusually explicit in expounding the moral implications of the *Tale of Nectanabus.* First of all, he explains how Nectanabus was a false creator who, in his unnatural prognostications, cut himself off from his true creator.

> Thogh he upon the creatures
> Thurgh his carectes and figures
> The maistrie and the pouer hadde,
> His creatour to noght him ladde,
> Ayein whos lawe his craft he useth,
> Whan he for lust his god refuseth,
> And tok him to the dieules craft.
>   (2339–45)

Second, though he may have seemed wise in saving his neck by fleeing Egypt, in truth, he simply abandoned his kingdom to his enemies by being no king at all. He turns his kingship into a self-imposed exile. As Genius puts it, "Ferst [he] him exilede out of londe / Which was his oghne" (2348–49)—a stupid thing for a king to do. Rather than protecting him, his disguise simply negates his true being. Every good king should know that his kingdom will always be under attack. It is his duty to defend his place, not flee from it. Having abandoned his true domain Nectanabus commits a further degradation. He betrays the office into which he was born: "from a king [he] made him to ben an underling" (2349–50). Not only does he make an underling of himself, instead of engaging in noble, truly kingly activities, he devotes his whole talent (of which he has a bountiful portion) to the petty deception of a queen in order to satisfy his mundane lust (2351–54). The ultimate vanity of his behavior is seen in his death, a pitiful fall from an alien tower at the hands of his own son, a son who, though he will in his turn apparently become master of the world, will also die miserably far from his homeland. Just as Telegonus' attack on Ulysses' tower epitomized that king's vanity, Nectanabus' fall from Alexander's tower stands emblem to his folly, a fall which began when he abandoned his kingdom and assumed a disguise in the first place.

In his sorcerous miscreation, in his loss of his kingdom through self-imposed exile, and in his concentration of his talents on the seduction of another's wife, Nectanabus stands as cogent warning to Amans. Amans too has wandered far from his true country. Like Nectanabus and like Alexander, he has made himself captive to his fantasy in hope of prolonged delicacies. Nor can he yet see the inevitable self-destruction such make-believe holds in store for him. The *Tale of Nectanabus* at least gets Amans to think far enough to inquire of another mode of governance, however. Book VI concludes with Amans' requesting information on Aristotle, the teacher of Alexander who replaced the vain Nectanabus. He has heard that Aristotle instructed Alexander in "al that to a king belongeth, / Whereof min herte sore longeth / To wite what it wolde mene" (2413–15). His hope is that such instruction will help him find relief from the pains of his sorrowful heart. Perhaps it might even reconcile Will and Reason. Genius responds by praising Wisdom (2421 ff.) and expressing his own longing to have better understanding of philosophy, "for it helpeth to comune" (2431). Genius' stories, it would seem, have at least piqued Amans' imagination to wonder if there might be something beyond his folly. He would learn of true wisdom and the philosopher king, whose actions lead to self-fulfillment, rather than the fantasy of a sorcerer, whose actions offer only the illusion of success. He has made progress, it would seem, despite the infatuated protestations of his resistant will.

What follows in Book VII is a positive statement on training oneself in proper governance. There the theoretical basis of common profit and good kingship is fully explained. Gower's Genius, like his namesake in the *Roman de la Rose,* will speak on wisdom even though it surpasses his understanding. As the Latin epithet to Book VII explains, "Naturam superat doctrina [Doctrine precedes Nature]." And although Genius is a faculty of nature, he appreciates that which rises beyond him and will do his best to help Amans approach that lore despite his own limitations as guide. Philosophy explores one's true lineage and helps him discover both his beginning and his end. As such it will help Amans to forgo his fantasy and regain control of his fate.

BOOK VII

the education of a king

GENIUS CONTINUES his apology on limited understanding into Book VII. He is "somdel destrauht" at having to go beyond his competence to explain how a king should be trained. But he agrees to undertake the task, first, for the sake of gladness, "for it is glad . . . to hiere of suche thinges wise" (10–12); second, because it will help Amans "the time [to] lisse" (13); and finally, because wisdom is of value to one who wishes to advance "in loves cause" (17). Genius' triple rationale merits attention as it affects the shape of the poem's psychological plot. First, he talks of wisdom for gladness' sake. The Boethian premise that wisdom and happiness are different names for the same thing will be amply demonstrated in the discussion and tales which follow. The wise man is happy, and the only truly happy man is wise. In his pursuit of folly, Amans is miserable. He has yet to find an activity worthy of his talents, one which will enable him to conjoin will with wit and reason. Second, Amans needs to find release from the exigencies of time. He seems trapped by temporalities which frustrate him continually and bind him like a "caitif." He tries to get beyond time through his imagined lover's bliss with its illusory paradise, but external time interrupts his fantasy, as it always does, to leave him more bound and frustrated than before. Talk of wisdom helps, of course, to pass the time in an agreeable way. But since Truth, the object of Wisdom, goes beyond temporalities, pursuit of Truth establishes the only certain way "the time [to] lisse." Finally, we shall discover that Wisdom does indeed advance "loves cause," if by love one means chaste love rather than concupiscence or selfish love (unchaste love), which Genius classifies in Book VIII under the heading of incest. Wisdom helps one discover the proper object of his affection. All three reasons help the will to understand Nature and Fortune rightly and thus to approach a sense of self commensurate with its attendant realities.

Structurally, then, Book VII is the most important in the *Confessio*. It turns the plot around by treating openly what had earlier been expressed through innuendo. Instead of confession we now, at Amans' own request, get homily.

Genius begins by defining the fields of study in a liberal arts education. Such are the approaches to wisdom which a "king" should take. They are objective enumerations of the realities of creation classified according to the three Aristotelian divisions of knowledge—Theoretique, Rhetorique, and Practique. Theoretique is subdivided as Theology, Physics, and Mathematics, various aspects of which Genius considers at some length. Such material is unbiased; it is material which a king must be able to see and accept on its own terms. It stands in contrast to the lore of one like Nectanabus for whom such teaching provided a means to manipulate illusion rather than approach God's Truth. Genius' discussion is impressive in its balancing of the aspects of creation. It offers the medieval humanist's view of reality. One sees mankind surrounded by symmetries, harmonies, proportions, and regulations to which he may relate beneficially if he chooses to do so. From Astronomy, a subdivision of Mathematics, he learns how the stars pertain to each other and to men and things on earth. From Physics he learns of the universal desire of all created things to maintain proper place and discover their "oghne kind." All facets of creation are interrelated as the parts of a cosmic community. Indeed, man's very body is itself a community with reason as king, the stomach as cook, the heart as "chief lord," and the liver, lungs, gall, and spleen as servants each with a special office to perform (463–89).

Though each aspect of creation has its own office, man, being both soul and body, has a uniquely subtle role. His position is complex in that he must relate both earthward and heavenward and try to maintain a balance even though the two directions "nevere stonde in evene" (506). Earth is "mannes weie" (550), so he must understand it well, even though heaven is his end. The mathematical sciences help man reclaim a larger perspective beyond the minuscule passions which so often blind him. Rhetoric offers a similar help to man since it is the study of the language which "the hihe makere of natures" (1508) gave to men alone above all other earthly creatures. Language, Genius explains, when properly understood and used, can, like mathematics, enable man to view the realities of creation from a lofty height: "word above alle earthli thinges / Is vertuous in his doinges" (1547–48). Study of words and meanings is especially important to a king who must learn how to discern and communicate things rightly.

Practique differs from the first two subdivisions of knowledge in that it is the science of human behavior itself. It encompasses three points: Etique, by which the king learns to govern himself; Inconomique, by which he learns to govern his household; and Policie, by which he learns to govern his realm at large. Since man in his personal, domestic, and social nature performs activities analogous to each other, Genius concentrates his discussion on Policy, for that offers the broadest definition of self, that is, the king in terms of his whole kingdom. As Genius discusses Policy, we shall regularly be made aware of the ethical or "economical" dimensions of his point as well.

Genius begins by talking about law. Law is, of course, what the distraught Amans has lost. Genius explains that though one finds in the king's realm many kinds of people (clerks, knights, merchants, common people, and, within the city, craftsmen), for all of them, law provides a universal.

O lawe mot governe hem alle,
Or that thei lese or that thei winne,
After thastat that thei ben inne.
                    (1696–98)

There must be one law for all men.[1] It behooves the king, then, to
understand not only the multitudinous offices within his domain but
also the regulations to which all adhere. The order of nature will show
him something of the harmony and proportion necessary for a complete life. It also shows him the importance of relating to things both
outside and within himself. One of Amans' problems has been his
reluctance to live under a single rule. Though he may see the virtue of a
point in the abstract he always makes of himself an exception in the
application. The consequence is not so much an affront to law as an
alienation of self from natural order.

Genius enumerates five points of policy—Truth, Liberality, Justice,
Pity, and Chastity—which the "Philosophre" enjoins a king "to kepe
and holde in observance, / As for the worthi governance / Which
longeth to his Regalie" (1707–9). This five-point format, to which the
last two-thirds of Book VII is devoted, recalls the structural principle of
the Prologue and first three books of the *Confessio,* where Genius had
exorcised sins according to their five points. Here the effect is opposite,
however, as Genius now deals with positive rather than negative
maxims of behavior. Moreover, his material is presented as a sermon
rather than a confession. Amans does not speak until the end of the
book. The sermon functions in the *Confessio* in some ways comparable
to the Parson's sermon at the end of Chaucer's *Canterbury Tales.*
Though Gower still relies on "fables," as the Parson does not, the
exemplary stories deal more explicitly with moral abstractions than
previous tales did. Like the examples of Chaucer's Parson, the tales of
Book VII reach magnetically into preceding tales of the *Confessio* with
remarkable perception. In the *Mirour,* each of the five children of a
given vice had an appropriate remedy. Here in the *Confessio,* the five
points of Policy stand as remedy for all vice: Sin and good kingship are
antithetical concepts (cf. *Tripartite Chronicle*: "The sinner cannot be
ruler"),[2] and these five are the points of right rule.

The most fundamental point of Policy is Truth, for if men do not find "Truth" within their king (or, by extension, within their reason), "it were an unsittende thing" (1736). An "unsittende thing" is a thing without proper place, something alien, or something which might provoke revolution or displacement of right order. ("Sitting" or "standing" metaphors are prominent throughout the *Confessio,* but especially in the conclusion, as part of Gower's apparatus to define or locate man's proper domain.) Truth is "the vertu soverein of alle" (1776). Without it, Reason is overthrown and the king is false. If the throne falls vacant, the kingdom staggers headless.

The first exemplary tale in Book VII, the *Contest of Darius,* pertains to Truth. Taken from "the Cronique" (in reality 3 Esd. 3–4), it is first of several examples of good and bad kingship. Darius, king of Persia, loved wisdom, we are told, and surrounded himself with wise men. On one occasion he put this question to three of his wisest: Which is strongest—Wine, Women, or a King? Arpaghes argued that a king is most powerful, since man is the most noble of creatures, having powers of reason, and a king rules over men. Manachaz argued on behalf of wine, since wine has powers of transforming lewd men into wise, making blind men see, conquering reason, and the like. Zorobabel argued on behalf of women, since they give birth to kings and vintners, can conquer men with their love, and, as the life of Alceste illustrates, possess such devotion and goodness as to die on their husband's behalf. But then the story takes an unexpected turn. Having argued on behalf of women, Zorobabel introduces a fourth, unexpected candidate— Truth, which he says is most powerful of all. Nothing may overcome Truth: "who that is trewe, / Him schal his while nevere rewe. . . . The trouthe is schameles ate ende" (1961–65). Zorobabel is most commended for his answer and receives his prize.

The story is not simply a tale about Truth; it embodies a model of the whole progress of the *Confessio Amantis.* Truth comes as an unexpected candidate, outside the original bargain. It is like Genius' lecture on Wisdom, which neither he nor Amans could have anticipated at the outset of their contract. Yet here in Book VII Truth wins the day as the game of the lover's confession shifts to include this profession of Truth. This pattern is seen again at the end of the poem as Amans gives up his illusions, looks directly at himself in the mirror, and, in the face of Truth, abandons his self-indulgent hopes for singular profit. As Amans shifts from protestation on behalf of his lady love to his prayer for common profit and England, our *"confessio amantis"* ends on an unexpected turn: charity displaces cupidity; Truth, the unannounced candidate, claims the field.

Liberality, the *Mirour's* antidote to Avarice, is the second point of policy. As in the Prologue, the end of Book II, and the beginning of Book V, where he had dealt with Avarice, Gower takes occasion to remind us that once "the worldes good was ferst comune" and enjoyed for "comun profit" (1991–93). But such liberality ceased when men started envying each other's goods and tried to draw everything to themselves "for singulier beyete" (1996). Kings had to be established to protect men from their own avarice. Such a derivation of royalty is a definition in itself. That is, kingship is the maintenance of common profit through liberality.

> So sit it wel in alle wise
> A king betwen the more and lesse
> To sette his herte upon largesse
> Toward himself and ek also
> Toward his poeple.
>   (2014–18)

The king should look after both himself and his people. He must not be too niggardly, hoarding too much to himself, nor too prodigal, giving too much away. He must know his place ("so sit it wel") and train himself in discretion. Genius emphasizes the danger which flattery poses for the king. If he does not judge astutely, he will not know where to bestow his largess. Examples in this section are so extensive and precise that one wonders if they might not have had a special pertinence in Gower's mind to Richard himself, who surrounded himself with notorious flatterers. A good king must be able to accept criticism, if it is justified, and he must be capable of making discreet distinctions, witness the tale of Julius and the poor knight: A poor knight approaches Julius Caesar in hope of recovering his rights; at first Caesar ignores him, so the knight chastises him, explaining how he fought by his side and had even been wounded, yet had received no thanks. Julius, recognizing that the knight speaks truth, bestows upon him enough goods to last him the rest of his life. Julius does not turn the knight away for having spoken directly to him; neither does he give him too much to make up for his error; rather, he gives him "good ynouh" (2105).

As a second example, Genius explains how a poor knight named Cinichus demanded great gifts of Antigonus and was refused, for the demand exceeded the knight's merits; when the knight sarcastically asked then for "bot a litel peny" (2125), he was again refused, for that was too small an acknowledgement. A king must learn to measure what is right. It behooves each man "to helpe with his oghne lond" (2139), and it behooves the king to support such pleas when they are reasonable. Gower follows something of the same logic in *Tripartite Chronicle* when he chastises Richard for not supporting his critics, the noble Swan (Gloucester), the Bear (Thomas, Earl of Warwick), and the Horse (Richard, Earle of Arundel), but rather, playing the part of fox, or worse, of mole, destroyed them while adhering to flatterers like the Earl of Oxford.[3]

Flattery, Genius insists, is a cardinal threat to both king and flatterer. Genius shows in his *Tale of Diogenes and Aristippus* how the flatterer sells himself into slavery: Diogenes and Aristippus graduated from "Scole" together; the former went home to dwell in his house beside a bridge "to studie in his Philosophie" (2245); the latter went to court to advance himself through flattery and "wordes softe" (2251). But in this instance "court" equates with "exile," for the price of membership at court is one's integrity. When the two classmates meet later in life beside Diogenes' bridge, Aristippus mocks the humble philosopher, suggesting that if he had gone to court he too could have become a great man. Diogenes replies that if Aristippus could "wortes pyke" (2302) he might not have become a slave to flattery. The point seems to be that Diogenes possesses his home and garden, with access to the outside world by means of his bridge, while the schoolmate, guided not by his own sovereignty but the tyrant's whim, possesses nothing.

Yet Genius knows that the world is likely to praise Aristippus over Diogenes and thus pose all the greater threat to the king.[4] Though the voice of the people may be the voice of God, the voice of the mob is usually fickle. Genius explains how a Roman emperor, as a precaution against self-flattery, had a fool ride beside him in his victory processions to remind him in his glory that Fortune could overturn him at any time and that one had best "know thiself" (2389) and let not pomp or pride turn his mind. Genius explains further how one of the emperor's first acts upon being "entronized" (2416) was to have his masons measure him for his sepulcher. That dreary business should help to deter his being fooled by flattery. Like the king of Hungary in the *Trump of Death,* he knew that death was a sure corrective to human arrogance. A discrete king should learn to handle flatterers as Caesar did: When one kissed his foot, revering him as a god, and then sat beside him saying, "If you are a god I have worshipped you aright, but if you are a man we share one nature," Caesar replied, "Blind fool, if I am a god you do wrong to sit here, and if I am a man, you were foolish to revere me as a god."

Genius concludes his discussion of flattery with an account of Ahab and Micaiah from the Bible: Ahab sends flatterers to King Josaphat in hope of getting him to rescue him from Benedab. Micaiah warns that the king is surrounded by flatterers, but Josaphat ignores his prophecy and goes to war. He is defeated in battle and the kingdom is divided. Genius' wording of Micaiah's prophecy is noteworthy:

> Goth hom into your hous ayein
> Til I for you have betre ordeigned.
> (2662–63)

The "hom" metaphor recalls the initial tale in Book VII exemplifying flattery, that of Diogenes and Aristippus. Josaphat does not go home, but, following the advice of the flatterer Sedechie, pursues his war and dies in exile, leaving his people "astray" in exile too. It seems, then, that not only does the flatterer commit himself to exile but so too the one who is flattered, who, lacking discretion, flatters himself with the flatterer's advice. But the story does not end there. We learn that despite Josaphat's vain pursuits, God looks after the people and helps them "hom ayein in goddes pes" (2683). Here, as in so many of Gower's stories, God's fundamental benevolence toward man maintains at least a semblance of common profit despite the folly of capricious rulers.

The discussion of liberality, discretion, and flattery, bespeaks, as I have suggested earlier, Gower's concern with proper governance in England and his worrying over the shortcomings of Richard, the boy-king.[5] It also reflects upon that other irresponsible youth, Amans, who has such trouble being a stable person. Regularly he flatters himself with thoughts of his lady, the result being that he, like other flatterers, is left in exile. As he misuses his eyes, ears, and thought to gratify his willful fancy, he is guilty of indiscrete judgment and willful manipulation of Truth. Unlike Julius Caesar, he refuses to accept criticism. He follows the path of Aristippus rather than Diogenes in all matters pertaining to his lady (fantasy). Thus, in his courtship of Venus he ends up far from home, lying apart in the wood, which is indeed, an "unsittende thing!"

Genius begins his third point of Policy, Justice, with a reiteration of the importance of law in defining relationships between the king, his subjects, and the land itself. He starts by emphasizing that a king must have a strong, personal sense of justice. Although he has great power, he must not oppress his people. He must "himself ferst justefie" (2730) to God "in his degre." Then he must see to it that his laws are just and applied by just judges to rich and poor alike.[6]

> If lawe stonde with the riht,
> The poeple is glad and stant upriht.
> Wher as the lawe is resonable,
> The comun poeple stant menable,
> And if the lawe torne amis,
> The poeple also mistorned is.
>
> (2759–64)

Good laws keep peace; but if they are not kept, then "ther is no comun profit soght" (2828). Breach of good law culminates on the large scale in peasant revolts and insurrections, and on the small, in self-pity and the abuse of Will, Wit, and Memory.

Genius' chief example for this point of Policy is Lycurgus, whose laws were so true and well understood that he could remove himself personally from the scene without jeopardizing the state. Lycurgus is the model prince, his kingdom the model home. His rule is such that no barriers stand between his people and the "trouthe of governance" (2925). Instead, "every man hath his encress" (2927).

> Richesse upon the comun good
> And noght upon the singuler
> Ordeigned was, and the pouer
> Of hem that weren in astat
> Was sauf.
>
> (2930–34)

His people enjoy peace without war, love without envy, and live free from internal strife "so that in reste / Mihte every man his herte reste" (2935–36).

Such a kingdom stands in sharp contrast to Amans' chaos. Before Lycurgus retires from Athens he reiterates his goals:

> my will hath be
> To do justice and equite
> In forthringe of comun profit.
>
> (2955–57)

He claims no personal credit for the laws; they were "altogedre of goddes sonde / And nothing of myn oghne wit" (2962–63). They are so true that they do not depend upon an individual personality or figurehead. Lycurgus' disappearance is no exile or abandonment of responsibility like that of Nectanabus. Rather, it represents the removal of willful emotion which so often causes disruption of the common good. His intent is that of "rihtwisnesse." Since Athens had sworn its oath to abide by the laws until Lycurgus returned, and since he never returned, the Athenians remained bound to good law "which was for comun profit set" (3007). For Lycurgus, law rather than whim bound his state together.

> And in this wise he hath it knet;
> He, which the comun profit soghte,
> The king, his oghne astat ne roghte;
> To do profit to the comune,
> He tok of exil the fortune,
> And lefte of Prince thilke office
> Only for love and for justice,
> Thurgh which he thoghte, if that he myhte,
> For evere after his deth to rihte
> The cite which was him betake.
>
> (3008–17)

This abandonment of selfish interest so that the "comune" might profit is the primary lesson Amans must learn in Book VIII as he moves beyond his self-pity. It is perhaps a paradox that one returns home from exile by exiling egotism, but that seems to be the only way to "knet" well the garment of happy estate.

To exemplify Pity, the fourth point of Policy, Genius begins with Christ, who took such pity upon mankind that he assumed human flesh. He then speaks of Constantine whom he had discussed at the end of Book II, whose pity for the children and mothers of his kingdom caused him to put personal needs aside. But as he gets further into his discussion of this kingly virtue, we see that Pity, like Liberality, is a virtue which requires discriminating judgment. Truth and Justice are superlative virtues. One cannot be too True or too Just. But one can be too Liberal or too Piteous. Thus, after explaining how mercy and pity must govern a king's behavior, Genius cautions against confusing cowardice, weakness, or indecision with Pity, just as he cautioned against prodigality and flattery in his discussion of Liberality.

Genius' first extended example of a piteous king is the story of

Codrus, a king who like Christ or Constantine so loved his people that he willingly would die to save them. In contrast to Codrus he presents the foolish king Rehoboam, Solomon's son, who ignored the wise advice of his old counselors to follow the avaricious ways of his young counselors who advised him to tax his people pitilessly, even though there was no need for additional revenue, his father's temple having already been completed. In response to the pitiless tax the people revolted and took another king, Jereboam, thus irreparably dividing the kingdom. The story is another which perhaps stands as a warning to Richard II, whose rejection of mature counselors for young seemed in Gower's eyes to be pressing the kingdom to the point of a second revolt. The unrest caused by Richard's taxes, especially in London, gave Gower great concern. The account of the folly of Rehoboam exemplifies sin as mother of division. His loss of his people stands in contrast to the governance of Lycurgus, whose wise laws and lack of personal aggrandizement assured him of never losing his people. Pitilessness costs Rehoboam his kingdom where Pity would have maintained it. We shall see the Pity motif again in our discussion of Apollonius in Book VIII.

The final point of Policy, Chastity, has frequently been touched upon in the *Confessio*. As Gower uses the term, Chastity enjoys a broader definition than that which we normally give it. Chastity is the proper maintenance of just marriages. It is a virtue which depends in part on what one is married to and what the rationale behind the marriage is. Genius introduces his discussion with a general admonition against lechery, the seventh of the deadly sins which Genius has been exploring throughout the poem. This discussion of Chastity, which the *Mirour de l'Omme* names as the antidote for Luxure, thus stands as a culmination to the previous discussions of sin. It also resolves many of the ambiguities we have noted thus far in the character of Genius. The *Mirour* considers five points of Chastité—Bonnegarde, Virginite, Matrimonie, Continence, and Aspre (hard life)—all five of which are exemplified in Genius' discussion of this virtue here at the end of Book VII.

Genius begins with an appeal against adultery. Though nature made

males to go with females and though desire makes the male seek many
females, bigamy is not the "weie of kinde."

> For whan a man mai redy finde
> His oghne wif, what scholde he seche
> In strange places to beseche
> To borwe an other mannes plouh,
> Whan he hath geere good ynouh
> Affaited at his oghne heste,
> And is to him wel more honeste
> Than other thing which is unknowe?
> (4218–25)

Though the rationale of the passage at first seems uncomfortably like
that of old Januarie in Chaucer's *Merchant's Tale*,[7] the ease with which
marriage provides sexual bliss is not Genius' point. Rather he is concerned with the relationship between home and true possession. "Bor-
rowing" wives from one's neighbor in "strange places" inevitably leads
to fruitless fantasy, conflict, and alienation. Where one's wife is, there
home is. A chaste man seeks proper, not alien marriages. And it is
man's nature to be monogamous. Genius' stand on monogamy may
come as a surprise after his various efforts to encourage Amans toward
vigorous love, but Genius well understands the virtue of common
profit and the importance of right marriages if the fruits of common
profit are to be born. Fruition, not sex, is the end Genius serves.

A proper marriage is rational and discrete. It fulfills both the laws of
love and of reason. It must not belie the partner's dignity nor one's
own. The prince must be careful that he does not become besotted in
his marriage, thereby changing "for the wommanhede / The worthiness of his manhode" (4255–56). That would indeed be adultery (cf.
Matt. 5:28). Genius explains that woman is not to blame for man's wild
sexual fantasy—that "fool impression of his ymaginacioun" (4271–72);
the fault lies rather in man's misuse of his will. We have seen Genius
insist again and again that creatures are born to love; that is their

proper nature. He now makes an important qualification, however, one which sets his rule quite apart from Cupid's.

> It sit a man be weie of kinde
> To love, bot it is noght kinde
> A man for love his wit to lese.
>   (4297–99)

A man indeed should be vigorous in love; his stomach, kidneys, liver, and so on, have their rights and need their exercise. But not at the expense of his wit, for then the king is overthrown and the whole estate ruined. Man's place (i.e., where he "sits" or "stands") resides in the "worthiness of his manhood," his virtue, which nature has uniquely bestowed upon him through the gift of reason. For a man to abandon "his astat / Thurgh his sotie effeminat, / And leve that a man schal do" is as stupid as wearing hose outside one's shoes (4303–6).

Genius offers several examples of foolish kings who lose their estate through love foolishness, the principal of which is Solomon. Though Solomon was wise to begin with, his cupidity ruined everything.

> That every worthi Prince is holde
> Withinne himself himself beholde,
> To se the stat of his persone,
> And thenke hou ther be joies none
> Upon this Erthe mad to laste,
> And hou the fleissh schal ate laste
> The lustes of this lif forsake,
> Him oghte a gret ensample take
> Of Salomon, whos appetit
> Was holy set upon delit,
> To take of wommen the plesance.
>   (4469–79)

Solomon forgot his wisdom, and instead of beholding himself within himself, he turned his lusts to women of alien lands ("Sarazines"); his fantasy led him to "ydolatrie" (4497). His is the arch example of loss of estate through misrule of his psychic domain. His femininity causes him to lose not only his rationality but also his kingdom which, once divided, falls. One finds support for Gower's position on rulers who are lovers in *Vox Clamantis,* where he emphasizes that Venus and knighthood are antithetical concepts. For a man to be Venus' knight is not only uncomely, it is more idiotic than the idiot.[8]

Book VII concludes with three tales devoted to "the remenant of vice" (4588), namely "lecherie," that seventh of the sins which Genius has yet to parse. The tales exemplify the various aspects of lechery— fornicacioun, stupre (rape), avolterie, incest, and foldelit—as well as their remedies. Each, moreover, explores the making or destroying of kingship, thus exemplifying further the five points of kingly policy.

The *Tale of Tarquin and Aruns* consists of two related parts: 1] the fall of the Gabiens, and 2] the rape of Lucrece. Tarquin and his son Aruns are evil rulers who gain power through treason and tyranny. In the first episode we see how they undermine a community and destroy it. Aruns, by means of deceit, infiltrates the city of the Gabiens. Having wounded and beaten himself, he pretends that his family has turned against him and sorely abused him. The Gabiens confuse sentiment with pity and admit him to their city. He immediately communicates the success of his infiltration to his father who sends a return message: "crop the lilies." Aruns interprets the message to mean cut off the heads of the Gabien princes, which he does, and another impregnable tower falls from within. Decapitation is apt punishment for the foolish princes, since they did not use their heads when they admitted Aruns in the first place. The effect of their error, however, is terrible indeed, for without good leaders the whole town is at the mercy of Tarquin who now attacks and destroys the city. All the citizens, regardless of "degre," are slain "withoute reson or pite" (4699). This detail of the slaughter of the citizens is Gower's addition to the story as he took it from Ovid's *Fasti.* The change is another instance of his belief in the interconnectedness of man's welfare. When the king errs, the people suffer.

Between the destruction of the Gabiens and the rape of Lucrece, Gower places an important interlude. Aruns and Tarquin assemble in

Rome for a solemn sacrifice at the Temple of Phebus. A hideous serpent comes out, devours all the sacrifice, and quenches the fires. The act is interpreted to mean that the sacrifice of Tarquin and his son is wasted because their sins have been so "abhominable." The abomination lies in their usurpation of kingship for singular profit. Phebus announces "with gastly vois" (4721) that whoever kisses his mother first will avenge the wrong. Unseen of others a knight named Brutus falls to the ground and kisses the earth.

> For he knew wel in his entente
> How therthe of every mannes kinde
> Is Moder: bot thei weren blinde,
> And sihen noght so fer as he.
>   (4742–45)

Brutus knows himself well enough to appreciate his origins and true attachments. He is farsighted, a wise one who perceives common nature and can detect abominable sin. It is too bad for the Gabiens that they had no Brutus among them. But though Aruns still has evil to do and will crop the lily of the good Roman citizen Lucrece, that city will not fall. Brutus, who keeps his priorities in right order, will see to that.

As the story continues, Aruns and his cousin Collatin are encamped near Rome, conducting further war. They make a bet on who has the most loyal wife. To prove the winner, Aruns and Collatin slip into the city at night to spy on their women. Collatin wins the wager, since his wife Lucrece, though industriously involved with her domestic "werche" as a good wife should be, speaks of her eagerness that the siege be ended so that her husband might come home. Little does she know that the siege of her fortress has just begun. Collatin surprises her by jumping from his hiding place to embrace her, thus answering her wish that he return. As she blushes with pleasure, Aruns is smitten with "thilke blinde maladie, / To which no cure of Surgerie / Can helpe" (4855–57). The parallel with the Gabien situation is evident. To what extent is Collatin guilty of his own downfall? Like the Gabiens, he took Aruns in and even showed him the way to his wife, a wife whom he was abusing by using her in a game to flatter his ego.

When Aruns returns to camp he "pourtreieth hire ymage" (4876) in his heart. The description of his infatuation is a rehearsal of his own downfall as he puts the hose over the shoe, so to speak, and muses on the "fool impression of his ymaginacioun" (cf. 4271 and 4303 ff.). As he recalls the features of her face, her womanly beauty, her yellow hair, her dress, her lovely voice, and how she wept, he reminds us of Amans and his three cooks—Looking, Hearing, and Thought, which enable him to fornicate with his fantasy in "foldelit." It is interesting to note that in Ovid, Aruns has his fantasy while looking at Lucrece in Rome.[9] Gower brings him home to his closet (albeit on the battlefield), to heighten the notion of his overthrow by "ymaginacioun." He hides himself away and dreams. That Aruns becomes a wild man in his lust is no excuse. Though desire may be natural, irrationality is not.

In his madness Aruns slips back to Rome and gains admittance to "Collatines In" through friendly manners and the fact that he is "cousin of house." Gower's repeated emphasis on Aruns' familial relationship with Collatin (4776, 4921) is calculated. It completes the totality of Aruns' lecherous guilt by involving him in incest as well as all other aspects of Lechery. More important, it spells out most precisely the doom of his own house. In Ovid, the relationship is less clear, with only a single oblique reference suggesting that Aruns and Collatin were of kindred blood ("sanguine junctus erat": Fasti II. 88). After the rape we learn that Brutus, who comes with Collatin to investigate what happened, is also "cousin" to Lucrece (5014). (No mention of his kinship is made in Ovid.) Gower draws the parallel to set Aruns' behavior more sharply in contrast to that of the more wise cousin. As Lucrece unexpectedly commits suicide, Brutus "toward himself his herte kepte" (5083); he takes the knife and swears revenge. He keeps his head and his own counsel where Aruns lost his, and though Lucrece dies, the city of Rome will be purged. Brutus, "with a manlich herte" (5093), goes to the people who rally and expunge the trecherous lily-croppers once and for all:

> Awey, awey the tirannie
> Of lecherie and covoitise!
> (5118–19)

So cry the people, and Tarquin and Aruns are exiled. The city takes "betre governance" (5123). In terms of Gower's motif of kingship and common profit, exile is the appropriate fate for Tarquin and Aruns, rather than death, since loss of estate through effeminacy is exile by definition.

The exile of Tarquin and Aruns recalls the fate of Mundus after his rape of Paulina in Book I; that tale offers an important contrast as well. Unlike Collatin, Paulina's husband was a moving force capable of righting disorder. Collatin, on the other hand, is weak. He plays games with Aruns at his wife's expense rather than being a true counselor to her. Thus Lucrece, without a true husband's support, commits suicide, while Paulina, in her comparable situation, found reassurance and confirmation of her community through her husband. It is Brutus, rather than Collatin, who "keeps his heart" and knows his true family ties (earth and Rome) well enough to act out of his own counsel while others stand amazed. Genius does not say so, but the implication seems to be that Brutus is the "betre governance" which restores Rome as a family. He certainly is the one who manifests Truth, Liberality, Justice, Pity, and Chastity in his actions.

The second of the three concluding tales in Book VII is the *Tale of Virginia*. Designed to show that justice and lechery hold no company (5125), the tale offers another example of a king who loses his kingship through lechery. Though Gower follows his source (Livy) fairly closely, he makes subtle changes which lend focus to his theme. For example, in Livy, Apius is one of the *decemvir*.[10] Gower first calls him "governour of the cite" (5133) and thereafter, "king." (He would keep his reader mindful of right governance of one's estate by consistent use of terminology.) When Apius falls in love with Virginia it is because fame of her beauty has reached his "Ere," another instance in which Gower slightly alters his source to tie the story in with earlier motifs. Gower's concern becomes even more apparent when the people plead with Apius for the sake of Virginia: They invoke "the comun lawe" (5188) on

Virginia's behalf and reason that she especially should be protected, since her father is fighting "for comun riht" and "the profit of hem alle / Upon the wylde feldes" (5192–93).

Apius, of course, pays no heed to their appeal to common profit. Unlike Lycurgus, he sets himself above law and would manipulate the legal structure to his personal likes. But ultimately the voice of the people restores right order—a law beyond the false king's whim. After Virginius escapes, the people rally and "of on acord upriht" return "at ones hom ayein" (5282–83) to Rome and depose the tyrant. At the end, when Apius is finally brought to justice, Gower omits his suicide. Instead he has the people, whom he calls the "comun feere," depose "here wrongfull king" (5295) through "comun conseil" (5290 ff.). In Gower's version of this popular medieval story, it is clear that not only does lechery not pay but also that the good king should work for the common benefit of his people else they revolt in a bewildered effort to restore the common good which is their right. Like so many other tales in this section of the *Confessio,* this tale stands as a pointed warning to kings against selfish rule and bad counsel.

The moral which Genius draws from the *Tale of Virginia* is built on a pun: "And thus thunchaste was chastised" (5301). The pun pertains significantly to Gower's emphasis in Book VIII on incest (incastus) as the epitome of all sin. A chaste person is a chastised person, one whose virtue is well guarded. In the *Mirour,* the defense against Fornicacioun is Bonnegarde. The last tale in Book VII, the *Tale of Tobias and Sara,* is developed around this concept of Bonnegarde. Earlier Genius had introduced the idea with his story of the pagan King Amalech's almost successful defeat of the Israelites (4406–68). The Israelites were too much for Amalech until his counselor Balaam suggested he send a bevy of beautiful women among them. The Hebrews became so infatuated that they became weak and were easily defeated. Then Phinees saw the problem and beheaded two of the offenders as an example to the rest to keep better guard over their sex life. The sight of such justice quickly turned the Israelites back to their proper defenses. As we have repeatedly seen in the *Confessio,* the good king must guard well his senses and his reason; otherwise he will be exiled and his citadel destroyed.

In the story of *Tobias and Sara,* Genius' "conclusion final" (5310), Sara is wed by six successive husbands who look upon her as an object to satisfy their lust. All six are successively destroyed by the fiend Asmod for their lechery as soon as they touch her. Then Tobias marries her. Unlike the previous six, he is not "assoted . . . upon hire love" (5322) but is guided by Chastity and the Angel Raphael, who has taught Tobias to be "honeste" (5359). Though he is a lusty fellow, he also honors reason. Thus,

> Thobie his wille hadde;
> For he his lust so goodly ladde,
> That bothe lawe and kinde is served,
> Wherof he hath himself preserved.
>
> (5361–64)

His will is not repressed; but neither is law. He has both his pleasure and just law. As Genius later explains,

> For god the lawes hath assissed
> Als wel to reson as to kinde,
> Bot he the bestes wolde binde
> Only to lawes of nature,
> Bot to the mannes creature
> God yaf him reson forth withal,
> Wherof that he nature schal
> Upon the causes modefie,
> That he schal do no lecherie,
> And yit he schal hise lustes have.
> So ben the lawes bothe save.
>
> (5372–82)

Through his chastity and well-guarded reason Tobias ends up in possession of his citadel and his happiness. He is personally preserved, and his marriage is saved.

But despite all the examples of good kingship and the exposures of false kings, Amans does not seem to have advanced very far in his understanding. As he explains,

> The tales sounen in myn Ere,
> Bot yit myn herte is elleswhere,
> I mai miselve noght restreigne.
>   (5411–13)

With his heart "elleswhere" and his wit unable to find proper restraint, he is still in exile and torment. He egotistically asks for talk of "my matiere / Touchende of love, as we begonne" (5422–23). Of course, the whole of the seventh book, though it began as an apparent digression, repeatedly spoke directly to Amans' "matiere" of love. In fact, it spoke in no uncertain terms of all categories of lechery and their evil effects upon one seeking a stable life. But "my matiere," as Amans understands it, is "Placebo" to his fantasy. So, although Genius has already given the topic of love thorough treatment (especially carnal concupiscence) and has defined in no uncertain terms his position on the relationship of reason and desire, he agrees to speak on one last facet of Venus' love, that is, "love which is unavised" (5433). The resolution will grow out of one last argument on learning to see well. By explaining the blindness of cupidity Genius hopes to open Amans' cupidinous eyes. Only then might there be hope of regaining his proper kingship and a passage home.

BOOK VIII

the Return home

BOOK VIII IS A STUDY in the rediscovery of right relationships. After Amans requests discussion of "my matiere touchende love" (VII.5422–23), Genius suggests they talk more about "love which is unavised" (VII.5433). "Unavised" means "not carefully looked at." As a perceptual term it equates with "mislok," the word Genius had used when he first began his shrift of the confused Amans (I.334; cf. I.418, 445). The Latin epigram which begins Book VIII glosses the condition as *cecus amor* (blind love).[1] Although Amans has been widely instructed in the moral code of his society, his most crucial problem is still one of perspective. He persists in looking at the world (or rather, his mistress) in the wrong way. The eighth book thus does not begin with words about "mi lady," the matter which Amans understands as "touchende [his] love"; instead, Genius touches upon love in a broader sense. He explains elements of God's domain, that place where all creatures should situate their love if they would find bliss.

The myhti god, which unbegunne
Stant of himself and hath begunne
Alle othre thinges at his wille,
The hevene him liste to fulfille
Of alle joie, where as he
Sit inthronized in his See,
And hath hise Angles him to serve,
Suche as him liketh to preserve.

(1–8)

The verbal metaphors of place and situation forcefully indicate the divine sense of domain. God, the true king, *"stant of himself"* and *"sit inthronized in his See"* (italics mine) with his community of the blessed around him. His throne is all creation's center. Reasonable creatures should seek God's enlightened home, each according to his created nature if he would be "avised" in love and know his own place with Truth at the center.

In contrast to true vision and steadfastness, Genius describes the apostasy of Lucifer, who blindly fell through selfish love and "dedly Pride" (23) into perpetual darkness (i.e., blindness). His fall presides as archetypal model behind Amans' own exile as he lies "caitif" in the woods, overthrown "withoute breth" (cf. I.119), wishing ever "after dethe" (I.120), and calling to Venus and Cupid, who led him up that crooked path. The ambiguous love-journey which had so engrossed Amans in the early books receives precise clarification in the Latin epithet at the beginning of Book VIII; "Cecus amor dudum nondum sua lumina cepit, / Quo Venus impositum deuia fallit iter." Blind love indeed has no light of its own and leads what might have been bright into dark confusion. Amans' fall, like that of the fallen angels, was precipitated by the blind leading the blind.

After explaining Lucifer's loss of place, Genius proceeds to the origins of mankind, who was created to "cresce and multiplie" (29) and thus restore "the nombre of Angles which was lore, / Whan thei out fro the blisse felle" (32–33). This genealogy helps explain how it is that man finds himself in a position between heaven and earth, yet bound to both. It clarifies where man should place his love, but also reveals why he is so susceptible to wandering. When Adam and Eve stumbled and were cast out of Eden, they were hopelessly miserable. Then it was, however, that their earthly nature helped them rediscover their purpose, even though they had fallen.

> Adam and Eve . . . were aschamed,
> Til that nature hem hath reclamed
> To love, and tauht hem thilke lore,
> That ferst thei keste, and overmore
> Thei don that is to kinde due,
> Wherof thei hadden fair issue.
>
> (51–58)

The passage summarizes a motif of "kynde" which we have seen operative from the beginning of the *Confessio*. Perverters of "kynde love," like Mundus, Narcissus, Albinus, Crassus, Jason, Nectanabus, and Apius, end up wretchedly, while those who learn to abide by nature, like the king of Hungary, Constantine, Diogenes, Bardus, Brutus, and Tobias, recover or maintain their estates with a satisfying equanimity. "Kinde love," combined with Reason, offers "fair issue" indeed, despite the fall. It reminds man of his created potential and helps him repair the breach caused by sin. No wonder Genius is so prominent a figure in the *Confessio*. Nature's guardian shrives Amans through the very process of experience to reknow "kynde love" and resanctify his broken marriage with the Creator.

Genius next proceeds to explain the marriage laws in an effort to help Amans think more perceptively about the kinds of attachments he makes. Though Genius' remarks originate in observations on earthly marriage, that perspective leads him to general rules of marriage which take their meaning from common profit, that area of natural experience which links creature with creature according to natural laws. When there were few people on earth it was necessary for kin to marry kin. In the first age even brothers and sisters married. But as folk of the world increased, by the third age "Sosterhode of mariage / Was torned into cousinage" (103–4) and cousins could marry cousins, but no closer kin. By Christian times the laws were such that one is allowed to marry no closer kin than the fourth generation removed.

> The Pope hath bede to the men,
> That non schal wedden of his ken
> Ne the seconde ne the thridde.
>   (145–47)

Genius' point seems to be that these laws keep men from becoming too nearsighted in love. They discourage factions. Rather than taking "what thing comth next to honde" (163), man must look to the larger community of mankind. The taking of love where one "take may" (152) is too easy; it is a "morsell envenimed" (195) which, like Narcissism, spoils common profit.

Amans fails to see any connection between his "matiere" and what Genius is talking about. He explains that his love has never been so wild that he would take from his kin nor even from a spiritual sister such as a nun. He becomes impatient with the whole procedure of the shrift, with all its irrelevant questions.

> Ye mai wel axe of this and that,
> Bot sothli forto telle plat,
> In al this world ther is bot on
> The which myn herte hath overgon.
>   (179–82)

Yet regardless of Amans' impatience, the questions now posed have closer bearing on his "matiere" than he wishes to allow. Precisely who is this "on" he so dotes upon? Is she some real person, or is she some fantasy he has conjured? Can this "on" ever satisfy the needs of his heart? Genius had first raised these questions in Book VII, when he explained how the lover's bejaping of his wit has nothing to do with real women or real situations but rather is a kind of fornication with one's fantasy.

> Withinne himself the fyr he bloweth,
> Wherof the womman nothing knoweth.
> (VII.4273–74)

Rather than a real woman, Amans is allured by the "fool impressioun" in his "ymaginacioun." That kind of fantasy was described in the *Roman de la Rose* as Narcissism. Here Genius explains it as incest. For what could be closer kin than the progeny of one's own brain?

Gower first explored this idea of incest in the *Mirour de l'Omme*, which shows Sin and her progeny of "les sept vices mortieux" to be products of incest. Derived from Latin *in-* (not) *castus* (chaste), incest designates unnatural spiritual love as well as sexual union. It is lack of proper chastisement. Gower apparently had the Latin derivation in mind when he provided the moral at the end of the *Tale of Virginia*, where the unchaste Apius was chastised. Similarly, in *Vox Clamantis*, he speaks of a man bemoaning his "incestuous wife" (i.e., unchaste wife).[2] The *Mirour* treats incest as unchaste behavior among prelates (9085–9192) and offers "La belle file Continence, / Naiscant du fine Chasteté" (17750–51) as its antidote. Of all sins, incest typifies preeminently crime against family and thus against community. It is implied in the selfishness of all sins. In fact, the word the Latin fathers generally used for sin—*cupiditas*—originates in the myth of Cupid, who incestuously loved his mother as if he were blind, the aftereffect being indeed the loss of his wits. Genius' discussion of incest is thus well timed and apt to help cure Amans' blindness. Amans must be chastened to value chastity.

Gower never specifically uses the term incest in the *Confessio* except in the Latin marginal glosses on the lechery of Caligula and Antiochus.[3] Instead, he speaks of "unavised" love, "mistimed" love, "unkynde" love, and, in the epigram to the story of Apollonius, of excessive and immoderate love. Although Genius is clearly talking about incest, and although Amans understands him only in the narrower sense, his

generalizations seem designated to encourage the reader to look on
this sin as the epitome of selfish, unnatural qualities of cupidinous love
in general. In Book VIII, two circumlocutions stand out particularly in
this regard: Genius objects to men who passionately "taken wher thei
take may" (152) and, again, to a man who knows no good "bot takth
what thing comth next to honde" (163). Such love is nearsighted,
oblivious of the true center of man's proper vision. After telling the
story of Apollonius, Genius observes that instead of taking whatever
love is close at hand, men should "tak love where it mai noght faile"
(2086). That love is of the "mihti god . . . inthronized in his See" with
whom Gower began Book VIII, the only "on" on which Amans should
set his heart. Genius' point seems to be that Amans should stop feeding
morosely on his emotions and look to something more important.

The *Tale of Apollonius* dramatizes the problem of incest superbly.
Antiochus is the man who indulges himself myopically, taking where
he may what is near at hand. But the effects are terrible. He becomes
worse than a beast.

> The wylde fader thus devoureth
> His oghne fleissh, which non socoureth.
>   (309–10)

Having abandoned his natural office of father, he corrupts his other
office, that of king, and adjusts laws to satisfy his "fol desir" (337). As he
acts "withoute insihte of conscience" (294), all his communal relationships are spoiled and he becomes an alien in his own home. To avoid
dealing with his inner anarchy, he becomes a tyrant, first over his
daughter who "couthe noght hir Maidenhede defende" (302) and then
over his subjects as he slays his daughter's natural suitors and puts their
heads on the town gates. Sin breeds sin: "with al his Pride" he slothfully
ignores his natural responsibilities ("Him thoghte that it was no Sinne"
[346]), lecherously gluts himself on his own flesh (310), enviously hides
his daughter from other men, and then becomes a murderer "full of
rancour and of ire" (500). He devotes "al his wit" (358) to thwarting his
subjects rather than to succouring them. He will have his daughter as

his own, though that act "non socoureth" (310). Ultimately he becomes too "unkynde," and God strikes him down with lightning.

Apollonius, on the other hand, shows what it means "to love in good manere." Though he begins as any lover, "musende on a nyht" over tidings of female beauty (380), he subsequently tries to maintain his reason and wit and grows coherently throughout the story, despite Fortune's adversities. The difference between Apollonius and Antiochus as rulers may be seen in part through the people's response to their rule. Apollonius always has full support of his subjects. When he is forced into exile the people of Tyre go into mourning.

> They losten lust, they losten chiere,
> Thei toke upon hem such penaunce,
> Ther was no song, ther was no daunce,
> Bot every merthe and melodie
> To hem was thanne maladie.
>
> (476–80)

They even let their hair grow and close "the bathes and the Stwes bothe" (484). And what is the reason?

> Helas, the lusti flour of youthe,
> Our Prince, oure heved, our governour,
> Thurgh whom we stoden in honour,
> Withoute the comun assent
> Thus sodeinliche is fro ous went!
>
> (490–94)

Apollonius' initial indiscretion costs his community sorely. But though he begins in error and exile, he works his way back, despite Fortune (or perhaps because of what Fortune teaches him). "Our Prince, oure heved, our governour" grows in all areas in which the king must be instructed (ethics, economics, and policy) to become true prince, head, and governor. The people accept the necessity of his having first of all

to protect himself; after Antiochus' death they pray for his return.
When finally he does get home with his whole family about him, there is
much bliss in the land.

> Tho was ther many a mowth to kisse,
> Echon welcometh other hom,
> Bot whan the queen to londe com,
> And Thaise hir doghter be hir side
> The joie which was thilke tyde
> Ther mai no mannes tunge telle.
>   (1894–99)

The king takes "his real place" (1902) and the queen is established in
her "chambre" and a "gret feste" is arrayed for everyone. At the
banquet, rather than explaining what the king thought or what the
queen did, Gower depicts health and community joy.

> Whan time was, thei gon to mete,
> Alle olde sorwes ben foryete,
> And gladen hem with joies newe:
> The descoloured pale hewe
> Is now become a rody cheke,
> Ther was no merthe forto seke,
> Bot every man hath that he wolde.
>   (1905–11)

The rosy countenance and fulfilled desire apply not only to Apollonius, his queen, and his daughter; they apply to the whole community. The body politic is at last whole and well. Honor has returned to
them all, and they share the full joy of their being. None can enjoy that
health until all are fit to participate in it. The image offers a splendid
example of Gower's notion that one increases through another's gain
and that the parts all need each other to achieve wholesome repose.

Part of Apollonius' ultimate success depends upon his admirable
fulfillment of Genius' five points of policy which should govern a king's

behavior. He adheres to Truth, accepting responsibilities and fulfilling promises. He exemplifies Liberality in providing wheat for the starving people of Tharse and in properly rewarding the physician Cerymon for saving his wife. He understands the importance of Justice and brings wicked Dionise and Strangulio to trial according to the laws and demands of their own land. He has Pity on the people of Tharse, first in giving them food and then in respecting their laws and judgment when their king has offended him. He adheres to Chastity, not only in the winning of his wife and in the care of himself and her memory after her supposed death, but also in the care of his daughter. He is confronted with a situation like that which confronted Antiochus. When Thaise sings to woo him from his melancholy, he feels strong love for her. But he does not impose on her. Rather than taking what is near at hand and thus losing his daughter, as Antiochus did, he recovers his daughter by loving chastely. Diana rewards him for his chastity by enabling him to recover his wife. In the end, he behaves in no way *incaste*.

Apollonius' story is admirably suited to the conclusion of the *Confessio*. So complicated is its plot that it ties together tales of marriage, wandering, and homecoming as well as tales of various sins such as incest, wrath, envy, perjury, and avarice, and also tales of virtues such as chastity, constancy, pity, perseverance, and good intent. But especially it reflects tales on good and bad kingship. It is remarkable to find so many contrasting examples of kingship within a single story: On the negative side, the wicked Antiochus, whose tyranny destroys his whole heritage, and the incompetent Strangulio, whose envious wife Dionise attempts to murder their benefactor's heir; and on the positive side, the good Artestrathes, whose pity and liberality rescue Apollonius, and the worthy Athenogoras, who marries Thaise—all these in addition to Apollonius himself.

The virtues of Artestrathes are particularly well drawn and stand as a foil to Antiochus in the education of Apollonius. Unlike the incestuous tyrant who thinks only of himself, Artestrathes seems primarily concerned with his people, both near at hand and far, and is capable of perceiving their individual needs and concerns. It is his public-mindedness as he attends the "comun game" of his subjects (678) which first introduces him to Apollonius. At the festival dinner Artestrathes is sensitive to the young Apollonius' noble behavior, notices his quietness, and moves him to head seat at "a Middel bord" (720). But instead of cheering Apollonius, the honor makes him brood all the more as he recalls what he has lost. So the king sends his daughter to cheer him. Instead it makes him cry. But the good king does not give up. He has his daughter comfort the stranger with music. This time the medicine works. Gower makes an interesting change in his source at this point.[4] Instead of having Apollonius scorn the woman's playing and boastfully show her how to do it (as he does in the source), he gives Apollonius a debonaire response. When she asks how he liked her music, he replies,

> "Ma dame, certes wel," he seide,
> "Bot if ye the mesure pleide
> Which, if you list, I schal you liere,
> It were a glad thing forto hiere."
>   (767–70)

The daughter is pleased with his tact and asks "of what mesure that ye mene" (773). Artestrathes is pleased too that Apollonius would show "som merthe," and when he learns how well Apollonius can play the harp, instead of being jealous for his daughter, he allows Apollonius to become teacher, a teacher of "mesure." "Mesure" is indeed a "glad thing forto hiere" (770), for as Apollonius benefits himself by helping another, it profits the whole court. Recall Gower's observations on good harping as a requisite of proper rule in the *Mirour de l'Omme*, which was cited earlier in the discussion of Arion at the end of the Prologue. Here, Gower returns to the idea to bring his entire poem to its end.

Artestrathes' prudence and thoughtful governance is most evident when he has to deal with his daughter's request to marry Apollonius. In Gower's source the daughter, when approached by the suitors, replies with a riddle, saying that she will marry the one who was shipwrecked, a riddle which quite confuses her father until Apollonius explains. The

riddle in the source is a felicitous touch in that it makes more emphatic
the parallel with Apollonius' first courtship when he encountered
Antiochus' riddle. Gower draws the parallel in another way. He makes
the daughter more willful and self-indulgent, describing in some detail
the love-sick feelings in her "ymaginacioun" (850). When she has to
choose amongst the suitors she flatly states that she wants Apollonius,
who is not even officially one of the suitors. Gower's reason for the
change is probably to set off the motif of movement from will to reason,
a motif we have already seen in a negative way with Antiochus, and now
put positively in the growth of both Apollonius and his bride-to-be. She
learns to fit into the measures of wise governance. Partly she grows
because of Apollonius' good influence as a harp teacher, and partly
because of Artestrathes' care and tact in educating her. Unlike Antiochus, Artestrathes is the model of a virtuous father. Rather than
scolding or being shocked when the daughter becomes willful, Artestrathes keeps his own counsel, then approaches Apollonius, the efficient cause of the willfulness, for direct consultation. Upon finding that
Apollonius has acted honorably, and wishing to please his daughter,
Artestrathes next approaches the queen. The queen has reservations
about the matter for fear that it might cause "debat" and "desese," but
after a normal amount of motherly worrying she too agrees. They then
go back to the daughter and plan the announcement. The wisdom of
three will provide wise counsel indeed. Artestrathes does not look upon
his daughter as an opportunity to acquire more wealth for himself. He
thinks rather of her happiness and future. He admires Apollonius not
for his "worldes good" (he assumes he has none), but because "he was
able to governe" (947). As a convincing touch to prove the wisdom of
Artestrathes' good judgment, Gower adds a description of the wedding
not found in the source in which all the people share in the joy and
which ends with the bedding of the couple and the conceiving of a
child, a natural proof of their happiness (970 ff.). As a king, Artestrathes stands in contrast to Antiochus; he is an example of good
governance which even Apollonius might emulate.

But in addition to exemplifying good kingship and condemning
incontinence, the plot of the *Tale of Apollonius* provides a model for

Amans at the end of his quest. Apollonius is a lover in exile who also is trying to regain his homeland. Fortune is a most bitter enemy, pursuing him with storms and assassins, stripping him of friends and possessions. She denies him his identity at every turn, making him a prince without a country, a husband without a wife, and a father without a child. Even so, he maintains his integrity. Although driven to the brink of despair, so far in fact that like Saul he strikes out, he recovers with the aid of his daughter. Thaise is his good seed. Like her father she too is victimized by Fortune, narrowly escaping murder only to end up in a brothel. But she, like her father, remembers her skill in music and science to save herself and also advance the community. She becomes a teacher instead of a whore.[5] Both she and Apollonius have learned to maintain their spiritual estates. The tale thus ends on a note of joy after woe: Apollonius finally achieves his happy homecoming. No more exile for him. He becomes king of all the lands he attended and governs them "of on assent."

Amans' homecoming differs from Apollonius' in that his exile is a spiritual exile. He has learned from Genius' examples, but at the same time he has not learned. He misses the point of Apollonius' story, though he does now ask directly for advice. He is at least that much closer to Truth, and speaks plainly: "What is my beste, as for an ende?" (2059). Genius with equal directness advises that he seek "trouthe" and "lete all othre truffles be" (2062). Genius allows that though he is Venus' priest, he has in this instance moved toward "Presthod" of a higher order (2075 ff.) and encourages Amans "to vertu more than to vice encline" (2082–83); he should "tak love where it mai noght faile" (2086). He calls Amans' cupidity sinful and without profit: "Thou art toward thiself unwis" (2094). The only "good counseil" is for him to reclaim his proper kingship before it is too late.

> For conseil passeth alle thing
> To him which thenkth to ben a king;
> And every man for his partie
> A kingdom hath to justefie,
> That is to sein his oghne dom.

If he misreule that kingdom,
He lest himself, and that is more
Than if he loste Schip and Ore
And al the worldes good withal:
For what man that in special
Hath noght himself, he hath noght elles,
Nomor the perles than the schelles.
                        (2109–20)

That was the lesson Apollonius learned as he came through many a
shipwreck and tempest; the real threat was loss of his spiritual kingship.
Though Amans never travels outside his England, his danger of loss is
every bit as great as was that of Apollonius.

In his confession Amans usually saw fairly clearly the nature of each
of the vices and the blindness of Cupid's love. But he always made an
exception when it came to his lady. He has trouble seeing well near at
hand. Genius explains to him that to the one who possesses true
kingship "al is to him of o value" (2121). It is time for Amans to
"withdrawe" from cupidity and special pleading. "Set thin herte under
that lawe, / The which of reson is governed / And noght of will"
(2134–36), Genius advises. He has given Amans plenty of examples,
but he can only show the way. Amans must make the decision himself.
He then poses his last question to Amans, the ultimate question of
Christian humanism: "Now ches if thou wolt live or deie" (2148). Will
Amans, like Diogenes, be the philosopher and reconcile himself with
life and death? Or will he, like Nectanabus, remain a cupidinous sorcerer, clinging blindly to illusion, fantasy, and upside-down definitions?

But Amans is not ready to make that choice. Although the prelimi-
nary questions have all been asked and illustrated, their meaning has
not yet come home. Again he dodges to protect his emotions. His
defense is the characteristic "but you don't understand" of lovers:

Mi wo to you is bot a game,
That fielen noght of that I fiele.
                        (2152–53)

Despite Genius' observation that if something is painful it must be bad (2096–97), Amans tenders his pain. He wants sympathy. Yet at the same time he begins to realize rationally that Genius' advice makes sense.

As Amans starts using reason, the point of view of the poem shifts. Instead of dialogue and debate between Genius and Amans, we now have first person narration. The effect is to make the debate seem to be going on within an Amans of past time, while at the same time adding distance of perspective as if he were looking down at himself.

> Tho was between mi Prest and me
> Debat and gret perplexete:
> Mi resoun understod him wel,
> And knew it was soth everydel
> That he hath seid, bot noght forthi
> Mi will hath nothing set thereby.
> For techinge of so wis a port
> Is unto love of no desport;
> Yit myhte nevere man beholde
> Reson, wher love was withholde,
> Thei be noght of o governance.
> (2189–99)

Reason in conflict with will—that is the conflict Genius has been emphasizing in various degrees of clarity from the beginning of the poem. Does the willful lover in truth want to sail into "so wis a port," or does he prefer the outrage of his passions? His is indeed a divided kingdom ruled by a tyrant usurper. It is noteworthy that Gower stages the scene as that of a man in confrontation with his own nature. Amans' persistent blindness, which once amused Genius, now sets a barrier between them: they fall "in distance, / mi prest and I" (2200–2201), the separation reflecting Amans' desperate willfulness. But fearing complete separation Amans addresses Genius with words "debonaire" and begs him to present his supplication to Venus. Genius agrees, providing Amans put it down in writing. This trope of writing might be understood as a step toward reordering the mind. Though the appeal is written with tears instead of ink and in its self pity is clearly by a man "noght of o governance" but rather "fulfilt of loves fantasie" (2211), it constitutes an objectifying of his dissatisfaction and in its very composition is thus a step toward coping with the divisions engendered by his fantasy. One voice pleads for release from love's cruelty, another for a lover's satisfaction.

The stanzaic complaint (2217–2300) stands in sharp contrast to Amans' emotional outburst in Book I when Venus first appeared. Although reason does not yet hold sway, she is at least present. His description of his malady (if not his analysis) is accurate, and although his desires are still at odds with their effects, he is beginning, in these twelve stanzas of rhyme royal, to impose order on them as a step toward reclaiming his kingship. The first stanza acknowledges how "bewhaped with sotie" (2219) his herte is and laments that his reason "can him noght defende" (2222). His error is clear enough if he would but see it. Having decided that his reason has nothing to offer, he seeks help outside himself "wherof I mihte amende" (2224). As far as his will is concerned, "amende" means "have my will"; for reason "amende" means "have release from cupidinous pain." In the second stanza he complains to Nature on grounds that love is natural and that every creature gets its chance to have a go. Besides, he allows, since he has but one desire it should be easy for nature to oblige. It seems that every creature has its bliss "bot I" (2230). His infatuation is like that of Aurelius in Chaucer's *Franklin's Tale,* who complains to Apollo that he wants his turn. The problem with such logic, of course, as Genius has frequently pointed out, is that the cupidinous lover's fantasy is *not* natural. Amans' minor premise is unsound. Though "the litel wrenne" may well have love "in his mesure" (2227), Amans' fantasy is without "mesure."

As Amans continues his *Supplicacion* to Venus he explains that Nature has taught him the way to love but not how to accomplish his desire. He cannot yet see that ultimately Nature will help him accomplish his desire once his desire becomes reasonable. But what is more strange, almost marvelous, Nature will help him to become reasonable by robbing him of his youth. Amans reiterates his inner conflict between reason and will, but sees himself overthrown in Love's wrestle as Pan was. In his frustration he rejects the help of his wits which only seem to contradict his fantasy—"bot non of hem can helpe after mi wille" (2248). Instead he prays to Jove, whom Genius had defined as "god of delices" (v.876), in hopes that he might drink from the sweet tun instead of the bitter cup which always seems to be his regardless of how often he tries. The world seems to be perpetually changing (2259); there seems to be only one constant, namely, "Danger in o place" (2264). Earlier Genius had suggested he turn to Ovid for advice in love's matters; Amans had declined the suggestion on grounds that the readings might contradict his desire. But now Amans finally recalls Ovid, especially his account of Cupid and Venus, noting that Cupid is a blind god "with many a fyri lance" (2270), and that Venus, especially when taking counsel with Saturn, as she was at the birth of Amans' love, never offers grace. But instead of heeding the obvious and rejecting the futility of his pursuit, he asks Venus' and Cupid's forgiveness and release from their anger so that Danger might be removed. In the last two stanzas, however, with their apostrophes first to Cupid and then to Venus, reason is at least present, albeit still subordinate to desire, as Amans asks either to be released from his pain or granted "salve such as I desire" (2290). He still claims to be guiltless in his "grene" lover's pain, yet he is ready for judgment: "mi love aquite as I deserve, / Or elles do me pleinly forto sterve" (2299–2300). He has had enough frustration.

The effect of Amans' prayer is immediate. Venus appears in less time than it takes to walk a mile. Amans is still in the woods where she left him at the outset of the poem, but this time as he falls to his knees before her and she asks him who he is, he replies "John Gower" (2321). The point here is not simply to let the world know who wrote the poem, though it does do that. Rather it marks a new beginning; Amans is beginning to sort out his rightful fate (cf. *sors,* discussed above, "Books III and IV"). He has come a long way from "a Caitif that lith hiere." His homeland has been identified. What remains is the repossession. Venus acknowledges the schizophrenic intention of Amans' "bille," but offers no help. She leaves the dispute to Amans and Nature. One of the options he had requested was, after all, to be made whole.

> And if thou woldest more crave,
> It is no riht that thou it have.
>
> (2375–76)

Amans must reconcile himself with Nature or be refused any consolation. He has no other "riht."

At the same time that Amans makes his appeal to Venus he also takes a closer look at her. He begins to see beyond her arbitrariness, an arbitrariness after which his own behavior had been patterned. He sees how "blindly the world sche diemeth" (2385), though that makes no difference to Venus. She is what she is. As she explains: "Thou wost wel that I am Venus, / Which al only my lustes seche" (2398–99). Conceivably she could have maintained her arbitrary character and still have granted Amans his fantasy. One wonders how Gower might have ended his poem if he had chosen that alternative in constructing his plot. He might well have followed the format of the *Roman de la Rose* and ended with irony. If he had allowed the consummation, however, poor Amans would probably never have been disenchanted and would have wound up as Chaucer's Januarie rather than "John Gower," still stroking his fantasy's swelling womb. With such a conclusion, Gower could have made many of the same points he does about will, desire, and reason. But he would have relegated to irony and obscurity his two most prominent motifs—common profit and kingship. From the outset, his poem has been committed to a Boethian conclusion with the wanderer becoming "avised" and returning to his homeland. That is the example he would set before his reader for common profit.

Venus disenchants Amans by getting him to look objectively at himself (something a Januarie type could never do):

> So sitte it wel that thou beknowe
> Thi fieble astat, er thou beginne
> Thing wher thou miht non ende winne.
>
> (2428–30)

The wise man must know discretely his feeble estate; he must recognize both his abilities and his limitations. Gower cleverly has Amans recount Venus' observations in retrospect throughout this section of the poem, as he ponders her whimsical rejection of his willful appeal. It is thus Amans himself who acknowledges, with keen awareness, that "old grisel is no fole" (2407). Venus advises him to make "a beau retret" (2416) and with some of the most poignant lines in the poem suggests—"foryet it noght"—how

> The thing is torned into was;
> That which was whilom grene gras,
> Is welked hey at time now.
> Forthi mi conseil is that thou
> Remembre wel hou thou art old.
>   (2435–39)

Time is "was." Amans, who had bound himself to fantasy-time, must reconnoiter with the present. That scout Gower sent out in the epigram to Book I has returned with a sour report. Acknowledgment that he is no lusty youth, that he is old, despite his "grene" words, causes Amans to faint, and brings him to the final step in his reeducation.

His swoon is more than disappointment over lost youth. Amans envisions a parliament of lovers led by Cupid and his captain *Yowthe*. These are the lovers whose stories Genius has told. They pass in review before him—first those caught up in the heat of their desire, then those betrayed by love who are in sorrow. Gower reiterates again and again such phrases as "I sih," "Min yhe . . . I caste aboutes," "I sih," "myn Ere it areche," and so on. Amans is seeing and hearing anew, and this time his wits behave reasonably, without the distension of fantasy. The noble young knights—Tristram, Lancelot, Galahad, Jason, Hercules, Theseus, Thelamon, Hector, Paris, Troilus—pass by "with here loves glade and blithe" (2539); but the lovers they lead are the ladies who will undo them—bele Ysolde, Gunnore, Creusa, Eolen, Phedra, Eseonen, Pantaselee, Eleine, and Criseide. The temporality of their bliss is jolting as one recalls Mark, Mordred, Medea, Deidamia, and so on, hovering on the fringe of one's memory. The recollection imposes a wider perspective of time and the immanent doom which the lovers' infatuation obscures from them. The offended members of their communities will strike back. The bliss of these blissful lovers is no true bliss. Next, in sad estate, the complaining lovers—Narcissus, Piramus, and so on, so many of whom end in suicide—appear in Amans' recollection. Their gloom likewise reveals the futility of their "noble" efforts in love. Even the four commendable women, whose faithfulness in love the whole world remembers—Penelope, Lucrece, Alceste, and Alcyone—offer little consolation to one seeking a lover's bed on earth.

The scene shifts from the company of *Yowthe* to a field "where Elde cam a softe pas" (2667). Amans takes some comfort to see that old men as well as young are afflicted with lovesickness. He is not alone in his predicament, even though he is old. It is curious that the examples in Elde's entourage are the historians themselves—David, Aristotle, Virgil, Plato, Sortes, and Ovid—rather than the protagonists of the various tales of love. Even among these wise old authors the love debate has continued, some advising that the lover has no cause "bot if he wolde himself benyce" (2769) and warning that old men should not be fools, while others defend lechery in old age. Perhaps the vision designates Amans' recognition of the complexity of moral issues in the debate. But mainly, he sees the futility of the lover's quest. In his swoon he incorporates the meaning of the past into his consciousness. As Gower puts it in *Vox Clamantis,* the wisdom of antiquity answers the needs of the present, once the present understands through its own experience the right use of memory.[6]

While Amans lies in his contemplative swoon, he notes that someone looking on might well doubt whether he will live. This ability to see himself objectively reflects a new use of his imagination which is different from his former narcissism. As he sees himself lying there, the blind god gropes his way toward him and extracts the "fyri Lancegay" (2798) with which he had earlier smitten him. Cupid then disappears. The rest is simple. As Amans comes out of his trance, Venus places an ointment on his heart, his temples, and his kidneys, implying the restitution of his three personal estates (the kingdom of his soul, the sanctuary of his intelligence, and the residence of his passions). Though it is not the love ointment he originally sought, it proves the more generative in that it gives him back himself. Venus also hands him a mirror that he might recognize the old man he has become. This time he does not swoon. He looks directly at himself, reason returns, and he is made "sobre and hol ynowh" (2869). The "Somerfare" (2856) is over. The seasonal reference ties his plot up with that whole genre of *chanson d'aventure* literature so popular in the latter fourteenth century, where the wanderer sets out on a summer's day to seek his fortune only to end up chastened by the prospect of Elde and Death. (Cf. *The Parlement of the Thre Ages* and *Piers Plowman*.) As he looks with "myn hertes yhe" (2824) upon his faded countenance and "yhen dymme and al unglade" (2826) a profound reconciliation with time takes place.

> Mi will was tho to se nomore
> Outwith, for ther was no plesance;
> And thanne into my remembrance
> I drowh myn olde daies passed,
> And as reson it hath compassed,
> I made a liknesse of miselve
> Unto the sondri Monthes twelve,
> Wherof the yeer in his astat
> Is mad, and stant upon debat,
> That lich til other non acordeth.
>
> (2832–41)

As he recalls the seasons and their various fruits, one is reminded of the third Latin epigram in Book VIII, with which this penultimate section of the poem began:

> Sicut habet Mayus non dat natura Decembri,
> Nec poterit compar floribus esse lutum.
> [What May has, Nature gives not to December,
> Nor can mud be compared to flowers.]
>
> (II,450)

"John Gower" is returning to the community of ordinate nature. Thoughts of the larger cycle of the year, its orderly progression, and of what may properly be compared with what, bring him around. As he likens himself to the natural cycle he recalls his "wittes straied" (2860) and bids them come "hom ayein" (2861). With wits returned, reason can address him the "rihte weie" and remove the "sotie / Of thilke unwise fantasie, / Wherof that I was wont to pleigne" (2865–67). Venus laughs at him and asks what love was. But Amans cannot answer: "Be my trouthe I knew him noght" (2875). His fantasy has gone so far from him that it is as if Cupid had never been.

Genius gives Amans absolution—a "peire of bedes," with the motto *Por reposer,* and Venus tells him to return to his books where moral virtue dwells (2925). He should pray for peace and let reason be his guide (2913 ff.). Then she returns to the stars. Genius also seems to depart with her. But has he in truth disappeared? Winthrop Wetherbee notes in his discussion of the classical Genius figure, the *deus humanae naturae,* that in his capacity as tutelary presence in the soul he may be compared with the *speculum,* "the secret perception of divine order and purpose hidden deep in the soul, by which man's deepest spiritual insights are rewarded."[7] In the *Confessio Amantis,* Genius has been replaced by the mirror; that is, he has been reincorporated into his proper dwelling place, Amans' contemplative mind.

As he looks in the mirror, beads in hand, Amans discovers that he is for the first time in the poem free and on his own. For a brief but telling moment he stands in amazement: has all his labor, all his lust, come to this—an old man, his reflection, and some beads? Then, like Troilus at the end of his romance, he smiles at it all. The smile is the final clue to his release. In that moment,

> Homward a softe pas y wente,
> Wher that with al myn hol entente
> Uppon the point that y am schryve
> I thenke bidde whil y live.
>
> (2967–70)

The reiteration is complete: With Genius intact, Amans has become whole. Now, as "John Gower" poet, he turns his attention away from the forest to look toward his larger domain.

The concluding prayer for the State of England grows naturally out of the romance plot as Gower fuses his great social theme with Amans' story. It is the "point" for which he was shriven. The prayer stands in striking contrast to the infatuated pleas of Amans in his precious "sotie." Having regained his sense of personal kingdom he now prays, as poet, for common profit, right use of memory, and good governance.

> For if men takyn remembrance
> What is to live in unite,
> Ther ys no staat in his degree
> That noughte to desire pes.
> (2988–91)

He reviews the three estates for which we should pray—the "Clergie" who should help us to procure "oure pes toward the hevene above" (2999), the laws which protect the "commun right," and the "chevalerie" which uphold the laws. We must be especially watchful against "singular profit" (3039) which brings "divisioun" (3041) where all should "ben al on" (3045). But mainly, we must pray for good kingship, for the king stands above clerk, knight, man-of-law, merchant, and laborer. Here in his résumé Gower centers his attention on the principal generalizations from Book VII. He would pray that the king "first un to rihtwisnesse entende" (3069) so that his life might be amended. Second, he would have him govern without "tirandise" (3076).

> For if a kyng wol justifie
> His lond and hem that both withynne,
> First at hym self he mot begynne,
> To kepe and reule his owne astat,
> That in hym self be no debat
> Toward his god.
> (3080–85)

If the king follows God he will find grace sufficient to govern in prosperity, for his "poeple schal nought ben oppressid" (3103) and his name shall be blessed. We saw this principle in effective operation in the *Tale of Apollonius*. It applies with equal validity to the tale of Amans. And it could likewise apply to the tale of Richard II, if the king would have it so.

The culminating prayer thus ties explicitly the conclusion of the poem to the Prologue, as well as to history. Recall in the Prologue that Gower asserted the need for individual integrity, that only when men adhere to common profit can the state survive. But the reverse is true also. Here at the end of the *Confessio* we see the importance of the state to the individual. At the end of *Vox Clamantis* Gower had observed: "Si perstet, persto, si cadat illa, cado" (If she—i.e., England, the land where I was born ["origio meun"]—if she stands firm, I stand firm; if she falls, I fall).[8] Thus we see the compelling import of the prayer. England and Amans could be the same body.

The journey which Amans undertakes through his confession forms a circle, a return home, as its eightfold structure implies.[9] As he completes his book Gower returns to his opening lines, explaining again how he undertook to make his book "in englesch" (VIII.3108; cf. Prol. 17 ff.). He then brings his plot personally home. He, as a poet now in old age, will write no more of love but will seek charity, the love which will not fail.

> Bot thilke love which that is
> Withinne a mannes herte affermed,
> And stant of charite confermed,
> Such love is goodly forto have,
> Such love mai the bodi save,
> Such love mai the soule amende,
> The hyhe god such love ous sende
> Forthwith the remenant of grace;
> So that above in thilke place
> Wher resteth love and alle pes,
> Oure joie mai ben endeles.
>   (3162–72)

Gower's peroration reminds us of Chaucer's Retraction or the conclusion to *Troilus and Criseyde,* insofar as each moves beyond artiface to an expression of faith in that body beyond self and state which makes all whole. Although such passages often make modern readers cringe, in terms of Gower's motif of common profit such a conclusion is necessary to the rationale of the poem. The poet, a king in his own right, acknowledges the divine center of his personal sovereignty. His conclusion brings home structurally the poem's central motif. After expressing personally his faith in the ultimate community, "Gower" has nothing more to say. His *Confessio* is complete.

Notes / Index

NOTES

Preface

[1] "Lak of Stedfastnesse," lines 19–20, *The Works of Geoffrey Chaucer*, ed. F. N. Robinson (Cambridge, Mass., 1957), p. 537. All subsequent references to Chaucer come from this edition and will hereafter be identified only by title and line number.

[2] Cf. my headnote, taken from *Mum and the Sothsegger*, ed. Mabel Day and Robert Steele, Early English Text Society, OS 199 (Oxford, 1936), p. 2, line 52. For general discussion of events of the later fourteenth century, see May McKisack, *The Fourteenth Century 1307–1399* (Oxford, 1959); Anthony Tuck, *Richard II and the English Nobility* (London, 1973); Alec Reginald Myers, *London in the Age of Chaucer* (Norman, Okla., 1972); G. M. Trevelyan, *England in the Age of Wycliffe* (London, 1899); and Robert E. Lerner, *The Age of Adversity: The Fourteenth Century* (Ithaca, N.Y., 1968).

[3] *Mum and the Sothsegger*, passus I. 1–8.

[4] See G. Mollat, *The Popes at Avignon: 1305–1378* (New York, 1965), pp. 14–25, for discussion of John XXII's fiscal policies and authoritarian character. For discussion of theories behind papal policies based on a hierocratic system with the pope on top see Michael Wilks, *The Problem of Sovereignty in the Later Middle Ages* (Cambridge, 1963), esp. pp. 15–64, 254–87. For

discussion of conflicts between the pope and clergy over taxation, see Palmer A. Throop, *Criticism of the Crusade: A Study of Public Opinion and Crusade Propaganda* (Amsterdam, 1940), esp. pp. 237–61. See also W. E. Lunt, *Financial Relations of the Papacy with England*, 2 vols (Cambridge, Mass., 1939–62), and "Papal Taxation in England in the Reign of Edward I," *English Historical Review*, 30 (1915), 399–406, for discussion of antagonism between papacy and England on taxation.

[5] For an excellent summary of Wyclif's positions in his attack on church hierarchy and the sacraments, see E. A. Block, *John Wyclif: Radical Dissenter* (San Diego, Calif., 1962). For a summary of the official church opposition to Wyclif's teaching, see Joseph Dahmus, *William Courtenay: Archbishop of Canterbury, 1381–1396* (University Park, Pa, 1966), pp. 47–49, 80–82. See J. A. Robson, *Wyclif and the Oxford Schools* (Cambridge, 1961), esp. chaps. 8, 9, for a judicious assessment of Wyclif's theological positions in the context of current theological disputes. For a somewhat outspoken discussion of Wyclif as a disappointed academic whose egotistical opportunism and physical frailty led him into progressively extreme and embittered po-

sitions, see K. B. McFarlane, *John Wycliffe and the Beginnings of English Non-conformity* (New York, 1953).

6   Dahmus, *William Courtenay*, p. 181.

7   See Chaucer's *Friar's Tale*, iii(D)1571 ff., where the unscrupulous summoner sets his whole intent upon robbing the poor widow Mabely of twelve pence. The widow might be understood as a figure of holy church being assaulted by avaricious churchmen.

8   For discussion of the effects of the commercial revolution on the ethical sensibility of the later Middle Ages, see Lester Little, "Pride Goes before Avarice: Social Change in Latin Christendom," *American Historical Review*, 76 (1971), 16–49; and John Baldwin, "The Medieval Merchant at the Bar of Canon Law," *Papers of the Michigan Academy of Science, Arts, and Letters*, 44 (1958), 287–99.

9   In addition to the outcries and political satire in various parts of *Piers Plowman, Wynnere and Wastoure*, and *Mum and the Sothsegger*, see Rossell Hope Robbins' recent bibliographical index and commentary entitled "Poems Dealing with Contemporary Conditions," in *A Manual of the Writings in Middle English: 1050–1500*, ed. Albert E. Hartung, vol. v (New Haven, 1975), especially items 15 ("Evil Times of Edward ii"), 26 ("Song of the Husbandman"), 30 ("Satire on the Consistory Courts"), 31 ("Satire on the Retinues of the Great"), 37 ("Song on the Times of Edward ii"), all twenty-four of the poems listed from MS Digby 102 (p. 1418), 80 ("The Sayings of the Four Philosophers"), 81 ("The Wickedness of the Times"), 82 ("A Satire of Edward ii's England"), 83 *("De Veritate et Consciencia")*, 85 ("The Insurrection and Earthquake of 1382"), and others on the Peasants' Revolt such as 254 ("The Great Rebellion"), 255 ("John Bull's Couplet"), 256 ("Letters of the Rebels"),

257 ("The Course of Revolt"), 258 ("The Yorkshire Partisans"), 259 ("Student Abuse of the Mayor of Cambridge"), and 260 ("A Song of Freedom"); 86 ("On the Times of Richard ii") 87 ("On King Richard's Ministers"), 96 ("Against Simony"), 97 ("Against Worldly Clerics"), 100–107 against the Friars, 109 ("Pierce the Ploughman's Crede"), 110 ("Complaint of the Plowman"), 119 ("Why I Can't Be a Nun"), 208 ("Summer Sunday"), 209 ("The Death of Edward iii"), 210 ("The Fall of Richard ii"), and 241 ("Advice to Prelates").

10   See May McKisack, "Edward iii and the Historians," *History*, 45 (1960), 7 ff.; John Barnie, *War in Medieval English Society: Social Values in the Hundred Years War, 1337–1399* (Ithaca, N.Y., 1974), pp. 66–67; Richard Barber, *The Knight and Chivalry* (New York, 1970), pp. 306 ff.; A. Graf, *Roma nella memoria e nelle immaginazione del medio evo* (Turin, 1923), pp. 17–23.

11   See the first recension of *Confessio Amantis*, line 37, in *The English Works of John Gower*, ed. G. C. Macaulay (Oxford, 1900), i, 31. The title "New Troy" or "Troinouvant" to refer to London was popular from the latter days of Edward iii's reign to the end of the fourteenth century.

12   *Tractatus contra Benedictum*, iii, as noted by Beryl Smalley, *English Friars and Antiquity in the Early Fourteenth Century* (Oxford, 1960), p. 29.

Introduction

1   "John Gower in His Most Significant Role," *Elizabethan Studies and Other Essays in Honor of George F. Reynolds* (Boulder, Colo., 1945), p. 61.

2 *John Gower: Moral Philosopher and Friend of Chaucer* (New York, 1964), p. 135.

3 Ibid., pp. 178–79.

4 See Wilks' excellent discussion of the ideal Christian commonwealth *(Societas Christianus)* in *The Problem of Sovereignty in the Later Middle Ages*, pp. 15–64. See also A. H. Chroust, "The Corporate Idea and the Body Politic in the Middle Ages," *Review of Politics*, 9 (1947), 423–52; and E. Lewis, "Organic Tendencies in Medieval Political Thought," *American Political Science Review*, 32 (1928), 849–76.

5 All references to the *Mirour de l'Omme* and the *Vox Clamantis* are taken from George C. Macaulay, *The Complete Works of John Gower*, 4 vols. (Oxford, 1902), and will hereafter be cited by title and line reference only in the context of my argument.

6 Cf. *Vox Clamantis* VI.vii.545–80. For Gower's interest in kingship early in his literary career, see *Mirour de l'Omme* 22228–23208. Cf., Fisher, *John Gower*, pp. 97–99, who suggests a latent Marxism in Gower's distrust of kings and moneyed classes, and George R. Coffman, "John Gower, Mentor for Royalty: Richard II," *PMLA*, 69 (1954), 953–64, for delineation of Gower's exhortations to Richard, especially in *Super Principum Regimine* and *O Deus Immense*.

7 Gower is not original in this particular stance but reflects a strong current of reaction against absolutism which characterized thirteenth- and fourteenth-century political scientists. See Wilks, "Princely Liberty and the 'Vox Populi,' " in *Problem of Sovereignty*, pp. 184–99. Wilks cites Marsilius of Padua, *Defensor minor* xii. I, on the conception of the ruler as a delegate of the popular will; Durandus of St. Porciano, on the natural right of each man to act as his own emperor and on the contingent proposition that the source of

the emperor's power is thus the popular sanction of such well-governed men; or William of Ockham, *Octo questiones* ii.8, on the proposition that a grant of authority to a ruler by his people can also be revoked on grounds of public expediency.

8 Compare Thomas Aquinas, *De Regno* I.i.4 and I.i.9, where the argument on behalf of monarchy as the best kind of government is advanced through analogy with the body's having one head or the idea of reason ruling an individual. Gower's attitude toward monarchy resembles that of Aquinas in other points as well: e.g., see *De Regno* I.6.49, where Aquinas argues the right of the *populus* to depose a tyrant if he rules badly on grounds that their contract of obedience no longer holds once the ruler has broken faith; or the idea that although a benevolent king may be the best kind of ruler, a tyrant is the worst *(De Regno* I.iii.23). Like Aquinas he would define "good" and "bad" in terms of the commonwealth, believing that the less a ruler heeds the common good to seek his own private good, the more unjust his rule becomes (cf. I.iii.24). Similar attitudes may be found in Gilbert of Tournai's *Eruditio regum*, Tholemy of Lucca's *De regimine principum*, Aegidius Romanus' *De regimine principum*, Dante's *De Monarchia*, and Thomas Hoccleve's *De regimine principum*.

9 See Gotz Schmitz, *The Middel Weie: Stil- und Aufbauformen in John Gowers "Confessio Amantis"* (Bonn, 1974), pp. 29–54, who discusses Gower's plain style as a feature of the poet's poetics and rhetoric.

10 Cf. *Vox Clamantis*, VII.xxv.1467, where Gower sees simplicity of intention as a criterion of virtue: "Corrigit hic mundum, qui cor retinet sibi mundum [This man corrects the world who keeps his heart pure]."

11 See *Vox Clamantis* I.Prol.57–58, where Gower identifies himself with John of the

Apocalypse on the Isle of Patmos, the headnote to Book II, and II.Prol.83–84, where he discusses the naming of the poem. Gower takes the phrase *vox clamantis* itself from the Gospel of Mark 1:3, where the voice crying in the wilderness is identified with John the Baptist. The phrase originates in Isa. 40.3. Cf. Matt. 3.3 and John 1.23.

[12] The dedication to Thomas of Arundel was added after Henry had become king, at the time of the addition of the *Tripartite Chronicle* to the *Vox Clamantis*. But even though he had Henry's favor, I find it remarkable that Gower would be so daring in his dedication. One wonders what Arundel would have thought of his excoriation of the pope and his predecessors in the Canterbury See. His attack on the corruptions of the church are unremitting. He had, of course, supported Thomas during his exile with Henry in France and saw in him, as he saw in the new king, the hope of reform.

[13] "Gower in His Most Significant Role," p. 59.

[14] In addition to the *Mirour de l'Omme* discussed above on p. 2, see *Vox Clamantis* II.iv, v, on the interconnectedness of man's fate with his personal behavior; VI.viii, on man's personal kingship and the importance of self-governance; VII. ii, on man's seeking after false possessions, thus dispossessing his soul; VII.vi, where all wickedness in the world is attributed to man; and esp. VII.viii ff., on man as a microcosm which if misgoverned by the will turns all topsy-turvy. Man, not God, is the cause of his own plight: "In meritis hominum solum deus aspicit orbem, / Et sua de facto tempora causat homo" *(Vox Clamantis* VII.xxiiii, 1381–82). The idea is recurrent throughout the *Confessio Amantis.*

[15] Cf. Donald G. Scheuler, "Some Com-

ments on the Structure of John Gower's *Confessio Amantis,*" *Explorations of Literature,* ed. Rima Drell Reck, LSU Studies, No. 18 (Baton Rouge, La., 1966), p. 21; and William George Dodd, *Courtly Love in Chaucer and Gower* (Cambridge, Mass., 1913), p. 82. Even as astute an observer of the poem as C. S. Lewis *(Allegory of Love* [Oxford, 1936], pp. 198–222, who was the first to remark on Gower's skillful craftsmanship, takes a "half glad" pleasure in censuring the "unsuccessful coda," the Prologue, the abusive digression on the pagan gods, and the encyclopedic matter of Book VII (p. 222).

[16] Not only did Gower carefully revise the poem at least twice in his three recensions of the *Confessio,* adding and deleting materials from one recension to the next, the Fairfax 3 manuscript, which Macaulay suggests reflects Gower's final version of the poem, contains many corrections in wording, capitalization, spelling, and even phrasing, which could only have been made by the author himself.

Prologue

[1] All references to the English text of *Confessio Amantis* are taken from G. C. Macaulay, ed., *The English Works of John Gower,* Early English Text Society, Extra Series Nos. 81–82 (Oxford, 1900–1901), and will hereafter be cited by book and line reference only.

[2] The debates at Oxford and Paris on Aristotle and the Muslim commentators which led to the condemnations of 1277 brought with them a powerfully revitalized interest in the writings of Augustine which assumed a prominence even greater than before and which continued throughout the fourteenth century. St. Augustine was preeminently the patristic

authority for Bonaventure, Grosseteste, Duns Scotus, and Ockham, as well as Holcot, Bradwardine, and Wyclif. *De Trinitate* explores most elaborately his theory of the analogies between man's mind and the triune Godhead and provided the starting point for other treatises on the faculties of the soul such as St. Anselm's *Monologion*, which also greatly influenced later medieval theologians, especailly the Victorines and St. Bonaventure.

3 *De Trin.* IV.xxi.30.

4 Ibid., XIV.iii.5; XV.viii.14.

5 Ibid., XIV.vii.9.

6 On Will (Love) as combiner and unifier, see *De Trin.* XI.xi.18, XIII.xx.26, XIV.vii.9, though allusions to this property of Will occur throughout the treatise.

7 See *De Trin.* XIV.vii.10, XIV.xii.15–16. On sin as parody of virtue, see XI.5 et passim.

8 Macaulay, *English Works*, I, 1. Since the Latin epigrams are not numbered along with the English verses I shall hereafter indicate their location by volume and page number in Macaulay's two-volume edition. The translation of this epigram has kindly been supplied by Frederick W. Locke. All translations of Latin and Old French not otherwise identified are my own.

9 I borrow the term "bookish" from C. S. Lewis, *The Discarded Image* (Cambridge, 1964), p. 11. See Donald R. Howard's excellent discussion of medieval attitudes toward books with special reference to Chaucer in *The Idea of the "Canterbury Tales"* (Berkeley, 1976), pp. 56–67. For a fourteenth-century explanation of why we should value books with reverence, see Richard de Bury's *Philobiblon*.

10 Cf. *Legend of Good Women* 26. Like Gower, Chaucer sees "the doctrine of these olde wise" (*LGW* 19) preserved in books.

11 For a survey of contemporary at-

titudes toward Richard II, see Louisa D. Duls, *Richard II in the Early Chronicles* (The Hague, 1975).

12 "Habent enim ex antiquo statuto et de facto non longe retroactis temporibus experienter, quod dolendum est, habito, si rex ex maligno consilio quocunque vel inepta contumacia aut contemptu seu proterva voluntate singulari aut quovis modo irregulari se alienaverit a populo suo, nec voluerit per jura regni et statuta ac laudabiles ordinationes cum salubri consilio dominorum et procerum regni gubernari et regulari, sed capitose in suis insanis consiliis propriam voluntatem suam singularem proterve exercere, extunc licitum est eis cum communi assensu et consensu populi regni ipsum regem de regali solio abrogare, et propinquiorem aliquem de stirpe regia loco ejus in regni solio sublimare" (*Chronicon Henrici Knighton, Monachi Leycestrensis*, ed. Joseph Rawson Lumby [London, 1895], II, 219).

13 I, 6–7. Translation by Alfred Geier.

14 I am indebted to an anonymous reader for this suggestion.

15 *Vox Clamantis* III.xv.1267. Gower repeatedly evokes the ancient maxim *vox populi, vox dei* in *Vox Clamantis* and the *Mirour de l'Omme* (cf. 10315 ff., 18445 ff., and 19057 ff.). In the *Vox Clamantis*, for example, he insists that he writes what the people's voice declares (III.Prol.11) and at the end (VII.xxv.1469–70) that what he has written is the voice of the people: "Quod scripsi plebis vox est, set et ista videbis, / Quo clamat populus, est ibi sepe deus [What I have written is the voice of the people, but you will also observe that where the people cry out, in that place God is often to be found]." Gower is not, of course, referring to democracy but rather to that native instinct for common profit which all men, by their given nature, share.

16 Cf. the opening of *O Deus Immense* with its attack on wayward kings (*quidam morosi Reges*) who destroy peace with strife and set all at odds.

17 The principal apologists include such writers as Augustinus Triumphus (d. 1328) in his *Summa de poteste ecclesiastica, Tractatus contra articulos inventos ad diffamandum Bonficium* (a defense of Boniface VIII), *Tractatus de potestate collegii mortuo papa,* and *Tractatus de duplici potestate praelatorum et laicorum;* James of Viterbo (d. 1308) in his *De regimine christiano;* Aegidius Romanus (d. 1316) in his *De ecclesiastica potestate;* and Alvarus Pelagius (d. 1353) in *De planctu Ecclesiae.* See Wilks, *Problem of Sovereignty,* pp. 1–11, on Augustinus Triumphus, and his useful Appendix 3 ("Notes on the Publicists and Anonymous Works"), pp. 548–59, which catalogues the publicists and their opponents and provides succinct observations on their works and main theological positions.

18 The principal works written in opposition to the publicists are John of Paris (d. 1306), *De potestate regia papali,* with its attack on Boniface VIII; William of Ockham (d. 1349), especially his *Tractatus contra Johannem XXII, Tractatus contra Benedictum XII, De imperatorum et pontificum potestate,* and *Octo quaestiones de potestate papae;* Marsilius of Padua (d. 1342–43), *Defensor pacis;* and John Wyclif (d. 1384), esp. his *Trialogus, De ecclesia,* and *De papa.* See Wilks, Appendix 3, for an index of specific points in the controversy. John of Paris defined Ecclesia as the company of the faithful (*De potestate regia,* chap. 3) and argued that to think of her as a worldly power is to commit the *error Herodis (De potestate regia,* chap. 9); for Marsilius the church is a "purely spiritual sacramental community," a "purely spiritual congregation of believers connected by no ties but

their common faith and participation in the sacraments" (Wilks, p. 92).

19 See Margaret Aston, "The Impeachment of Bishop Despenser," *Bulletin of the Institute of Historical Research,* 38 (1965), 127–48; May McKisack, *The Fourteenth Century, 1307–1399* (Oxford, 1959), pp. 427–33; E. Perroy, *L'Angleterre et le Grand Schisme d'Occident* (Paris, 1933), pp. 166–209; G. M. Wrong, *The Crusade of 1383, Known as that of the Bishop of Norwich* (Oxford, 1892); and G. Skalweit, *Der Kreuzzug des Bishops Heinrich von Norwich im Jahre 1383* (Königsberg, 1898). Ashton also cites the London Ph.D. thesis of A. P. R. Coulborn, "The Economic and Political Preliminaries of the Crusade of Henry Despenser, Bishop of Norwich, in 1383" (1931), which is summarized in *BIHR,* 10 (1932–33), 40–44.

20 Palmer Throop, *Criticism of the Crusade: A Study of Public Opinion and Crusade Propaganda* (Amsterdam, 1940), p. 4.

21 Aston notes that after Charles entered Bruges and confiscated the goods of the English merchants the wool traffic at Calais almost ground to a halt, dropping from eighteen thousand sacks in 1381–82 to about two thousand in 1382–83, "Impeachment of Despenser," pp. 133–34.

22 See McKisack's succinct discussion, *The Fourteenth Century,* pp. 429–30.

23 The phrase is Aston's, p. 135.

24 *Rotuli Parliamentorum* iii.140.

25 "Et sic secretus thesaurus regni qui in manibus erat mulierum periclitatus est" (*Chronicon* II, 198).

26 *The Fourteenth Century,* p. 431.

27 "Dicebatur enim quod quidam de commissariis suis asserebant, quod ad eorum praeceptum angeli de caelo descenderent, et animas in purgatoriis locis positas de poenis eriperent, et ad coelos absque mora deducerent" (*Chronicon,* II, 199).

[28] "Impeachment of Despenser," p. 128.

[29] It is noteworthy that the chronicler Henry Knighton is even more outspoken against Lollardry than he is against the Norwich Crusade. He devotes most of the latter part of his chronicle to an account of Wyclif's heresies and the evils of their influence. His position on both the crusade and Lollardry is similar to Gower's and reflects the common concern of an educated man writing at the same time that Gower wrote.

[30] *Polemical Works* ii.592, 595, 603, 610 ff., 624, as cited by McKisack, *Fourteenth Century*, p. 431.

[31] Gower's call for reform while relying on God for judgment reminds one of the position of another lawyer, Bracton, who argued that an official who fails to fulfill his office ceases to have right to that office, but advises that his subjects should trust God to punish the offender and annihilate his rule rather than taking the matter into their own hands. See Fritz Schulz, "Bracton on Kingship," *English Historical Review*, 60 (1945), 153.

[32] Although manuscript illuminations do not always reflect the author's intent, Gower so carefully supervised the composition of this particular manuscript that it is likely that the drawing, like the various corrections of the text, fell under his supervision. As artwork, the illumination is not very skillful. It can hardly have been done by one who has mastered a pattern book. Maybe Gower did it himself.

[33] The end note to the *Confessio* concludes: "Tercius iste liber qui ob reuerenciam strenuissimi domini sui domini Henrici de Lancastria, tunc Derbeie Comitis, Anglico sermone conficitur, secundum Danielis propheciam super huius mundi regnorum mutacione a tempore regis Nabugodonosor vsque nunc tempora distinguit. Tractat eciam secundum Aris-totilem super hiis quibus rex Alexander tam in sui regimen quam aliter eius disciplina edoctus fuit. Principalis tamen huius operis materia super amorem et infatuatas amantum passiones fundamentum habet. Nomenque sibi appropriatum *Confessio Amantis* specialiter sortitus est" (Macaulay, *English Works*, ii, 480). See also *Vox Clamantis*, vii, esp. lines 5–6, 106–12, 136, 353–54, and 1379. (I.e., Nebuchadnezzar's monster provides the controlling metaphor for the conclusion of *Vox Clamantis* as well.)

BOOK I: Pride

[1] Some portions of my argument here have appeared previously in the "Introduction" to my edition of *Confessio Amantis* (New York, 1968), pp. xi–xii.

[2] Macaulay, *Confessio Amantis*, i, 37.

[3] Cf. *Vox Clamantis* II.ix.451 ff. on the importance of knowing one's limitations, where we learn that Reason should yield to Faith and that man should entrust to Faith what he cannot entrust to Reason. To know one's "compas" is the starting point of all responsible moral judgments.

[4] "Truth: Balade de Bon Conseyl," line 10.

[5] Here again, some portions of my argument are taken from the "Introduction" to my Gower selection, pp. xii ff. For a different view of the role of Venus in the *Confessio* from the one I argue, see Patrick Gallacher, *Love, the Word, and Mercury: A Reading of Gower's "Confessio Amantis"* (Albuquerque, 1975), pp. 108 ff. Gallacher suggests that Venus represents "the ideal conception of sexuality, who, by demanding that Amans search out his 'trouthe' in confession, relates the ideal to the acknowlegment of a total world order."

6 *Allegory of Love,* p. 200.

7 See Thomas J. Hatton's discussion of the two Venuses in medieval allegorical tradition, "The Role of Venus and Genius in *Confessio Amantis*," *Greyfriar: Siena Studies in Literature,* 16 (1975), 36–37. Hatton observes that "Amans' problem is not to stop loving but to start loving in the right way." It is not love "that destroys human souls but misdirected and inordinate love for the wrong things."

8 *Metalogicon* I.11, as cited by Winthrop Wetherbee, *Platonism and Poetry in the Twelfth Century* (Princeton, 1972), pp. 94–95.

9 *Platonism and Poetry in the Twelfth Century,* p. 95.

10 Plato, *Timaeus* 45b–47c, explains why the eye is man's principal sense organ and the ear next in importance. These two wits enable man to perceive number, motion, harmony and rhythm, those properties of nature which help him to maintain order in his soul. Plato ignores the other three wits entirely as agencies for illuminating the soul, although later (61d–68d) he discusses all five as part of man's physical mechanism for understanding physical phenomenon. His premises constitute one basis for medieval preoccupations with vision and harmony. Genius, in the best Platonic tradition, exorcises only these two of the Lover's five wits. For as Gower explains in the fourth Latin epigram in Book I of the *Confessio:* "Visus et auditus fragilis sunt ostia mentis [Sight and fragile hearing are the doors of the mind]."

11 Cf. Ovid *Metam.* IV.772–803. Gower is apparently using additional sources, however. He names Medusa's sisters, as Ovid does not, though he calls Stheno, "Stellibon," and Euryale (whom he calls "Suriale"). Moreover, he combines the story of the Graeae, who share one tooth and one eye, with the story of the Gorgons.

Macaulay (*English Works,* I, 468) notes that this confusion appears in Boccaccio, *Genealogiae Deorum Gentilium,* x.10, which Gower may have known. Whether Gower follows Boccaccio or not, the mingling of the two stories is fortuitous for Gower's purpose in demonstrating the evil of "mislok" and the wisdom of looking well.

12 Eric W. Stockton, *The Major Latin Works of John Gower* (Seattle, 1962), p. 387, n. 13, observes that the pun on *mundus-mundare* was a favorite with Gower. E.g., in *Vox Clamantis* VII.v.365–66: "Mundus enim sibi dat nomen, set mundus haberi / Ex inmundiciis de racione nequit [The world, to be sure, has given itself the name of being pure, but it rightly cannot be considered as free of impurities]"; or in *Vox Clamantis* VII.xxv.1467: "Corrigit his mundum, qui cor retinet sibi mundum [The man who keeps his heart pure sets the world right]"—Stockton's translations, pp. 262, 287.

13 See Gallacher's interesting discussion of overtones of Mary and the Annunciation in the story of Paulina, *Love, the Word and Mercury,* pp. 32–37.

14 "Lak of Stedfastnesse," line 2.

15 *De Civitate Dei* I.19.

16 See *Vox Clamantis* III.xxiii for discussion of the double guilt of the priest who sins.

17 Cf. *Vox Clamantis* VI.xvii, where Gower instructs King Richard in the virtue of death as prompter of just perspective for a king. Mindful of death and his kinship with humanity, the king of Hungary loves his people as a king should. See also *Vox Clamantis* VI.xviii.

18 Gallacher relates the importance of keeping one's word to the Verbum tradition, suggesting that there are perhaps overtones of the Annunciation in the resolution to this tale where the remarkable grace comes out of a sort of *fiat mihi secun-*

dum verbum tuum, as the king's words are held true and create a new social order (*Love, the Word and Mercury,* p. 40).

BOOK II: Envy

1 A similar reordering of the children of Vice occurred in the first book of the *Confessio* as well, where Gower concluded his discussion of Pride with Nebuchadnezzar's vainglory, which had been the first of Pride's children in the *Mirour.*

2 "Trivet's Life of Constance," ed. Margaret Schlauch, in *Sources and Analogues of Chaucer's "Canterbury Tales,"* ed. W. F. Bryan and Germaine Dempster (London, 1958), p. 170.

3 It is curious that Gower did not look upon Henry iv's ascension or its possibility prior to the fact as an act of Supplantation. The difference between Henry's ascent to power and that of Boniface lies in both motive and situation. Celestine was a good pope; Richard was a bad king. If the king fails to be a true king, then he is no king at all. (Cf. Bracton, Text A 16.22–24, in Schulz, "Bracton on Kingship," p. 153.) To Gower's way of thinking, Richard would be the supplanter. He supplanted himself with his irresponsible whims and by ignoring the needs of the people. Henry thus filled a vacuum rather than perpetrated a revolution. Cf. Gower's *Tripartite Chronicle* on God's abomination of an evil ruler.

4 Macaulay's notes on the historical inaccuracies of Gower's version are useful here (*English Works,* I, 490–91).

5 Like Constantine, Peronelle, at the end of Book I, embodies all five children of the virtue which is antidote to the vice her story summarizes (i.e., Humility to Pride). She shows Devocioun rather than Hypocrisie toward her father and king, Paour rather than Vain Gloire in these same relationships, Discresioun rather than Surquidrie as she volunteers to help her father, Vergoigne (modesty) instead of Avantance as she reminds the king of his promises, and Obedience rather than Inobedience as she waits her turn and obeys her superiors.

6 See *Vox Clamantis* iii, chaps. 1–5, and esp. chaps. 6, 9. Perhaps one effect of Gower's choice of Boniface viii as villain of the preceding tale was to provoke the consciousness of his audience into reflection upon the namesake-successor to Boniface, the present pope, Boniface ix, whose machinations in the 1390s to get England back into war against France and whose eagerness for revenues and new taxes to support his own war against the French Gower thoroughly abhorred.

7 Gower's position on the Donation of Constantine and the papacy's subsequent claim to worldly power shares much with that of Dante in *De Monarchia.* See *De Monarchia* ii.11, where Dante reminds the reader that Christ Himself recognized the rights of Caesar's jurisdiction, and the whole of Book iii which is devoted to the proposition that temporal world rule comes directly from God, not the papacy. See esp. iii.4, with its argument that ecclesiastical claims of worldly power are sins against the Holy Spirit; iii.9, which insists (contrary to Boniface viii's bull *Unam Sanctam*) that the two swords of temporal and spiritual power are not in the hands of the church; and iii.10, which contests Constantine's right to donate imperial power to the church. Dante concludes with the argument that it is impossible for the church to receive or give temporal authority (iii.14), that the form of the true church is the life of Christ, not some imperial policy (iii.15), and that God

is the only ruler over both spiritual and temporal realms (III.16). Cf. *Inferno* XIX, where Dante finds in the third bolgia (Simonists) of the eighth circle a place reserved for Boniface VIII, whose name rises from the hole in the rock as Pope Nicholas III thinks Boniface has come even before his time.

BOOKS III *and* IV: Wrath *and* Sloth

1 *Vox Clamantis* V.i–v.

2 *Ricardian Poetry*, p. 109.

3 See especially Genius' exhortations to Nature's creatures to reproduce themselves in such passages as *Le Roman de la Rose* (ed. Ernest Langlois), lines 19505–906.

4 Ibid., 4429–4628.

5 See *Vox Clamantis* VI.xiii, for example, where Gower exhorts Richard to be warlike as his father was, a plunderer of foreign lands but a protector of his own.

6 For an excellent discussion on the popularity of Alexander in the fourteenth century, and more particularly on his use as an exemplum of tyranny, see William Matthews, *The Tragedy of Arthur: A Study of the Alliterative "Morte Arthure"* (Los Angeles, 1960), pp. 68–93. Matthews considers Gower's use of Alexander exempla on pp. 75–76, 90–92.

7 See *Ovide Moralisé*, ed. De Boer (Amsterdam, 1936), IV.x–xiii, where Alcyone's excessive grief, which leaves her totally at Fortune's mercy, is compared to storms at sea tossing her soul like a ship without sailors, since her senses have stopped guiding her properly. When she is turned into a bird she remains bound to the world, always to be buffeted by wind and cold.

BOOK V: Avarice

1 Gower's intense concern with the corruptive effect of Avarice on fourteenth-century society is not unique but rather a shared concern of his day. See Morton Bloomfield, *The Seven Deadly Sins: An Introduction to the History of a Religious Concept* (East Lansing, Mich., 1952), p. 95; and Lester K. Little, "Pride Goes before Avarice: Social Change and the Vices in Latin Christendom," *American Historical Review*, 76 (1971), 16–49.

2 I take my count of ten from Genius' summary of Avarice's company, v.7617–23, where he lumps Stealth and Micherie together.

3 *Vox Clamantis* I.xiii.880 ff.

4 *Le Sept Sages de Rome*, ed. Gaston Paris (Paris, 1876), pp. 40–44. The various Middle English versions of the story speak of the villain as "sire Cressus" and "Cressus the riche man," conflating the idea of avaricious man with the myth of the rich Croesus, king of Lydia (cf. the early fourteenth-century "Auchinleck MS," i.e., Adv MS 19.2.1, No. 155 of the National Library of Scotland, and the early sixteenth-century Balliol College Oxford MS 354). The mid-fifteenth-century Egerton 1995 MS of the British Library calls him "king Crassus." The fifteenth-century Arundel 140 MS of the British Library calls him "Crayfus." See *The Seven Sages of Rome* (Southern Version), ed. Karl Brunner (London, 1933), esp. pp. 87–96.

5 *O Deus Immense*, lines 21–22 (G. C. Macaulay, ed., *The Complete Works of John Gower*, vol. IV, *Latin Works* [Oxford, 1902], 362), "Rex qui plus aurum populi quam corda thesaurum/Computat, a mente populi cadit ipse repente."

6 Benoit de Sainte-Maure, *Le Roman de Troie*, ed. Leopold Constans (Paris, 1904), I.781. Subsequent references are to this

edition and are cited by line number in the context of my argument.

[7]   Macaulay notes the detail, calling it "a pretty touch" (*English Works*, II, 499).

[8]   A convenient example of the icon may be found in Emile Mâle, *Religious Art in France of the Thirteenth Century: A Study in Mediaeval Iconography and Its Source of Inspiration*, trans. Dora Nussy (New York, 1913), p. 380, reprinted from the *Hortus Deliciarum*.

BOOK VI: Gluttony

[1]   *Love, the Word, and Mercury*, p. 83.

[2]   Macaulay, *English Works*, II, 192, opposite VI.915 ff.

[3]   Ibid., p. 201, opposite VI.1262 ff.

BOOK VII: The Education of a King

[1]   Gower's attitude toward the supremacy of the law and the need for one law and one rule beyond the whims of individual rulers reflects the arguments of his day. Bracton insists that the law resides beyond the king (*lex supra regem*) with the king under God and the law (*sub Deo et lege*), that he is bound by laws he has given (*leges suum ligant latorem*), and that the law makes the king a king and that he owes the law a gift of obedience to the law in return (Schulz, "Bracton on Kingship," *English Historical Review*, 60 [1945], 156–69. Schulz traces the notion back to antiquity). Cf. Gilbert of Tournai, *Eruditio regum et principum* II.i.1 ([*rex*] *non recte regendo nomen regis amittat*), an attitude found in Bracton and reiterated by Aegidius Romanus, *De regimine principum* I.i.12, and Alvarus Pelagius, *De planctu Ecclesiae*, chap. 62. See Wilks, *Problem of Sovereignty*, pp. 200–229. And see Dante, *De Monarchia* I.5, on the need for one law governing all men.

[2]   *Cronica Tripertita* III.486 (Est qui peccator, non esse potest dominator").

[3]   *Cronica Tripertita*, *Latin Works*, pp. 314–42.

[4]   Cf. *Vox Clamantis* VI.xxi, where, lamenting the loss of virtuous men like Socrates and Diogenes, Gower sees the vain Aristippuses of the world usurping man's kingdom.

[5]   Cf. *Vox Clamantis* VI.vii–xviii, where Gower, in a "letter" addressed to the young king, warns against flattering courtiers. The king must first govern himself. He must avoid war and love his people with pity and liberality, be just and truthful. Gower clearly had his five points of policy in mind long before he began working on the *Confessio*.

[6]   It is noteworthy that Gower includes his discussion of kingship in *Vox Clamantis* in the sixth book, the book devoted to law. See especially the eighth chapter in this regard.

[7]   Recall Januarie's decision to marry, since sex in wedlock is "so esy and so clene, / That in this world it is a paradys" (E.1264–65).

[8]   *Vox Clamantis* V.i.31–32. Cf. VI.xii.

[9]   *Fasti* II.761 ff., ed. Sir James George Frazer, Loeb Classical Library (Cambridge, Mass., 1957), pp. 112 ff.

[10]   Livy's *History* III.xliv. See Edgar F. Shannon's edition and discussion in "The Physician's Tale," *Sources and Analogues to the "Canterbury Tales,"* ed. W. F. Bryan and G. Dempster (New York, 1941), pp. 398–408.

BOOK VIII: The Return Home

1   Macaulay, *English Works*, II, 386.

2   *Vox Clamatis* VII.v.437–38. "Hic gemit incestum corrupte coniugis, alter / Delusus falsa suspicione timet. The discussion of sin's incestuous progeny in the *Mirour de l'Omme* occurs in lines 205–76 (where Sin and her son Death engender the seven deadly sins).

3   Some portions of my argument here have appeared previously in the "Introduction" to my edition of *Confessio Amantis*.

4   See Macaulay's discussion, *English Works*, II, 536–38, 539–40.

5   The alternative path was the more likely, as Gower well knows. In discussing the corruption of England in *Vox Clamantis* Gower laments that Penelope is dead and Justine too, and Thaise, instead of teaching, lies flat on her back (VI.xxi.1331–34).

He goes on to add that women nowadays seek five men where formerly one served for mutual love and companionship. The point here is that Apollonius' Thaise is no unregenerate Woman of Samaria but rather knows proper rule; England should look to her as teacher, adhering to the original story, rather than perverting her office.

6   I have in mind here the opening lines of *Vox Clamantis* I.Prol.1–2: Scripture veteris capiunt exempla futuri, / Nam dabit experta res magis esse fidem.

7   *Platonism and Poetry in the Twelfth Century* (Princeton, 1972), pp. 183–84.

8   *Vox Clamantis* VII.xxiv.1300.

9   On traditional connotations of "8" as a sign of blessedness, return home, new beginning, and peace of mind (i.e., completed Boethian journey) see my "Number Structure in *St. Erkenwald*," *Annuale Mediaevale*, 14 (1973), 12–13.

INDEX

also Fantasy
Sovereignty, 12, 43, 49, 145, 184
Steiner, George, ix
Super Principum Regimine, 189n6

Tantalus, 102, 123
Tarquin and Aruns, 153–56. *See also* Lucrece
Tasso, ix
Telephus and Teucer, 90
Tennyson, Alfred, x
Tereus, Philomena, and Procne, 104, 123
Thelamon and Eseonen, 178
Theseus, Ariadne, and Phedra, 38, 104, 178
Thisbe and Pyramus, 86, 179
Thoas: and fall of Troy, 101, 103, 107
Tholemy of Lucca, 189n8
Three Estates: failure of Second Estate, xii, xiii, 13–19, 71–73, 99–102; failure of First Estate, xii, 10–13; Third Estate, xiii–xiv, 19–20; mentioned, xii, xix–xx, 21, 93, 179–80, 182
Three Questions, Tale of, 55–58, 68, 76, 77, 195n5
Time: degeneration of, xiv, 3–4, 8, 10, 20–21; as psychological space, xv, 1, 2, 4, 11, 35, 90, 183; sin descended from Siecle, xx; isolation in, 2, 5; as process, 2, 6, 11, 31, 32, 34, 55, 140, 178, 180, 183; Creator beyond time, 3; poetry as liberator from, 5, 6; poetry as regenerator of, 6, 22–23; present time as inverted tree, 12; dramatic irony as feature of human time, 60; time as tyrant, 139–40. *See also* History
Tiresias, 52, 84, 85, 86
Tobias and Sara, 157–58, 163
Tower: metaphor of wisdom and stable mind, 106–8, 120–21, 122, 129, 132, 137, 153
Travellers and the Angel, Tale of, 60–61
Tripartite Chronicle: appended to *Vox Clamantis* after Richard's overthrow, xix, 142, 145, 190n12, 195n3, 197n2–3
Tristan, Isolde, and Mark, 178
Trivet, Nicholas, 63, 65, 67, 69, 195n1
Trump of Death, Tale of, 49–52, 58, 68, 130, 146, 163, 194n17
Truth, 47–49, 57, 140, 142–44, 149, 162

Tuck, Anthony, 187n2
Tyranny, 56, 64, 86, 87, 89, 90, 145, 154, 156, 166, 169, 174, 182

Ulysses and the Sirens, 40
Ulysses and Telegonus, Tale of, 130–33

Venus: parody of Lady Philosophy, 29–32; distrust of Amans, 30; sends Amans to Genius, 32; her double nature, 33, 84, 193n5; Genius' ambivalent relationship with her, 34, 84, 104, 134; her promiscuity, 104; she returns, 176–78; eases Amans' kidneys, 179; gives Amans a mirror and disappears, 180–81; mentioned, 1
Virgil, ix, x, 179
Virgil's Mirror, Tale of, 106–8, 116, 122, 163
Virginia and Virginius, Tale of, 156–57, 163, 165
Vox Clamantis, xvii, xix, xx, xxiii, 5, 13, 22, 80, 88–89, 96, 100, 103, 132, 153, 165, 179, 183, 189n5, 189n6, 189n10–11, 190n12, 190n14, 191n15, 193n3, 193n33, 194n12, 194n16–17, 195n6, 196n1, 196n3, 196n5, 197n4–6, 197n8, 198n5–6, 198n8
Vulcan and Venus, 103, 104

War, 89, 91, 99, 146
Wetherbee, Winthrop, 34, 181, 194n8–9, 198n7
Willfulness: source of wonders, xi, 41, 132; characteristic of Richard II, xi, xii; efficacy of will, xv; fourteenth-century preoccupation with will, xv–xvi; free will, xv, 75; will as protagonist, xvi; well-governed will, xvi, xvii, 122; need for commitment to society, xvii; historical effects of evil will, xx–xxi; will and dramatic irony, 61–62, 64, 71; fate and will, 71, 75, 88–89, 132, 133; idle will, 82, 87; tyrant will, 82, 87–88, 128; insatiable will, 83; education of will, 139
Wilks, Michael, 187n4, 189n4, 189n7, 192n17, 197n1
Wrong, G. M., 192n19
Wyclif, John, xii, xiii, xv, 14, 107, 187n4–5, 191n2, 192n18
Wynnere and Wastour, xvi, 188n9